Maritime Ireland

AN ARCHAEOLOGY OF COASTAL COMMUNITIES

Maritime Ireland
AN ARCHAEOLOGY OF COASTAL COMMUNITIES

Aidan O'Sullivan & Colin Breen

TEMPUS

We dedicate this book to our parents, John and Kathleen O'Sullivan and Anne and Gerry Breen in gratitude for all they have given us

First published 2007

Tempus Publishing Limited
The Mill, Brimscombe Port,
Stroud, Gloucestershire, GL5 2QG
www.tempus-publishing.com

©Aidan O'Sullivan & Colin Breen, 2007

British Library Cataloguing in Publication Data.
A catalogue record for this book is available from the British Library.

ISBN 978 0 7524 2509 2

Typesetting and origination by Tempus Publishing Limited
Printed in Great Britain

Contents

List of illustrations

Colour Plates

Preface

Maritime archaeology is a subject with huge potential for discovery and research in Ireland, but this also means that it is in its infancy. In this book we have tried to sketch out a general outline of Ireland's maritime cultural heritage, as well as the questions and gaps in our knowledge. Hopefully, with more maritime archaeological investigations some answers will emerge and some gaps will start to be filled in and we hope that this book points scholars in some useful directions.

In the meantime, we acknowledge the inspiration and work of our friends and colleagues. In particular, we would like to thank Rory Quinn, Tom McErlean, Rosemary McConkey, Dan Rhodes, Ted Pollard and Wes Forsythe, Centre for Maritime Archaeology, Coleraine; Brian Williams, Environment and Heritage Service; Donal Boland, Dr Niall Brady, the Discovery Programme; Fionnbarr Moore, Karl Brady, Connie Kelleher of the Underwater Archaeology Unit, Dept of Environment; Muiris O'Sullivan, Gabriel Cooney, Barry Raftery, Graeme Warren, Robert Sands, Dorothy Kelly, Joanna Bruck, Tadhg O'Keeffe, Stephen Harrison and Sharon Greene, UCD School of Archaeology; Emily Murray and Finbar McCormick, School of Geography, Archaeology and Palaeoecology, Queen's University Belfast, Peter Woodman, John Sheehan and Colin Rynne, Dept of Archaeology, University College Cork; John Waddell, Billy O'Brien, Liz FitzPatrick and Kieran O'Conor, NUI Galway; Moira Ní Loingsigh, Cork; Dr Patrick Wallace, Director, National Museum of Ireland; Eamonn Kelly; Beatrice Kelly and Ian Doyle of The Heritage Council.

We also thank our colleagues who have provided us with articles and information in advance of publications, or whose work we draw down heavily from, including Claire Cotter, Margaret McCarthy, Graeme Warren, Niall Brady, Jonathan Wooding, Tom McErlean, Wes Forsythe, Nigel McDowell, Gail Pollock and Emily Murray.

We thank Peter Kemmis Betty of Tempus for his endless and almost inexhaustible patience. This book has taken longer than we, and he, expected, but we hope that it has been worth the wait.

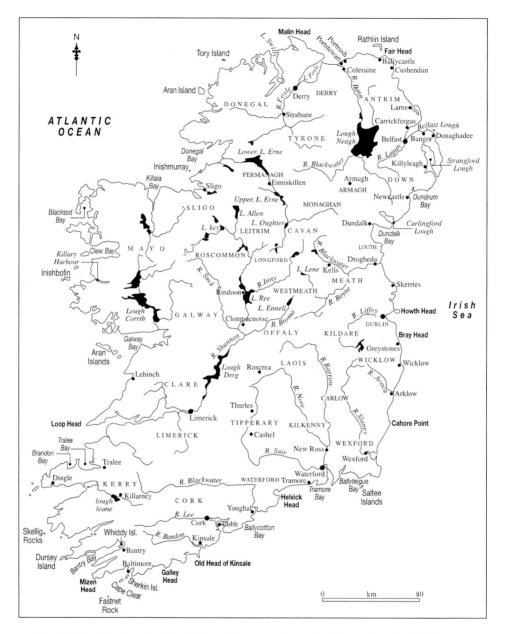

1 Map of Ireland showing location of places (bays, estuaries, etc) and key archaeological sites mentioned in this book

1

Introduction

INTRODUCTION

Ireland is a maritime island lying off the north-western European seaboard, surrounded by seas that link it with the wider world. About 10,000 years ago, Ireland's first human settlers – Mesolithic hunter-gatherers – came here by hide-covered boats or canoes and started to live by its shoreline, gathering shellfish and other marine foods. Since those first arrivals, people have lived, worked, travelled and buried their dead along Ireland's coastal landscapes. They have used the sea and its shoreline as a source of food and raw materials, a source of livelihood, as a means of travel and communications, and as a place to build communities. In this book, we hope to tell some of the stories of the many different peoples that have lived by and worked the sea, from prehistory to modern times.

These stories are rooted in the maritime landscape of the coast and the many pieces of physical evidence that these past peoples left behind (1). Archaeological traces of these coastal dwellers are rich and diverse, including dwelling places, rubbish heaps or middens, fishing structures, harbours, piers and boats. However, it is only in the last two decades that Irish archaeologists have begun to seriously think about such stories and the wider cultural heritage of the coastal zone in Ireland. This is in contrast to the Mediterranean, Scandinavian and North Atlantic archaeological traditions, where scholars have accomplished marvelous archaeological and bioarchaeological results by the careful, multidisciplinary investigation of coastal settlement sites.

REMEMBERING IRELAND'S MARITIME TRADITIONS

You would have thought that writing an overview of maritime archaeology in Ireland should be a relatively straightforward process. It is, after all, an island, which has been subject to up to ten thousand years of human activity, much of it concentrated along the coast, and it has been a focus for continual trade and communications in a European and Atlantic world for millennia. Yet, given this longevity of human coastal activity and associated archaeologies this has not been an easy task. It has been compounded by a relative paucity of information, little understanding or recognition of past maritime traditions and an established marked lack of enthusiasm for investigating Ireland's past from a maritime or sea-based perspective.

Of course, since the earliest origins of Irish archaeology, antiquarians and scholars have shown some interest in aspects of coastal sites. Indeed, in the nineteenth century, scholars such as George Petrie, T.J. Westropp and William Wakeman visited the Aran Islands and Inismurray. They described the coastal promontory forts and monastic enclosures, but they also often depicted the contemporary populations as living primitive lives that they saw as being rooted in antiquity. This 'othering' of island populations went hand-in-hand with Irish nationalist beliefs that the western seaboard and its Atlantic islands were places where an ancient, surviving Gaelic culture could be used to reinspire a cultural revival in Irish society. Through the twentieth century, archaeologists continued to work on coastal archaeological sites, exploring the organization of island monasteries, the chronology and function of coastal promontory forts and the role of so-called 'kitchen' middens (shell middens) that they found in sand dunes. Indeed, for a time, Irish archaeologists were showing great interest in sand dune occupations and shell middens, with significant publications by W.J. Knowles, and later by Brunicardi and the Rev. Hewson. However, there was rarely ever a sense that this was regarded as coastal or maritime archaeology, but rather a study of people living oddly and at the edge of normal life – scholarly work that was apart from the classic monument studies that have dominated Irish archaeology.

Traditionally, Irish society generally has looked inwards to its rural landscapes, seeing agriculture as being of key cultural and economic significance. By contrast, it has to be said that our Atlantic neighbours, from Iberia, France and Britain across to Newfoundland, see their national identities as being firmly rooted in the traditions of the sea and built national economies structured around its marine resources. This is partly rooted in scholarly activities at crucial times of state and identity formation in Ireland; the nineteenth century cultural nationalist emphasis on the saints and scholars of Ireland's 'Golden Age'; the fact that the seminal Harvard Archaeological Mission of the 1930s concentrated on prehistoric and early medieval sites inland, and perhaps too the sense that 'outsiders' (i.e. the 'English', or variants of the same) were responsible for the development of our maritime ports and fleets.

The sea – although a powerful trope in the Irish imagination – has largely been associated with arrivals of 'outsiders' whether real or imagined, with the advent of new ideas, technologies and cultures from without. Since the earliest antiquarian studies in the nineteenth century, the peoples thought to have 'arrived' here from across the sea included the pseudo historical, mythical Milesians; the 'invading' Celts (still a particularly deeply-rooted popular idea, despite a generation of research that shows there was never a 'Celtic invasion'); the onslaught of the Vikings; the arrival of Christianity from Gaul and the peregrinations of the early Irish saints, Anglo-Norman colonizers and upwards to the Spanish Armada and later French fleets that were involved in various rebellions. Indeed, historic shipwrecks were seen by some Irish scholars as the archaeological heritage of other peoples (i.e. the Armada shipwrecks belonged to the Spanish, rather than the Irish). On the other hand, the sea was seen as the means by which our people left; emigrating to Britain, Australia and America. Exile, departure, and loss – all were associated with the actual ships and ports that bore our people away (no doubt, future Irish identities will be shaped by stories about other people's arrival and departure from airports!). In any case, it was often a story about maritime movement and arrival, but rarely was there recognition of everyday activity of coastal dwellers – of the lives, traditions and economic activities of people who lived by the sea through all these historical events.

It could also be argued that the social and political construct of the contemporary Irish state and its continued coexistence with Northern Ireland was also partly responsible for this antipathy. Prior to Irish independence in 1922, the coast, its towns, villages, British economic and military interests largely controlled harbours and estuaries. The presence of extensive post medieval fortifications around the coast bear testimony to this overt military presence and the dominant symbolic and visual role they played in the landscape. These monuments and their associated large navies and mercantile fleets were later to become associated by Irish nationalists, and consequently by the public with the island's colonial past and thus representing a cultural separateness which was disengaged from the national social perceptions of heritage.

This resulted in many of the former centres of colonial activity like forts, towers and batteries becoming culturally invisible or even non-places in the landscape. 'Forgetting', in the end, is as deliberate and dynamic a process as 'remembering'. As a consequence, many of the other cultural traditions of the coast also become marginalized through association. This process of forgetting was also coupled with abandonment of islands and the repatriation of their maritime communities to the mainland and beyond. The abandonment of the Blasket Islands, that most iconic of Gaelic Irish islands, was ironically accomplished at the same time as its Gaelic Irish cultural identities were promoted in schools. Even during periods of economic recovery, the large-scale migration to the urban centres and emigration out of the country marked a sustained period of depopulation of the coast with little official interest in its sustainable development.

Instead in the early years of the Free State, cultural heritage was more associated with the 'Celtic' and Christian past than with everyday coastal activities. There was a very noticeable introversion where the government in the 1930s, largely directed by Eamonn De Valera, both physically and metaphorically turned their backs on the sea in an attempt to 'recreate' a Christian rural society that was largely self-sustainable. At the same time, links to the sea were deliberately cut, the government sold off merchant fleets and an attempt was made to separate Ireland from its closest maritime neighbour, Britain. Indeed, people from fishing communities today would argue that government policy, influenced by EU conservation and agriculturally-oriented economic policies, has continued to lead to a gradual downgrading of the commercial and fishing marine sector.

In the 1990s, government and heritage bodies, university archaeology departments and commercial companies across the island developed a growing interest in maritime and coastal archaeology. Much has been achieved, from coastal surveys of regions to inventories of shipwrecks around the entire island. The Discovery Programme's pioneering Shannon estuary inter-tidal survey between 1992-2000, directed by Aidan O'Sullivan revealed the existence of Neolithic and Bronze Age submerged landscapes, occupation sites and trackways on its foreshore, as well as a range of medieval and post medieval fishing structures, piers and reclamation walls. This project confirmed the huge archaeological potential of Ireland's intertidal zone, which had hitherto been overlooked. Since the 1960s, there has been an awareness amongst the diving community of our shipwreck resource. In 1997, the National Monuments Service established a National Maritime archaeological survey in the Republic. This has initially focused on an exhaustive literature and desk-top survey, providing the basis for an inventory of shipwrecks around the coast – suspected to consist of tens of thousands of sites. More recently, the state's Underwater Archaeology Unit has made serious progress at providing a full inventory of shipwrecks and other maritime structures.

Northern Ireland's archaeological community have very successfully progressed maritime archaeology as a discipline, as can be seen in both university and heritage agency initiatives. In 1993, The Maritime Archaeology Project was established by the Environment Service, and was based at the Institute of Irish Studies in Belfast. Using documentary and cartographic sources and some excavations, this project directed by Colin Breen prepared an inventory of at least four thousand shipwrecks lying in Northern Ireland waters. A long-term intertidal survey was also carried out on Strangford Lough, Co. Down between 1995-2000 by Tom McErlean, Rosemary McConkey and Wes Forsythe and colleagues. Arguably, this provided the first maritime cultural landscape study of part of Ireland's coastline. In both Northern Ireland and the Republic, both commercial archaeologists are highly active. However, it remains to be seen whether the professionalisation of maritime archaeology in both parts of Ireland will help, or perhaps partly hinder, a public awareness of the potential richness and role of coastal archaeology. It could also be argued that this growing professional archaeological activity has 'chilled' the potential contribution of local communities, or at the least has not necessarily enabled local communities to explore for themselves their own coastal cultural heritage.

This is despite the fact that up to half this island's population live within ten kilometres of the coast and few are further than a few hours' travel to it. In contrast, in Britain local historical and archaeological groups have been much more involved in coastal archaeological survey and monitoring. Perhaps coastal archaeological monitoring schemes involving local communities are something that could be usefully developed in Ireland (especially considering the potentially destructive, and largely unwitnessed, impact of coastal erosion on thousands of Ireland's coastal archaeological sites). In a sense, we have decided to aim this book at a general or popular audience because of this, in the belief that it is only by encouraging and informing local communities of the excitement of coastal archaeology that further discoveries will be made.

In this introductory chapter, we will set the scene by describing some ways of thinking about coastal archaeology. Above all, we are interested in exploring how people perceived and understood the sea and used this knowledge and understanding to order and constitute the landscapes and societies that they lived in. While as archaeologists we work with the material remains of the past, it is not these places and objects alone that we are interested in, but in the living, breathing people that made, used and discarded them. So firstly, we will try and think about how communities derived their social identity and sense of belonging by their daily engagement with these dynamic environments. We will also consider the places where these people lived and worked, showing how communities worked within the physical realities (in terms of its topography, weather, tides, currents, etc.), of the Irish coastal landscape as well as the diversity of resources (salt, fish, marine mammals) available in different places.

IRELAND'S COASTLINE — ITS PHYSICAL AND ENVIRONMENTAL CHARACTER

Ireland's physical topography and island character have long been shaped by the sea; from the geological origins of its limestones and shales formed on the bed of a shallow tropical ocean aeons ago to its present-day maritime climate and weather (2). What is Ireland's coast like? Firstly, it is enormous. Although it is a small island, with its complex, fractal-like network of headlands and inlets, Ireland has a longer coastline (c.7,500 kilometres) than most European countries (certainly longer than France and Spain). Indeed, this island has one of the highest ratios of coastline to land surface of any in the world. It also possesses a coastline of astonishing diversity, with high cliffs along the west, earthy bluffs down the south-east, sand dunes everywhere, estuaries and both sandy and rocky sea-loughs at most points of the compass. It is quite varied too in terms of regions. The rugged fractals of the western Atlantic seaboard can be contrasted with the generally low-lying sandy coast of the east coast. Ireland's coastal landscapes, both natural and cultural, are built on a base of varying geology and topography.

Most of it is hard and rocky, as can be seen along the high cliffs of the west, south-west and north coasts, as well as their islands – where mountains and uplands often grade rapidly into the sea, sometimes leaving bays and inlets either side of long peninsulas (such as along the sandstone mountains of Cork, Kerry). These bays form sheltered harbours and are often places of long-term human settlement. The best known archaeologically is Strangford Lough, Co. Down, where extensive sand-flats are exposed at every low tide (3). Recent intertidal archaeological surveys have uncovered hundreds of archaeological sites, ranging from fish traps and tidal mills, kelp walls and harbours and landing places. Similarly dramatic are the limestone cliffs of Clare and the Aran Islands, and the hard granites of Donegal. Another large part of the Irish coastline (c.3,000 km) is low-lying, either consisting of bluffs of glacially derived soils, shingle or sandy shores, such as down the east coast from Meath to Wexford, or it is sand dunes and machair plains (a distinctive soil dominated by wind-blown sand) that are found along the north-west coast (Mayo, Sligo and Donegal).

2 Ballycastle, north Mayo – Ireland's northwest coast with its rocky cliffs and small sandy bays (Aidan O'Sullivan)

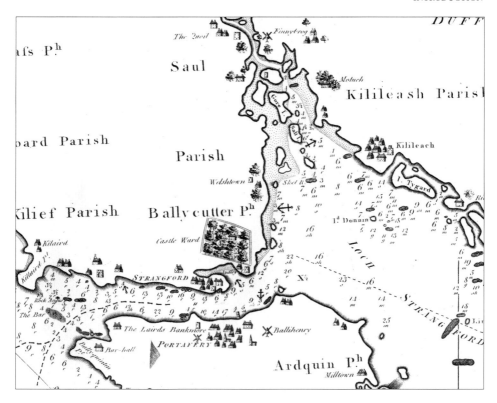

3 Detail of the Quoile estuary and Strangford Narrows (from Murdoch Mackenise's 1776 chart)

Estuaries are also a significant feature of the Irish coastline, where rivers ebb into the sea through vast areas of salt marshes, mudflats and beaches (*4*). Particularly significant estuarine landscapes are to be seen on the Shannon/ Fergus estuary, Castlemaine Harbour, Cork Harbour and Dundalk Bay, but also along many smaller rivers. Archaeological intertidal surveys on the Shannon estuary, in particular, pioneered the study of these landscapes and uncovered evidence for submerged forests, prehistoric marshland sites, Medieval fish traps and post medieval fish traps, piers and reclamation features. Finally, people have also modified the coast over generations, either by reclaiming and protecting it behind sea walls or by building towns and waterfronts along its edges. Indeed, our historical urban maritime archaeological heritage is probably both our richest and least understood.

Our coastal landscape is also a space where time has wrought more changes than those brought about by the processes of geology, coastal erosion and deposition. Much of Ireland's earlier coastal landscapes are now submerged under the sea. Over the last 10,000 years, the island of Ireland has slowly re-bounded from the original weight of the ice sheets that lay on it during the last Ice Age. This is not precisely the same everywhere, so that in the south-west the land is slowly tipping into the ocean, resulting in ancient ground surfaces now being

4 Shannon estuary – a marshland seascape of mudflats, salt marshes and reclaimed levels (Shannon estuary ports)

under water – meaning that is possible on the Shannon estuary at low tide to walk across peats and ancient submerged forests that once grew four and a half thousand years ago, but are now only to be seen at low tide. In contrast, the north-east part of the island is gradually rising upwards, so hundreds of metres inland from the present seashore, on the Antrim coastline for example, it is possible to see the terraces of ancient beaches (known as raised beaches) that were once lapped by the waves but are now in modern farmland. It need hardly be said the sea-level change is a complex process, much more complicated than will be presented in this book, but it is something that needs to be borne in mind when looking at archaeological sites. Indeed, recent archaeological, palaeogeographic and marine geophysical research indicate that submerged cultural landscapes may lie on the seabed around our coastline and that these may be amenable to investigation. In any case, we need to imagine that some coastal archaeological sites were once set in landscapes that were dramatically different to the modern coastline.

Living by the sea, people have also long had to contend with coastal weather (with its winds, rain and storms) and the movements of the sea itself (currents, waves and tides in particular). The Atlantic Ocean is of course one of the stormiest in the world and Ireland faces unprotected into its worst conditions. Winds drive salt and sand inland, hinder vegetation growth (the lack of trees across much of the west coast can be explained by wind, not rain) and cause communities to huddle into the shelter of bays and inlets. It also governs, along with currents and tides, when and how people move along the seaways. Prevailing winds are from the south to west, and in particular, although high winds can occur throughout the year, gales are most frequent in winter. Prior to modern ship technology, and the ability it has given seafarers to move against the wind and tolerate heavy seas, long-distance voyaging was a seasonal activity. Currents and wind conditions also have an impact on local navigation.

Bathed in the warming waters of the currents of the Gulf Stream, Ireland has better winters and a more moderate climate and might be expected at its latitude in the North Atlantic. There are also 'local' currents that are a product of the circulation of water around these islands and the coast of western Europe. One current moves up from the south-west and moves northwards along the west coast of Ireland. There are also currents that flow northwards up into the Irish Sea, and down from the north between Antrim and Scotland. Seasonal thermal sea fronts in these currents also influence sea life, particularly in terms of phytoplankton. In the summer time, the Irish Shelf Front causes the south-west coast of Ireland to have a very high population of seabirds, porpoises and dolphins. The Celtic Sea front off Wexford also supports the huge seabird populations of the region. There is also a significant front in the north part of the Irish Sea, between county Down and the Isle of Man, which supports a rich population of fish, seabirds and basking sharks. In the Middle Ages, climatic changes in the North Atlantic were to strongly influence the potential of this area for the movement of English and Irish fishing fleets.

Tidal conditions also are hugely important, particularly in terms of availability and character of food resources. The ebb and flow of the tides is governed by the waning and waxing of the moon, which moves water back and forth across the Atlantic. These tides vary according to the phase of the moon, with the great range or tidal amplitude occurring with the Full Moon and the New moon. Spring tides are those with the highest range, neaps are the lowest. In estuaries in particular, where the movement of the tides are constricted by land, the difference between high and low tides can be measured in terms of several metres. On the Shannon estuary vast areas of mudflats are thus exposed at low tide twice a day, enabling huge populations of seabirds and waders to feed on the nutrients left by both brackish and inflowing water. On open shorelines too, the tides expose a larder of shellfish and seaweed on rocks and pools that can be exploited by both birds and human populations.

Finally, all these factors – geological, geomorphological, ecological, climatic and oceanographic – strongly influence the character of coastal habitats and the environmental and economic resources they provide for people and animals. On cliff-tops and rocky islets, there may be enormous populations of kittiwakes, razorbills, guillemot and gannets. On the Blasket and Aran Islands, gathering seabirds and their eggs was an occasional food gathering strategy carried out by young men, who worked with ropes on the dangerous cliffs. Fishing was also carried out from the high cliffs using long lines. Seals can also be seen lying out sleepily on the rocks resting and digesting their food or frolicking in the water. These creatures have often been seen as eerily similar to human beings, and while they were occasionally hunted by Mesolithic hunter-gatherers, and they were certainly hunted for skins, meat and oil in the nineteenth century, they were also the focus of folk beliefs and legends. Rocky shorelines support crabs, barnacles, limpets and periwinkles, as well as edible seaweeds, waders and barnacle geese. They also provided seaweed for industry and agricultural fertilizer.

On sand dunes, coastal heaths and particularly the machair soils that are found on the north-western coast, there can be a thin, but nutritious growth of grasses and herbs. These can provide rich grazing land for cattle and sheep and until recently, coastal communities used them as commonage. People living on islands, bays and coastal plains are also used to the flotsam and jetsam brought in by the sea. Indeed, early Irish laws from the seventh and eighth century AD described the ownership of such harvests of the ocean. Particularly striking were the occasional stranding of whales, porpoises and dolphins, some of which may be described in early Irish annals. In the nineteenth century, the Blasket Islanders were familiar with the occasional deposition of timber, raw materials and exotic foods on their shores from local shipwrecks. While the islanders worked courageously to save unfortunate sailors, they also made good use of this gift from the ocean.

In estuaries, plant and nutrient-rich salt marshes and mudflats support teeming populations of seabirds, waders, fowl, eel and fishes and provide an attractive resource to people, while the grasses of the marshes have long been seen as rich grazing lands for cattle and sheep. In the nineteenth century, cattle herders were employed by local landlords to manage animals grazing on the marshes and also the 'corcass' – the reclaimed estuarine marshlands. Finally, we should remember the resources of the open sea itself. Sea-fishes that people have traditionally fished for out in the deep ocean include cod, plaice, herring and mackerel. There is also some historical tradition of whaling and hunting for the basking shark in Irish Atlantic waters. Closer in to the shore, in shallower waters, were herring, sprat, plaice and gurnard. Obviously, there is also a regional basis for fisheries. The Gaelic Lordships of the O'Sullivan Beares in the late Medieval period were located in the Beara Peninsula in south-west Ireland, a region of poor agricultural potential but rich maritime resources. Late medieval fleets fished for monkfish, cod, haddock, herring, pilchard, mackerel and plaice, and provided the basis of this lordship's wealth.

PEOPLES OF THE SEA?

Since people first came to Ireland they have inhabited coastal landscapes. They have lived beside the sea, using it as a source of food, raw materials and as a means of travel. However, people have also used the sea as a source of identity and belonging. Identity amongst coastal communities, as elsewhere, was fluid and mutable, negotiated by people themselves through their lives, and manipulated when the opportunity presented itself. Identity was socially and culturally constructed, deriving partly from ethnicity, gender and social class, but it was also constituted by practice; the routines of every-day life, the work that people did and their knowledge of, and daily engagement with, their environment (5).

Ethnic diversity amongst coastal communities has always been enhanced by the role of the sea as a nautical route between Ireland and the wider world. Previously, the fact of being an island has encouraged many to think of the sea as a boundary or even a frontier. However, while the farmer in the Irish midlands may not have often encountered foreigners (and even this is debatable), it can hardly be said of the coastal dweller, whether she was living on the late medieval Cork coastline or the vicinity of Viking Dublin. While prehistorians worry about the truth or otherwise of large-scale migrations, we are certain that throughout the Middle Ages different ethnic groups were moving around and interacting along the Atlantic sea-lanes.

At the beginning of the early medieval period, we know of constant cultural connections between Irish population groups and those of Scotland, England and Wales, while the occurrence of imported glass, pottery and other exotic items hints at further flung connections in western Europe and the Mediterranean. In the Viking Age, Scandinavian and Hiberno-Norse raiders, traders and settlers

5 Women gutting herring (UFTM)

were also moving around the Irish coast and establishing towns in Dublin, Waterford and Limerick. In the late medieval period, Anglo-Norman elites, along with their farming tenants and merchants established colonies in Ireland from their Severn estuary homelands, while English, Scottish and even Dutch settlers were introduced during sixteenth- and seventeenth-century plantations. Indeed, our coastal ports and towns of Ireland have had incredibly diverse ethnic communities since at least the Middle Ages (including Jews, Flemish, Huguenots, etc.), largely because of their extensive trading maritime contacts with France, Spain and other north-west European countries. Indeed, the sea has also long served to promote emigration from Ireland, as huge numbers left the island in the eighteenth and nineteenth century for new lives in Britain, America, Australia and the Caribbean. This global Irish diaspora has often then participated in, and sent home, new ideas to the homeland; diverse ideas ranging from politics to fashion and rock 'n' roll music.

Power, social status and the ensuing tensions between different social groups have also been played out against the backdrop of Ireland's coastal landscapes. Certainly, we can trace how control of the sea, and access to the rich economic resources it provided, has long been sought by the powerful. Early medieval promontory forts, for example, sited on commanding headlands with good views of landing places and seaways could be seen as symbols of local political power; designed to impress upon passers-by the high-status of the kings and nobles occasionally residing within them. In the Late Medieval period on the south-west and west coast, while Gaelic Irish lords did not have fishing fleets of their own, the O'Sullivan Beares, the O'Malleys and the O'Flahertys certainly exacted fishing dues and economic income from those continental fishing boats working their territorial waters. On the other hand, much of what we find as archaeologists along the Irish coastline materially represents the day-to-day work of ordinary people, who spent their lives fishing, gathering seaweed and grazing cattle.

Interestingly, we need also to consider the role of gender, age and kinship in our interpretations of coastal archaeology, particularly in terms of labour practices. It has been suggested that amongst Ireland's Mesolithic hunter-gatherers, the seashore was primarily a place for women and children, as ethnographic studies suggest that gathering was primarily done by women. In contrast, more recently fishing has been seen as a male activity. In some historical and ethnological contexts, men fix their own nets, tend their boats and avoid women on the way to sea. A woman's presence at the launching of a boat or on a boat was traditionally seen as bad luck. The sea was seen as feminine, as was the boat, but men worked the sea. The strong continuities and conservative traditions in maritime societies suggest that it is likely that throughout the medieval and early modern period, fishing was also divided into gender roles. Men would have fished by boats, made the fences and baskets and managed the traps out on the foreshore. Famously, it was young men who clambered down the cliffs of the Aran Islands, the Blasket Islands and St. Kilda off the Scottish coast, to take seabirds and their eggs.

However, this belies the work done by women along the seashore. Fishing, like any other economic activity, was in reality a co-operative venture in which men, women and children shared responsibilities. In recent historical times, women were largely responsible for gutting and processing the fish on the pier or harbour (a task rarely done by men). In a famous early twentieth-century photograph by R.J. Welch, we can see women working cleaning herring for curing on the waterfront at Ardglass, Co. Down. At Kilrush, Co. Clare, huge numbers of local women were involved in net-making, repair and the curing of fish. Throughout the nineteenth century, large groups of women worked as migrant labourers and moved around the Irish Sea region to work in the thriving herring industry. This must have been a difficult life. One perspective suggests that the collectivity of the women moving and working together must have provided some respite from the tight boundaries of social life in Ireland and allowed the women to develop independence and mutual strength. On the other hand, this was hard work and often poorly paid. The women spent much of their time away from their families and communities out of financial necessity. This displacement from community and associated imaginings becomes a predominant theme amongst the diaspora, and plays a central element in subsequent cultural constructs. Working with the sea then was difficult. It was work in a challenging and often dangerous environment, and we need to be conscious of this in case we over-romanticise coastal life in the past.

SEASCAPES, PLACE AND BELONGING

In recent years, archaeologists have approached the coastal zone using the idea of the 'maritime cultural landscape'. This approach emphasises the importance of integrating various disciplines in the investigation of the past perception, understanding and use of coastal regions from the seabed, across the foreshore and inland. It is certainly true that we need to think about entire coastal landscapes as texts wherein are written narratives of human activity on this island. Coastal landscapes, like other spaces, were more than environmental larders for the production of seafood. They were also storehouses of cultural values and traditions, places where ideas about community, ancestry, belonging and identity were constructed and enacted. People would have thought about and understood places along the coast in different ways. Indeed, we should also be aware that people would have used their knowledge of the sea to define themselves.

We need to think about the human shaping of these spaces. Ireland's coastline, as stated above, has been partly created by various natural forces – geological, climatic and environmental. Indeed, we might be tempted, when we look out at awesome Atlantic breakers crashing against western cliffs, or when we listen to the wilderness silence of an estuarine salt marsh, to think that our coast is essentially wild, untamed and 'natural'. In fact, our coastal landscapes have often been the product of centuries of human toil, drainage, building and exploitation. In their diversity, they reveal that people have constantly adjusted their lives to its rhythms, while also working constantly to adapt them to their needs. Examples of coastal landscapes actually made by people include the fields of the Aran Islands and the drained levels of the Wexford Slobs. Similarly, our machair plains have been largely created by centuries of grazing, whereby grasses were maintained by people and their animals.

Regional landscape perspectives also bring us closer to the reality of how coastal communities lived, worked and understood their worlds. Traditionally, archaeologists have seen coastal communities as specialized and paradoxically remote from significant social and economic changes. For example, archaeological studies of maritime islands used to see them as usefully bounded units of land, as 'island laboratories' wherein it was possible to trace the processes of social and historical change. More recently, archaeologists have approached islands in terms of 'seascapes' exploring islanders' connections and integration with other islands and the mainland. It is also true that coastal landscapes encourage us to think about movement and travel. In general, a person walking on primitive roads will travel about twenty miles a day. In contrast, people rowing a boat may travel up to forty miles, while a crew in a sailboat on a good day might travel eighty miles. Instantly, we can see that this shifts our perspective on distance. Coastal communities may have the ability to move easily up and down the coastlines, travelling much further and have more distant social and economic contacts than their inland cousins.

Even in coastal landscapes most lives are lived at the local scale. In the past, people would have been born in a particular place, would have lived out most of their lives there and upon their death, their family and friends would have buried them within sight of their birthplace. Obviously, there was the possibility for many of long-distance travel across the sea – we need only consider the movements of Norse settlers across the North Atlantic to realize this. However, most people would have had a close and intimate knowledge of a particular estuary, shoreline or island. Obviously, much of this fine-grained, detailed knowledge is lost to us. We can get a sense of this when we realise that on the Irish coastline in the recent past, every rock, pool, headland and geological oddity was given a name, or was associated with an event or incident (often a wreck or drowning).

Such local folklore is often lost to us as archaeologists. In the words of the novelist W.G. Sebald it reminds us that 'everything is constantly lapsing into oblivion with very extinguished life … in that the history of countless places and objects which themselves have no power of memory is never heard, never described or passed on'. However, archaeology itself is about remembering, or more accurately making a memory of such forgotten places. We do gain a sense of the role of history in the intimate, local knowledge of places and objects through people's use and re-use of material culture. At Ballymacaward, Co. Donegal, a burial mound a short distance from the sea was used for many generations, with early medieval burials placed in a mound that has been used in the Bronze Age and Iron Age. Similar senses of local memory making can be traced through exploring the inhabitation of an island, sand-dune or particular promontory across time. For example, we can see how sometimes medieval wooden fish traps were abandoned, but were then replaced by post medieval fish traps hundreds of years later. It is almost as if local fishermen used their knowledge of the archaeology of estuarine mudflats to choose the best place to build fish traps in the nineteenth century.

Indeed, we would argue that local knowledge was a significant source of social identity for people in the past. We can start thinking about how people's daily encounters with the hidden and intimate places of the coast – the salt marshes, creeks and channels of the estuary, the windswept islands of the west – would have influenced how they thought about themselves and others. Local fishermen working everyday out at sea would have experienced a sense of isolation and distinctiveness from the broader community. They worked the coastal landscape at the same time as it worked on them. Furthermore, they would have possessed a unique knowledge of places, an awareness of the dangers of rocks and pools, and an appreciation of how to move through and across treacherous marshes. So these same fishermen could have actively used their exclusive and specialist knowledge of places to create and sustain a unique sense of identity within that broader community. So, we should be thinking about coastal communities as seeing themselves different from those further inland. The classic example is that of historical fishing village communities, who have often been seen as close-knit, conservative and even secretive about some aspects of their work.

TIME AND TIDES

Working with the archaeology of dynamic coastal landscapes encourages us to think about time. It is true that our coast is not fixed, but constantly changing. While soil and sand is eroded from one place, they are deposited elsewhere. As cliffs and rocky shorelines are worn away, muds and silts are laid down in silent lagoons. In other words, time is all-pervasive on the coast – tides, currents, and weather – all changing constantly according to daily, monthly and seasonal rhythms. In thinking about how people inhabited and understood time in coastal landscapes, it is useful to think in terms of different temporal cycles and rhythms, all moving and working together.

We can identify in coastal archaeology long-term continuities, deep underlying structures and patterns of persistence and reiterative practices across the generations. In this book, there are many topics and ideas that will recur again and again. For example, we can point to the seaways between Ireland, Scotland

and south-west England, showing how important they were to Neolithic farmers, Bronze Age mariners, Romano-British traders, early Irish pirates and raiders, all working to the winds and currents between these islands. Indeed, John Waddell in writing about the distribution of prehistoric monuments and objects around the Irish Sea region has previously suggested that there were long-standing patterns of communication across this sea that may have had an impact on kinship links, political structures and even linguistic developments. Indeed, the 'Celticisation' of Ireland and the evolution of linguistically similar languages along this Atlantic shoreline in later prehistory may actually reflect long-standing maritime cultural connections, rather than any migrations of peoples with their spoken tongues.

Similarly, at a local scale, there appears to be an immense continuity in the activities that led to the creation of coastal shell middens. While these are traditionally seen as 'Mesolithic', we will explore the long-lived coastal activities and practices that led to the creation and accumulation of mounds of shells, stone, earth, bone and objects across at least six thousand years of Ireland's history. Middens vary in character; from small heaps of shells of a single species, to complex sites with intercalated layers of sand, stone and shells; to the massive mounds found around Cork Harbour, Galway Bay and Ballysodare Bay, Co. Sligo. Furthermore, radiocarbon dating shows that middens are chronologically complex and can be dated to the Mesolithic, Neolithic, Bronze Age, Iron Age, early medieval, late medieval and even post medieval periods. What we are certainly witnessing here is the movement of people to rocky foreshores and pools across thousands of years, for the gathering of oysters, mussels, periwinkles or other shellfish for food, fishing bait or even industrial reasons (i.e. production of dyestuffs). Interpreting coastal archaeology in terms of the *longue-durée* (long-term) enables us to identify these deep, underlying structures of life by the seashore. However, it would be a mistake to think of these as culturally or socially similar practices – the thinking, social context and economic needs behind these middens undoubtedly changed across time. Somebody eating oysters in a medieval town was most definitely not living a 'Mesolithic' lifestyle. Indeed, the seeming waxing and waning across time of the exploitation of such maritime resources in Ireland remains a subject of debate and puzzlement.

People living in coastal landscapes may work to different temporal rhythms than their country cousins, revealing perhaps the mentalities of coastal communities. On an estuary or along the seashore, time is measured by a different clock. There are the unique daily and monthly rhythms of the tides to consider, with its diurnal cycles of low and high tides, of neaps and springs tides. The passing of the seasons can also be recognised through observation of the rhythms of the natural world. A coastal dweller can observe the seasonal migrations of waders, ducks and geese – huge numbers of which over winter – by marshes, mudflats and coastal waterways. He can note also the seasonal movement of fish, from the herring of the deep sea to the summer arrival on estuaries of salmon, the autumn departure of eels. He can watch the seasonal changes in vegetation, knowing when to cut willow and reeds for basketry and thatch. People use their knowledge of these temporal rhythms to build an understanding of the world. So, for example, in recent west of Ireland folklore, the first Spring tide in May was known as *Rabharta Mór na n-Éan* ('the great Spring tide of the birds'), as it was believed that birds observed the height of this flood-tide before they built their marshland nests so as to put them out of reach of danger.

However, there can be problems with this. People are not passive creatures that simply react to environmental forces, but agents that try every day to make their own worlds. Across the generations, we can pick out periods of time of profound social and economic change in coastal landscapes. In the later Middle Ages, it is arguable that the Anglo-Norman colonisation of Ireland can be closely linked with the importance of the herring fisheries in the north Irish Sea, and it is potentially the case that it enabled its success. Similarly, the sturdy Martello towers around the Irish coastline represent a period of worry that people had that Ireland would be invaded during the Napoleonic wars of the early nineteenth century.

We can also think about coastal landscapes in terms of the short-term events. Above all, a shipwreck is the archaeological traces of a moment in time, when despite the best efforts of human ingenuity and technology, a ship is driven by currents and winds onto the rocks (6). Literally, it becomes at that moment a time capsule, preserving the social and ideological character of its crew and cargo in the sands. While all archaeological sites represent a moment in time, there are few

6 A Greencastle yawl

that so eloquently express the impact of a single event on people's lives. However, even that moment can also be understood in terms of long-term processes. Look at the map of Ireland's shipwrecks, which depicts individual moments of tragedy across literally hundreds of years. Yet see the density of wrecks off Dublin, Wexford and Dundalk, and consider how cumulatively they represent the long-term importance of those ports for Irish society.

CONCLUSIONS

In conclusion, looking at the physical character of the Irish coastline, and in considering questions about identity, landscape and time, we can see that there is a range of ways of exploring the archaeology of the Irish coast. We have chosen a traditional chronological approach in this first maritime archaeology of Ireland. However, throughout we also explore themes of settlement and dwelling, labour and economy, the symbolic role of the ocean, and the use of the sea for trade, travel and communication. We intend that these recurring investigations be seen as deliberately reiterative – but also that the same social and cultural explanations cannot be provided for seemingly similar patterns. In any case, in this book we hope to tell some of the many stories of past peoples that lived by the sea. We hope that it will encourage others to begin to explore archaeologies of this island's coastal communities.

2

Mesolithic hunter-gatherers: life and death by the seashore, 8000-4000 BC

INTRODUCTION

One day, 10,000 years ago, a group of hunter-gatherers lifted their paddles and beached their boat somewhere on the Irish coastline. Stepping out onto the shore, these men and women found themselves at the edge of a land with no other human occupants but with a rich environment and wildlife. Long used to living by the coast and knowledgeable of its spaces, rhythms and food sources, they knew that they could gather oysters, mussels, limpets and birds eggs along the shore, that they could trap salmon and eels in the estuaries, and collect flint and other stone pebbles from the beaches for their stone tools. Beyond the expanses of the coastal environments, moving into the woodlands and mountains, they would quickly discover and explore a land that was recovered from the last Ice Age, with woodlands of birch and Scots pine growing around reedy lakes and rivers.

We don't know where these first human settlers of this island came from, presumably from somewhere in the geographical areas now known as western Britain or western France, but it is certain that they came here by skin or bark-covered boats or wooden canoes. For thousands of years afterwards, between 8000-4000 BC, Mesolithic hunter-gatherers lived on and travelled across this island, moving through the woodlands in the summer, paddling along its rivers, gathering along lakeshores in autumn and returning to the seashore at various times of the year. Indeed, it is possible that some communities primarily either inhabited inland woods and river valleys, while others chose coastal landscapes. The men and women of these Mesolithic communities trapped, fowled and fished on rivers and the seashore and indeed, coastal foods were very important to them. This is because they inhabited a landscape remarkably restricted in flora and fauna. However, there were some large mammals present that could be hunted, such as wild pig, wild cat and mountain hare (while brown bear and wolves may have been less prey than predators).

This way of life and its patterns of movement involved more than an economic effort to 'exploit' food resources, it was also a way of life that revolved around people's interest in living a good life, in meeting up occasionally at good places to exchange news, stories, information, or to strengthen social bonds through sharing food, feasting, friendship and marriage. Although our archaeological evidence for the Mesolithic period is scanty enough, we nonetheless have good knowledge of coastal life, particularly from a few sites that have produced evidence for occupation activities, the exploitation of shellfish, fish and waterfowl, as well as the occasional butchery of stranded seals and whales. In fact, archaeologists now believe that the sea was of key importance for these Mesolithic communities, being seen as much more than a source of economic benefit, but also as a storehouse of cultural traditions and values and a place that was central to people's lives, symbolic beliefs and practices.

LIVING BY THE SEA IN THE MESOLITHIC

Mesolithic hunter-gatherers and their seascapes

Mesolithic archaeological sites in Ireland are mostly situated in coastal locations, being particularly densely distributed along the north-east coast (7). This is probably mostly due to archaeological research activities since the nineteenth century, which have tended to focus on such coastal locations. There is no doubt that both early and late Mesolithic peoples were also living and moving through the midlands, using the rivers in particular to move through a wooded landscape. Mesolithic occupation sites have been identified by lakeshores, on inland bluffs and in various other locations. Nevertheless, Mesolithic communities did attach a particular significance to the coast – and some key archaeological sites for understanding the Mesolithic in Ireland are coastal – such as Ferriter's Cove, Co. Kerry, Rockmarshall, Co. Louth, Sutton and Dalkey Island, Co. Dublin, as well as more recently discovered sites at Belderrig, Co. Mayo and on Rathlin Island, Co. Antrim.

However most of this abundant archaeological evidence for Mesolithic activity in coastal landscapes has been in the form of lithic scatters, it has often proved difficult to discover actual dwelling places or occupation structures. People moving seasonally through the land may have lived in simple shelters that were built quickly and that have left little archaeological trace other than spreads of charcoal and some worked stone. Mesolithic camp sites on the edge of the shore may also have been submerged since by subsequent sea-level rise, destroyed by storms and erosion or buried under layers of coastal alluvium. Even when Mesolithic occupation sites are discovered by archaeologists (such as at Ferriter's Cove, Co. Kerry) the evidence is usually limited to hearths, working surfaces, pits and postholes that are the product of many phases of occupation, as people returned several times over the centuries.

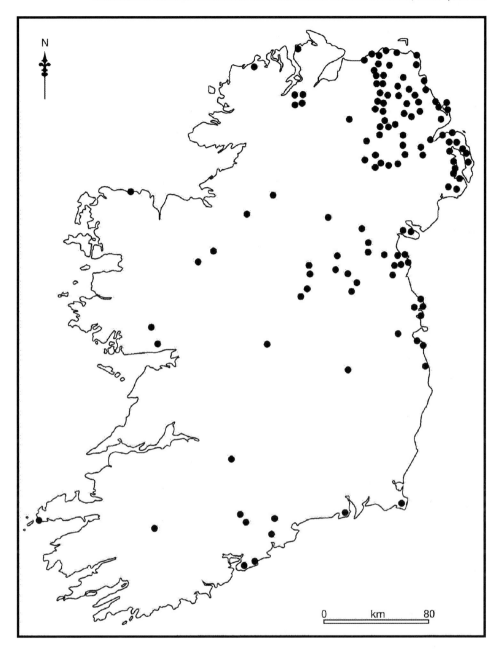

7 Map of Ireland showing locations of Mesolithic hunter-gatherer sites (after Stout 1997)

While archaeologists have traditionally investigated the functional, economic aspects of Mesolithic life by the seashore, it is worth also thinking about how hunter-gatherers lived by the ocean's edge in terms of cultural beliefs and practices. For Mesolithic hunter-gatherers in Ireland, the seashore was a place of social, ideological and economic importance. It was the place that sustained them, provided them with food, raw materials and other resources, while it was also probably a space of symbolic and ritual activity. We can begin by thinking about how life by the ocean, and its seasonal and environmental patterns, constituted and framed people's social lives. Seascapes are governed by seasonal, monthly and daily rhythms that depend on the tides in particular. For example, every low tide exposes a shoreline and rock pools in which many things can be seen and gathered before the flooding tide sweeps in and covers the shore. Mesolithic hunter-gatherers would have been aware of differences in tides (e.g. between the springs and neaps tides), and would have understood other things, such as ocean currents, winds and other weather changes.

Ethnographic studies indicate that hunter-gatherers dwelling by the seashore live in tune with the seasonal rhythms of the ocean, monitoring the migrations of seabirds, fish and marine mammals, or attending to the seasonal resources of shellfish, seaweed and driftwood. Indeed, there is evidence for seasonal activities amongst Mesolithic hunter-gatherers, even where it is clear that they lived by the shoreline all year around. At the Mesolithic midden on Dalkey Island, grey seal bones found during archaeological excavations may be evidence for the trapping of these marine mammals during the winter, when they typically congregate to bear their seal pups. At Ferriter's Cove, zoological analyses of fish bones recovered from the archaeological excavations indicated the presence of particular fish species, suggesting that people were fishing the seashore during the summer and autumn.

Mesolithic hunter-gatherers used the resources of the seashore in various ways. Apart from birds, fish and shellfish, other foods can be found there. It is possible that some edible seaweeds were used for food. It is also likely that dolphin, whale and especially sealskins were used for making clothing, caps or belts or the covering of boats and shelters. Graeme Warren has noted that we should not imagine their clothes as drab and discoloured, and that hunter-gatherers such as the Ainu people of Japan procure and prepare fish skins for clothing, for example, as salmon skins produce durable, silver-coloured leather that is startling to the eye. The feathers of seabirds may also have been used in hair or clothing decoration, while the purple dyes from dog whelk shells might have been used in tattooing the body and for decorating clothes. It is also likely that pebble of flint and other workable stone could have been gathered from the seashore or coastal cliffs. What is important to consider here is how seascapes clothed the people, fed them, provided them with raw materials of stone, skins and driftwood. This landscape was also to be important throughout their lives, and as we will argue below, at the end of their lives.

Indeed, accepting the importance of the ocean to Mesolithic hunter-gatherers in Ireland, it is hard not to conclude that their seascapes need to be understood in many different ways; social, economic and symbolic. We might remember that amongst virtually all hunter-gatherers, the landscape itself is imbued with symbolic, spiritual meanings and power and there is little distinction made between different forms of life; whether they be people, marine mammals, fish or birds. It might be suggested then that the daily and seasonal practice of gathering food on the coastal shore would also have been work imbued with social and symbolic importance. It has been suggested by some Mesolithic archaeologists working from ethnographic analogies, that the seashore was a place for women and children, while men would have been more active in hunting and trapping in the woodlands. There are obviously problems with this idea, not least the gender stereotypes it promotes and the lack of archaeological evidence that might be used to confirm it. However, it is certainly true that during the Mesolithic in Ireland, children would have grown up learning, whether it was from their mothers or fathers, the different foods, weather, tides and other phenomena associated with the sea.

EARLY MESOLITHIC MOUNT SANDEL AND THE SEA

The earliest known Mesolithic settlement on this island was located at Mount Sandel, Co. Derry, situated on the River Bann a few kilometres upstream from its estuary (8, 9). Peter Woodman's archaeological excavations of this early Mesolithic (i.e. the period between 8000-6500 BC) site in the 1970s indicated that people had returned to this place several times in the centuries following 8000 BC. They built and occupied several phases of fairly substantial circular huts, measuring 6m in diameter, with an internal space of 30m² and a hearth near the centre. These huts were constructed by placing thick saplings, up to 20cm in diameter, into angled postholes, lashing them together and then roofing the structure with rushes, turfs or perhaps even seal-skins. These were large structures and would have been snug and warm. Ethnographic studies suggest that the internal space of such huts would be occupied by a single, extended family. It is possible that the Early Mesolithic occupation site at Mount Sandel consisted of no more than 2–3 houses occupied at any one time. Each house may have been used by a band of 1–2 families, totaling perhaps 10–12 people in all, but it was a community who lived there in winter and summer and returned to the site frequently.

Inside the huts, there were several storage pits and hearths filled with occupation soil, hazelnut shells and burnt animal bone, indicating cooking and eating inside the shelters. Outside, there were several large pits used for rubbish disposal or for food storage. Other pits filled with burnt stone may have been used for cooking. Flint waste and implements were abundant on the site, comprising up to 44,386 artefacts, 3.3 per cent of them being what archaeologists call finished or retouched tools.

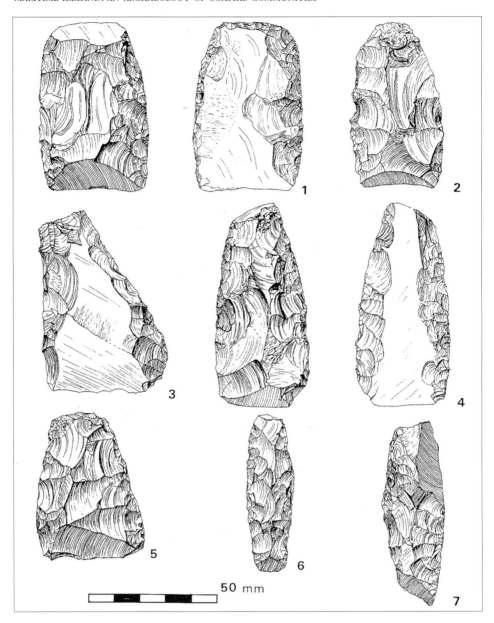

50 mm

8 Mount Sandel flint flake axes (after Woodman 1985)

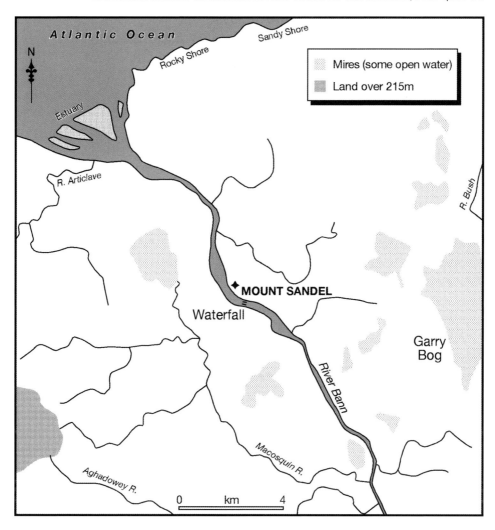

9 Map showing location of Mount Sandel in its wider landscapes. It is likely that hunter-gatherers traveled to the coast to trap fish and gather raw materials (after Woodman 1985)

The tools produced on the site form part of the characteristic flint technology of the Early Mesolithic in Ireland; narrow-bladed 'microliths' (meaning 'small stones'), produced by a technique known as indirect percussion (the use of a stone hammer with an antler or bone punch in the striking of the flint core).

These microliths would have been used in composite tools, being inserted and glued into wooden or antler handles. It is not known how they were used. They may have been arrow-tips, harpoons, knives or some type of tool used in the processing or grating of plant foods. Indeed, this latter tool would have been useful to a community who, at some times of the year, probably lived more off gathered plant foods than hunted meat. Other flint implements include scrapers, burins and awls – probably used for preparing skins, butchering meat, preparing edible plants for meals and the working of wood and bone. Several types of stone axes were found on the site. The different types of core and flake axes may have been used for cutting and planning wood, for dismembering meat, for food preparation and digging of plant foods. Some of the flint pebbles used for these tools were probably carried to the site from the coast, from a location only a few kilometres away.

Plant foods eaten on the site included hazelnuts (high in protein, starch and carbohydrates) gathered in the autumn, white water-lily seeds and pear/apple seeds. Wild pig dominated the animal bones, being largely of young pig that had been hunted during the winter. There was also some mountain hare and dog or wolf. Birds, waders and waterfowl were also being hunted or trapped, including birds that would have been taken from the seashore and waterways, such as mallard, teal, widgeon and red-throated diver. It is also likely that some birds, such as eagle may have been taken for plumage.

Fishing was very significant at Mount Sandel, and studies indicate that this was mostly for salmon, sea trout and eels from the river, although there was also indication of sea fishing for flounder and sea-bass from the nearby coastal estuary of the River Bann and further out on the inshore shallows along the northern Irish coastline. These fish could have been taken at certain times of the year, especially early summer and autumn and Mount Sandel with its location overlooking rapids in the River Bann, could have been a place where fish traps were built, maintained and used.

In conclusion, Mount Sandel is generally interpreted as the residence of a hunter-gatherer group who settled there throughout much of the year, living off the resources of the river, wetlands, uplands and coastal environments all situated relatively close by. It has also been used to suggest that in the early Mesolithic, hunter-gatherer groups may have had a near sedentary lifestyle, with places like Mount Sandel serving as almost permanent 'base-camps', while other smaller campsites may have been occupied on a more transitory, episodic basis. Other early Mesolithic sites have been discovered right on the coast, but the presence of sea fish, seabirds and even the pebble flint probably gathered from the seashore at Mount Sandel indicates that the maritime landscape was of key importance at the beginning of the story of human activity on this island.

LATE MESOLITHIC COASTAL SITES

Although we have no late Mesolithic (i.e. the period between 5500-4000BC) settlement sites like Mount Sandel, there are several coastal occupation sites that date to this period. Most are found at sites close to water, typically along rivers, lakes and coastal zones, indicating that fishing and use of coastal resources remained as important as before. Although not always easy to understand, it is clear that some parts of the Irish coastline saw a lot of Mesolithic activity over hundreds of years.

Late Mesolithic sites are easily identified partly because of the distinctive types of tools they produce. In the late Mesolithic, from about 5500 BC onwards, there is a technological shift towards a typically Irish (although it is also found in the Isle of Man) or insular technology, based on hard hammer technology and the production of heavy or robust blades (known by the very end of the late Mesolithic as Bann flakes). This technology, which is island-wide, may suggest a dynamic and active use of technology to construct social identities across the island's population (which may have been no more than a couple of thousand people).

Particularly interesting are the late Mesolithic sites found on what are known as raised beaches, particularly along the north-east coast of Ireland. Raised beaches appear to be the topographical remnants of a period when relative sea levels were higher in this region. These sites remind us of the scale of physical changes on the Irish coastline since early prehistory. Late Mesolithic coastal lithic scatters have traditionally been the main focus of archaeological investigation, going back into the 1930s and 1940s at places like Cushendun, Co. Antrim, Larne, Co. Antrim and around Strangford Lough. Originally these would have been occupation sites situated close to the shoreline, and thence they are often partly destroyed by erosion, with water-rolled lithics scattered through beach deposits, with little evidence for animal bone or economic activity. They are situated today on terraces set back from the shoreline, because sea level change in the millennia since has meant that sea levels are now much lower than they once were. Tom McErlean has recently reviewed all the shell middens around Strangford Lough. Although there are undoubtedly large numbers of Neolithic, Bronze Age and historic shell middens on the islands and around the edges of the lough, there is a strong sense from the distribution of Mesolithic lithics and the middens that many of them originated in the late Mesolithic (*10*).

On the other hand, there is also evidence that substantial parts of the original Mesolithic coastline are now under the sea – particularly along the west and southern coasts of Ireland, where Relative Sea Level changes since the last Ice Age, combined with dynamic coastal geomorphological developments may have lead to modern sea levels being at least 6-7m higher today than they were during the Mesolithic. It is likely that early prehistoric palaeoenvironmental deposits and archaeological sites lie submerged under the ocean. Indeed, intertidal archaeological surveys have identified both Mesolithic and Neolithic submerged peats and forests down the west coast and on the Shannon estuary foreshore – with stone axes and animal bone recovered from some. It is possible that multidisciplinary underwater archaeological and marine geophysical research could lead to the discovery of submerged Mesolithic landscapes and the sites that existed within them.

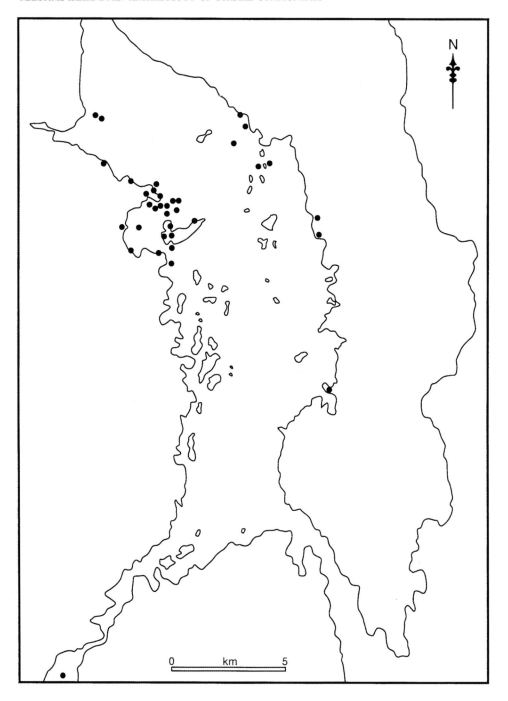

10 Distribution of shell middens and Late Mesolithic flint scatters around Strangford Lough (after McErlean, McConkey and Forsythe 2002)

LATE MESOLITHIC ESTUARINE FISH TRAPS ON DUBLIN BAY

It has also long been suspected that the coastal and riverine distribution of late Mesolithic sites in Ireland suggested fishing activities – with hunter-gatherer groups residing by the shore and using fish-spears, nets, baskets or fish traps to harvest the waters. Most of the fish bones found on late Mesolithic sites in Ireland are inshore species, such as mullet, wrasse, sole and tope – suggesting that they were taken from rocky shallows using nets or from estuaries using fishing structures. Until recently, we have had little sense of what such fishing equipment and structures looked like. Fish traps are barriers, either of stone walls or wooden fences, erected in riverine and estuarine waters. They usually are V-shaped in plan, guiding fish towards the apex of the fences where there may be a net or basket which is used to trap the fish. They exploit the tendency of fish to move up with flooding tides and to drop down the shore with the ebbing tide. One would expect to find the archaeological traces of such structures in the form of alignments of upright, wooden posts in original intertidal shore deposits.

Fish traps are known from around Britain and Ireland, where they have been mostly dated to the medieval or post medieval period. In contrast, the archaeology of The Netherlands, Denmark and France has included a range of wooden fish traps discovered in estuarine and coastal waters that have been dated to the Mesolithic. This archaeological evidence implies that Mesolithic hunter-gatherers were managing and exploiting fish in a fairly systematic way, gathering the raw materials, building the structures and maintaining them against the erosion and destruction by currents and waves.

Recently, archaeological excavations by Melanie McQuade for Margaret Gowen and Co. at North Wall Quay, in Dublin city have discovered spectacular evidence for Ireland's earliest fish traps (*11*). The site was located under reclaimed ground in the city's northern quays, but would originally have been on the silty foreshore of the estuary of the Liffey. There were at least five wooden fish traps, varying in size and form, broadly dating to a surprisingly early date range of 6100-5720 BC.

The most distinctive trap was a stake row of hazel posts, 25m in length, which was possibly associated with a woven basket of hazel and rushes that was circled by wooden stakes. Other post-and-wattle fences, platforms, a possible C-shaped trap (2.7m x 1m), stake rows and scatters of worked wood were found around the foreshore, suggesting both regular activity there, as well as a continuity of practice across time. It seems that a hunter-gatherer group living in the locality were gathering narrow hazel rods, trimming them with stone axes, and constructing a variety of fishing structures on the intertidal zone. There was little evidence for gutting fish on-site, although some crabs may have been accidentally trapped amongst the posts. Melanie McQuade suggests that the fish traps were used for catching flounder, plaice, mullet and other estuarine species, noting that these estuarine waters would have had a richer range of species than Ireland's

11 Mesolithic fish trap recently excavated at Dublin's North Quay (Melanie McQuade, of Margaret Gowen and Co. Ltd)

inland waters (where fish species would have been limited to salmon and eels). It is unclear where the users of these fish traps lived, but there is certainly late Mesolithic archaeology around Dublin Bay, as will be discussed below.

INTERPRETING LATE MESOLITHIC COASTAL SHELL MIDDENS

Late Mesolithic coastal occupation sites and shell middens, like those found around Dublin Bay, have also produced evidence for settlement and economy. These coastal occupation sites are usually identifiable through their 'rubbish heaps' – known to archaeologists as shell middens. These are small mounds or layers of shells, ash, sand, charcoal and bone, usually lying as complex, stratified lenses of dark, organic rich material in beach deposits. They range in size and composition, from discrete, thin lenses to large distinctive mounds of shells – the latter usually dating from later prehistory or the historic period. They are essentially dumps of food waste and other debris. However they were often used themselves as occupation sites, and even burial places, from early prehistory to the post medieval period.

In the late Mesolithic, it is thought that middens are evidence for the episodic use and occupation, for relatively short periods of time, of places along the coast and that they were associated with the gathering of food on the seashore and the working of flint and perhaps other organic materials. In essence, Mesolithic middens tend to be small, discrete dumps of shells that accumulate across time to cover relatively large areas of ground. These sites are usually interpreted as places used by small groups of mobile hunter-gatherers who may have been perpetually on the move. It is clear from these middens that gathering of shellfish for food or bait was an important activity on the shoreline adjacent to these middens. Shellfish recovered from middens include oysters; mussels, limpets, periwinkles and crabs gathered from the rocks; clams and cockles taken from the beaches and silts, while whelks and crabs may have been caught in baited basket traps. Some of this shellfish meat may have been for human consumption; or for baiting basket traps or hooked lines; or for producing dyes for decorating clothes.

It is likely too that edible seaweeds were cut with flint blades from the rocky foreshores at low tide, especially during the warm summer months when seaweed growth is at its height. The modern bushcraft expert Ray Mears has written that the best and most common edible seaweeds are rich in minerals, particularly iodine, and have notable amounts of protein and carbohydrates (although not all of this is digestible). Seaweeds are also astonishingly rich in vitamins. A modest 'serving' (i.e. 100g) of edible seaweed will provide you with over half your daily requirement of vitamin C and more than the daily requirement of vitamins A, B2, B12, sodium, potassium and magnesium, as well as amounts of chlorine, calcium and vitamin D. Obviously, such organic material will rarely survive in archaeological contexts. It is interesting though that some shellfish found in middens like Ferriter's Cove are too small to have been used for food. Some of these shells may in fact have been attached to the stems and leaves of seaweed and so may have been accidentally deposited in the middens as people brought seaweed itself up to the dwelling place.

LATE MESOLITHIC MIDDENS AT DALKEY ISLAND, SUTTON AND ROCKMARSHALL

On other middens, such as Dalkey Island, Sutton and at places like Cushendun, there is also evidence for exploitation of whales, dolphins and grey seals. It is difficult to know whether these were hunted or not. In the case of the whales, it seems more likely that creatures naturally stranded on the beaches were dispatched and butchered. No doubt, such an occurrence, the seeming offering of the whale's life to the people would have been an event redolent of myth and symbolism. Even the presence of massive whalebone lying for years after on the midden would have been a monument to that event.

Although few late Mesolithic middens have been excavated in Ireland, and only a handful have been subjected to multidisciplinary, scientific excavations, because of the lack of other excavations, they remain key sites for our interpretation of the period, Amongst the most significant middens to be excavated in the past are the sites at Rockmarshall, Co. Louth, Dalkey Island and Sutton, on opposite sides of Dublin Bay and Ferriter's Cove, Co. Kerry.

Dalkey Island is situated 400m off the coast on the south side of Dublin Bay, overlooked by the high hill of Killiney and is separated from the mainland by a narrow, but dangerous sound with a strong tidal current. It is a small island, but is habitable due to the presence of a natural spring and the island is also surprisingly strategically located on Dublin Bay and the Irish east coast, as can be seen by anybody approaching Ireland on the ferry to Dublin today. David Liversage's excavations in the 1950s revealed evidence for Mesolithic, Neolithic, Bronze Age and early medieval activity on a promontory at the island's north-west corner (12). In early prehistory, there was a sequence of midden activity and occupation here, just above the island's only sandy beach looking out towards the mainland. Two small archaeological excavations (sites II and V) produced late Mesolithic and Neolithic artifacts – and these discoveries have recently been reinterpreted by Barbara Leon.

Site V, tucked up against a rock outcrop at the promontory's north-west end, produced an extensive midden of limpet shells, as well as collections of flint artifacts (Bann flakes, scrapers, blades), cores, hammer stones, and a type of bevelled pebble tool that are often known as 'limpet scoops'. Other finds include a stone axe, a schist roughout and a grinding stone. There were also postholes under the midden, indicating that there had been structures there before its formation. The occupation activity could be dated to between 5970-5560 BC, down to very late in the Mesolithic at 4620-4250 BC. However, there was also activity on this site down to 3760-3370 BC, in the early Neolithic.

Site II was also situated on the terrace underneath the steep, rock outcrop. It was also an extensive midden of shells and occupation material stretching across the ground between the rock and the sea. Bones were recovered from cattle, sheep, seal, fish and birds, leaf-shaped arrowheads, a scraper, cores, hammerstones, stone axe heads and Neolithic pottery. A human burial underneath the shell midden was radiocarbon dated to 3350-2700 BC. The body was disarticulated, but the cranium was filled with periwinkles – despite the fact that the surrounding midden was mostly of limpets. The midden also sealed a cache of thirteen Mesolithic blades and flakes – that seem to have been deliberately and carefully deposited pointing downwards in a pit. This find certainly could be interpreted as a ritualised, structured deposit of objects into the ground. There were also stake holes from a structure that predated the midden. It is likely that the Site II midden is late Mesolithic in date, with earliest dates from 5980-5620 BC. However, there was at least some activity on this spot at about 1450-1050 BC, in the Middle Bronze Age.

The Dalkey Site II and V middens, rather than being a place inhabited continuously, may represent multiple, episodic activities on this terrace looking out into Dalkey Sound across thousands of years in the Mesolithic and the

12 Dalkey Island, Co. Dublin, location of Mesolithic and Neolithic occupation sites (Aidan O'Sullivan)

Neolithic. The island's occasional occupants trapped seals, pig, birds and fish and gathered limpets. They also brought beach cobbles of dolerite, schist, mudstone and shale and flint onto the island, probably from the beaches along the Killiney shoreline to the south-west, so as to make stone axes on grinding stones. They also deposited some of these stone tools, as well as other flakes and blades, in pits and caches, presumably as part of religious or symbolic practices on this distinctive island. We should probably imagine Dalkey Island then as a place used occasionally, perhaps seasonally and that it was slightly at the edge of things, where both 'domestic' and 'ritual' activities went on within sight of the mainland.

Looking from Dalkey Island to the north across Dublin Bay, it is almost possible to see the site of another late Mesolithic midden at Sutton. This was a large (although thinly layered) shell midden that lay along the southern shore of what would then have been the island of Howth. It is now at the end of the peninsula connected to the mainland because of sea level and coastal geomorphological changes. The midden was up to 100m in length, but lay to a depth of only 30cm. It produced evidence for the exploitation of at least twenty different types of shellfish, including limpets, whelks, cockles, scallops, periwinkles, oysters and mussels. There was also some evidence for occupation activities and lithic production on the middens. Animal bones recovered included wild pig, hare, wolf and fish. A range of radiocarbon dates between 4340-3810 BC indicate the probability of activities at the end of the Mesolithic, moving into the early Neolithic period.

From the Hill of Howth today, one can see the Cooley peninsula lying across the sea on the skyline to the north. There are late Mesolithic shell middens on the southern shoreline of these mountains, at Rockmarshall, Co. Louth. The Mesolithic sites are situated on a raised beach overlooking the broad expanse and extensive intertidal flats of modern Dundalk Bay. Frank Mitchell excavated three middens in this location. These excavations indicated that Mesolithic hunter-gatherers collected oyster, periwinkle, limpet, whelk, mussel and cockles – perhaps at various times of the year. There were only a few finds of flint flakes, blades, cores and bevel-ended beach pebbles. Midden III produced charcoal radiocarbon dated to 4570-4040 BC, with human bone from the midden dated to 4774-4366 BC.

LATE MESOLITHIC COASTAL OCCUPATION AT FERRITERS COVE, CO. KERRY

The late Mesolithic coastal occupation site at Ferriter's Cove, Co. Kerry was excavated by Peter Woodman in the 1980s and unlike many of the sites discussed above, was subjected to multidisciplinary scientific studies. The site was originally located on a level terrace or rock platform near a beach on a small bay at the western tip of Dingle Peninsula – right out at the edge of Atlantic Europe (13). Palaeoenvironmental studies indicate that the bay was then fringed by oak and hazel woodlands, with salt marshes in vicinity and a rocky foreshore and shallow bay that would have been rich in shellfish and other foods.

Radiocarbon dating and the archaeological and palaeoenvironmental evidence for episodic and seasonal occupation suggest repeated revisits to Ferriter's Cove in late summer and autumn. It is also likely that this was going on for perhaps hundreds of years (between 4600-4300 BC). From ethnographic studies, Graeme Warren has suggested that hunter-gatherers often have short generations, as little as twenty years, and they 'marry' young. A period of three hundred years might encompass as many as fifteen generations. We have evidence then that people stayed for only short periods of time, but also that they came again and again across the generations. So, we might take the long-term activity at Ferriter's Cove as evidence for Mesolithic hunter-gatherer's 'persistence of returning', for their sense of landscape, that this was a traditional place to come to and that this was passed down within the lore or stories of the people.

What did these people do there? Archaeological excavations show that while they camped beside this coastal inlet, they fished for young wrasse, whiting, tope and ray in the rock pools, inshore shallows and perhaps even offshore for the tope. Although there is no archaeological evidence for nets, some types of lines, or other catching and trapping mechanisms and maybe even boats must have been used to catch these fish. On the rocks jutting out into the sea, they made

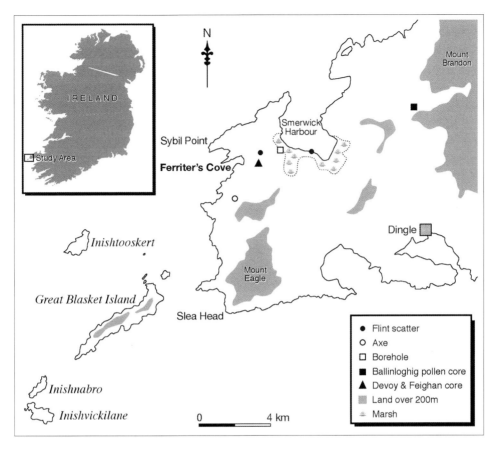

13 Location of late Mesolithic site at Ferriter's Cove at the end of the Dingle Peninsula, Co. Kerry (after Woodman, Anderson and Finlay 1999)

use of the abundant shellfish resources of dog-whelk, periwinkle and limpet, dumping the shells beside them as they roasted them on stones (perhaps to make them more palatable) and sat chatting and eating by fires (14).

Occasionally, they hunted in the woods for wild pig and hare, and sometimes they may have trapped guillemot and herring gulls along the coast. However, by and large, their diet was mainly based on marine resources, as has been confirmed by stable isotope analysis of a few human bones found on the site. The traces these hunter-gatherers left behind them were meagre enough. Indeed, the archaeological evidence suggests that the site was mostly used for short episodes of occupation, with its fire-spots, pits, stake-holes, discrete shell-dumps and spreads of burnt stone indicating that the most substantial structures there would have been merely fish-drying racks or windbreaks. This was a place then that was used by small groups of people for weeks or months, all the more interesting then, that it was returned to so often.

The Ferriter's Cove archaeological excavations also revealed that these hunter-gatherers were also exploiting local geological sources of stone (although some stone may have been carried onto the site), and their tools were made not from the more commonly used flint or chert, but from rhyolites, siltstone and volcanic tuffs. Yet, despite the constraints of these raw materials, these people were still using a typically Irish hard-hammer technology to produce much the same types of robust blades found on other late Mesolithic sites around the island. In addition, lithic analyses and refitting experiments on the lithics from Ferriter's Cove also reveal the spatial patterning of stone-working on-site and the use of a wider range of other tools, such as mudstone and shale stone axes, possible 'limpet-hammers' (modified beach pebbles) and possible spear points.

Interestingly, Ferriter's Cove also produced remarkable, slightly later evidence relating to the transformation of Irish society during the Mesolithic/Neolithic transition. The presence of surprisingly early cattle bone on the site towards the end of its use, radiocarbon dated to between about 4500-4200 BC, indicates that local hunter-gatherers were in contact somehow with very early Neolithic farming communities. Intriguingly, Peter Woodman suggests that the cattle bone may have been a 'prestige gift' indicating trading or social contacts across the seaways with farming communities in southern Britain or western Europe and that this process of acculturation could have begun the process which lead to the introduction of farming into Ireland at about 4000 BC.

14 Reconstruction drawing of Late Mesolithic oyster consumption (from McErlean, McConkey and Forsythe 2002)

LATE MESOLITHIC COASTAL OCCUPATION AT BELDERRIG, CO. MAYO

Recent excavations by Graeme Warren of UCD School of Archaeology at Belderrig, Co. Mayo have identified an important late Mesolithic site, where initial radiocarbon dates suggest that it was occupied around 4500-4300 BC (15, 16). The site is located today at the cliff-edge of a small bay on the north Mayo coastline – and is notable in part because of the scarcity of Mesolithic sites in this region. Originally, the site may have been located on land that sloped down to a riverbank, but subsequent sea level rise and coastal erosion may have altered the landscape to some degree. The site has produced some structures, a range of quartz and chert tools and manufacturing debris, as well as plant and fish remains. Preliminary analyses demonstrate the presence of conger eel and wrasse: both probably resulting from inshore fishing off the rocky coasts at Belderrig.

The stone industry relies heavily on local raw materials, especially quartz, some of which, at least, was procured from the beach. The late Mesolithic site at Belderrig is located in a landscape that subsequently was settled by Neolithic farmers who created the famous Céide Neolithic field-systems. Many discussions of the transition to farming at about 4000 BC have suggested that this key historical event involved Neolithic communities 'turning their back' on the sea, choosing to ignore rich marine resources that had been exploited throughout the Mesolithic and focusing instead on the exploitation of new domesticates. The Belderrig site offers a chance to examine these debates in detail on the Irish coast.

DID THE ROLE OF THE SEASHORE CHANGE IN THE LATE MESOLITHIC?

How are late Mesolithic coastal occupation sites, shell middens, raised beach sites and the Dublin estuarine fish traps to be interpreted? Peter Woodman has suggested that late Mesolithic communities may have become an increasingly mobile, low-density population, with an expedient subsistence strategy and an increased emphasis on movement through the landscape on a seasonal round. Woodman points out that during the late Mesolithic there is no evidence for basecamps or long-term residences and that we only have evidence for ephemeral, specialised short-stay camps such as coastal occupation sites, suggesting that sites were hardly occupied by a few people for more than a few days or weeks. It is possible that the late Mesolithic seasonal round was based on movement around distinct hunter-gatherer annual territories, perhaps similar in size to those proposed by the archaeologist Louis Binford for Nuniamut territories, in Canada. Small social groups, perhaps families or bands, may have resided by the coast during the spring and summer, and then moved inland in autumn to lakeshore sites, situated at recognised stopping points along river valleys, to fish for eels and salmon for periods of weeks or months. They would then either move into the uplands or go back down to the coast for the winter, when fishing and shellfish would still be available.

15 Late Mesolithic site excavations at Belderrig, Co. Mayo (Graeme Warren, AOS)

16 Late Mesolithic artefacts from Belderrig, Co. Mayo (Graeme Warren, UCD)

In contrast, other archaeologists have suggested that the Irish late Mesolithic was similar to that found elsewhere in northern Europe and that there would have been a growing population and a move towards *greater* social complexity and sedentism. The changing late Mesolithic landscape would have provided a wide range of resources, particularly in the wetlands and woods, and large social groups could have aggregated by the coast or lakeshore sites especially. The campsites that we find may only have been used by small hunter-gatherer parties travelling on scheduled visits for particular tasks. In the Scandinavian late Mesolithic or Ertebølle period, large coastal campsites were used by most of the community, whilst others went out on temporary tasks to campsites elsewhere. In other words, our difficulty in identifying large late Mesolithic base camps may largely be due to problems of archaeological visibility. Our coastal shell middens may merely have been situated at the edge of larger occupation sites (that may be difficult to trace archaeologically), above the beach or some short distance away.

DEATH AND THE SEASHORE IN THE MESOLITHIC

Reconstructing hunter-gathers' perception of the ocean

We have already suggested that hunter-gatherers perceive and understand the landscape as something that is imbued with symbolic and spiritual power, and that it is constitutive of people's sense of identity and belonging. Life itself is seen as a web of relationships between people, mammals, fish or birds and inanimate things – and people are not seen as being outside of this world. If in Ireland, with its distinctive flora and fauna, the seashore was of crucial importance in economic terms, then it must also have been so in symbolic terms. The sea was not only a source of food and raw materials, it represented life itself and 'the people'. We can begin to interpret these potential social and symbolic meanings, if we consider what archaeological evidence we have in particular for persistence of place and for the structured, deliberate deposition of Mesolithic human and animal bone in coastal middens, the caching of stone axes, flakes and cores in pits on coastal occupation sites and a range of other potential ritual practices.

Firstly, it is clear that mundane materials; stone tools, animal bones and other objects were not casually discarded, but were deliberately deposited in a careful way on occupation sites. At Ferriter's Cove, it is evident that there are several phases or events of dumping in pits and hollows, perhaps representing particular meals or periods of eating together. One hollow area in the dunes was filled with shells of periwinkle, dog whelk, limpets and mussels, fish and mammal bones, burnt hazelnut shells, crab claws, as well as human teeth. Because hunter-gatherers see profound connections between people, objects and the animal world, such associations are not problematic and make 'sense'. People would have seen human and animal bone, as well as objects and raw materials, as things that were closely connected.

There are also other types of deposit that seem even more clearly to be structured and deliberate. At Ferriter's Cove, a cache of stone axes were deliberately laid together in a pit, almost as if they were a reed-bound 'catch' of recently hooked fish lying beside each other on the ground. Similarly, at Dalkey Island, Mesolithic flakes were carefully packed in an inverted position into a pit on a terrace that was the focus of midden activity. Mesolithic hunter-gatherers may have placed objects and bones in the ground for some reason; to acknowledge the gift of food by the spirits, to placate nature's forces or simply to maintain the balance between the people and the world they lived in.

MESOLITHIC COASTAL CEMETERIES IN EUROPE

Recognising that the seashore itself was a space of some symbolic or metaphorical meanings for Mesolithic communities in Ireland, we can move towards interpreting the scanty evidence we have for human skeletal remains from coastal occupation sites. Rick Schulting has noted that there is good archaeological evidence for coastal cemeteries amongst late Mesolithic hunter-gatherer groups of Atlantic Europe, and at least 700 individual human burials are now known. These cemeteries are often spatially associated with coastal occupation sites and occasionally with shell middens and they have been found across a wide geographical area. In Scandinavia, there are Mesolithic cemeteries associated with coastal sites at Skateholm, (southern Sweden) and Vedbaek (Denmark). At Téviec and Höedic on the Armorican peninsula of north-west France, there were nineteen graves of thirty seven individuals in a coastal shell midden. At Cabeço de Pez, in the Tagus estuary region of Portugal, there were twenty seven graves in a coastal shell midden. It should be noted that burial practices vary widely across these regions, reflecting different cultural traditions, social practices and religious beliefs. There is also considerable evidence for variation in burial practice within these coastal burial grounds, reflecting the different social status and role of different members of the community.

Burials are typically laid out in single graves, but people are also buried in groups. Men, women and children can be found together. Dog burials on some European Mesolithic cemeteries may reflect a belief that ancestral spirits resided within these animals, while shamans may have been placed in shafts or were accompanied with antler bone headrests. The use of grave goods is also complex, with perforated shells, animal teeth, stone pendants, head dresses, bone pins, animal bone and stone tools often buried with the dead. Occasionally individual Mesolithic graves were used across time, being re-opened to receive another body, prefiguring in a sense, the megalithic tradition of the early Neolithic. Indeed, on the Armorican sites there is an intriguing symbolic link to be made between these small Mesolithic mounds of white shells associated with human remains and the subsequent larger Neolithic mounds of stone (i.e. passage tombs) that also received human bones.

MESOLITHIC HUMAN BONE FRAGMENTS IN SHELL MIDDENS

Interestingly, at the same time that Mesolithic inhumation cemeteries were in use, there seems to have been a parallel Mesolithic burial practice along the coast of Atlantic Europe involving the placing of *fragments* of human bone in coastal shell middens. These human remains are not randomly chosen, typically consisting only of skull, jaw and long-bone fragments, with pelvic, shoulder and trunk skeleton fragments usually absent. It is also interesting that there seems to be a distinction between cemetery sites and bone in midden deposits – only a fraction of known Mesolithic sites have produced both formal human burials *and* fragmentary skeletal remains. It is interesting to reflect then that Mesolithic human skeletal remains are also known from middens in Ireland (remembering how few have been excavated), namely at Rockmarshall, Co. Louth and at Ferriter's Cove, Co. Kerry. While these deposits in no way match in quantity the burials found elsewhere in north-west Europe, it is possible to use them to help us reflect on the ritual practices and cosmological beliefs of hunter-gatherers on this island.

On the Scottish island of Oronsay, Paul Mellars excavated several coastal shell middens occupied at various times of the year. Fifty five fragments of human bone – representing at least nine individuals – were found within them, mostly from one site known as Cnoc Coig, but also from middens at Caisteal nan Gillean II and Priory midden. These fragments included human teeth, cranial fragments and hand and feet bones, yet they exhibited no evidence for butchery or cannibalism. It has been suggested that bodies were exposed on the middens until flesh had rotted off, and that later when the bones were being gathered together for transport elsewhere, small hand and feet bones simply fell away into the shell heaps. There is also some evidence for a symbolic link being made between people and the sea, as human finger bones had been deliberately placed on the bones of a seal flipper (they are anatomically similar), perhaps signifying that these creatures were seen as ancestors, as was commonly believed amongst many coastal communities in modern times.

At Rockmarshall, Co. Louth, in Ireland, the late Mesolithic shell middens excavated in the 1940s by Frank Mitchell were situated at the edge of a glacial moraine overlooking a former coastal lagoon at the north side of Dundalk Bay. These shell middens produced charcoal and shells, mainly of oyster, periwinkle, whelk, mussel and cockle, as well as crab and fishbones. Other finds included lithics, mostly blades, flakes and cores. One of the Rockmarshall middens, was situated at a sheltered location on the back of the ridge, at a place where people could have sat and looked back up into the mountain valley above them. It produced a human femur that has since been radiocarbon dated to the late Mesolithic at 4720-4360 BC.

At Ferriter's Cove Co. Kerry, Peter Woodman's excavations also revealed evidence for human remains. One of the many interesting things about Ferriter's

Cove was the evidence that it had been a place of some importance over hundreds of years. Down through the generations, people would have returned to a place where their great-grand parents had been before. It is interesting then that several fragments of human bone, including pieces of jaw bone, legs, arms, feet, hands and teeth, were also found at the site, probably dating to the final phase of activity there. A long bone was radiocarbon dated to 4225-3950 BC, while a human tooth was dated to 4250-3980 BC. Cathryn Power has suggested that these remains derive from at least one adult aged 25-30 years old.

MESOLITHIC HUNTER–GATHERER COSMOLOGIES AND SHELL MIDDENS

It is possible that this scanty evidence for human bone merely represents the accidental accrual of human skeletal parts at places of long-term activity – although this would still require us to explain why human bodies are being laid out there. However, recent archaeological excavations on the banks of the River Shannon at Hermitage, near Castleconnell, Co. Limerick have revealed the people in the early Mesolithic were deliberately placing cremated human bone with stone tools in pits. In the late Mesolithic, it seems likely that the coastal foreshore – itself a physically liminal space between sea and land – was a place of great social, mythic and symbolic significance for the people. The maritime landscape was enormously important to them in terms of food production. Shell middens, because they were recognisable markers of the places used for social gatherings, the preparation and consumption of food, would have been key points of pause in this landscape of movement. However, it was probably also a landscape with a 'history', in that its distinctive physical features (beaches, creeks, promontories) could have been associated with past events and people. An association between shell middens and the past may also have led to their being used as places for formal, structured deposits. Certainly, it happened on some sites, such as Ferriter's Cove with its hoard of stone axes, or at Dalkey Island with its formal cache of flint flakes.

In Mesolithic Ireland, it is also worth noting that shell middens – being bright mounds of white shell, ash and charcoal – were the one topographical feature that could be easily recognised as having been made by human beings, amongst a people who were adept at reading the natural signs of the landscape around them (similarly, Mesolithic lakeshore platforms would have been also 'readable' to these people). It is also likely that these were places that people emotionally associated with a time of warmth, plentiful and varied food. So, we can imagine a band of hunter-gatherers returning to the seashore after a few months spent living in the river valleys and woodlands of the interior, seeing again the shells, stone tools and animal bones amongst the sands at the foreshore's edge, they would have felt like they were coming home.

Places like Ferriter's Cove and Rockmarshall, with their deposits of human remains, might have been seen as places of the ancestors – they were certainly places with temporal resonances. Late Mesolithic shell middens – although themselves quite small – did accumulate slowly over immensely long periods of time (literally over hundreds of years). They were significant places in the landscape then for generations of local people – which may have been why they were considered as appropriate places to deposit human bone. Amongst some recent hunter-gatherer groups, individuals choose the place where they wish their bones to be deposited, this often being a place they associate with happy times or with the family. We can imagine then that the bones of a loved one would be carried through the winter, before finally being put at the family midden in the springtime – or indeed at various times of the year.

How would people have felt about these human bones? Certainly amongst some hunter-gatherer groups (the Inuit of Greenland for example) human remains can have a polluting or sickening effect; but this can be prevented by their proper treatment, often involving deliberate lengthy exposure to cleanse them. Exposure on a midden might achieve this, and this in itself would lead to the accidental 'loss' of bones in the midden deposits. In Mesolithic Ireland, it may have been considered entirely appropriate for people to live with their ancestors' bones around them. In fact, the recognisable presence of grandmother's bones beside you may have been re-assuring. Amongst many hunter-gatherer groups, death is basically seen as a transformation into another state of being. Death is essentially something that is the same as this life, but it is an existence that is lived elsewhere. In other words, people buried at the seashore would have continued to do what they had always done there; gather shellfish, hunt seals, fish and birds. It is also worth pointing out that people may have felt that the ancestors were always around them, not situated back in the past. Perhaps, people believed that their ancestors were working in spirit beside them as they gathered food on the foreshore.

MOVING ACROSS THE WATER: BOATS AND NAVIGATION IN THE MESOLITHIC

How do hunter-gatherers use boats?

What were the boats used by Mesolithic hunter-gatherers and indeed the first farmers in the Neolithic like? It is obvious from the settlement of the island itself and from the evidence for the ongoing movement between these islands through early prehistory of people, animals (i.e. cattle) and objects (e.g. the stone axe trade), that both hunter-gatherers and farmers had access to ocean-going vessels. It is also more than implied, it is proven by the habitual use and inhabitation of offshore islands throughout the Mesolithic and Neolithic. For example, Rathlin Island in the waters between Northern Ireland and Scotland and the Isle of Man, Lambay Island and many other islands in the Irish Sea were clearly inhabited through early prehistory, as has been shown by recent archaeological research and excavations. Unfortunately, we are almost completely in the dark about the nature of boats that people used.

Archaeologists have generally turned to ethnographic evidence to guess at what types of boats hunter-gatherers used to colonise the island. It seems logical that the movement of peoples, but particularly cattle, sheep and goats, onto this island would have required a larger hide-covered craft, perhaps with a sail. Amongst the Inuit of the Canadian and Greenland Arctic regions, large boats propelled by paddles known as umiaks, constructed of wooden framing and skins, were used to transport family groups and cargoes. However, these craft may have been a relatively recent development in the Arctic regions. Faced with a lack of archaeological evidence, archaeologists have often claimed that Mesolithic hunter-gathers and Neolithic farmers in these islands might have used a skin or hide-covered craft that resembled the modern Irish currach. However, one might just as usefully state that the prehistoric stone axe is like the modern steel axe: an equally meaningless truism. In truth, we simply have no idea what these craft were like and in any case the Irish currach is not some age-old type existing outside of history; it was a product of particular social and economic conditions in the west of Ireland in the nineteenth and twentieth centuries.

There is also ethnographic evidence for the use of smaller craft known as canoes. In recent historical times, it is well known that bark-covered canoes and hide-covered kayaks were used by hunter-gatherer groups in the North Americas and Arctic regions to carry individuals or a small group of people, both for journeying and for seal-hunting. In Britain and Ireland, smaller craft such as the hide-covered, wicker coracles used on the Boyne for example, may somehow echo the types of smaller craft used in early prehistory. Unfortunately, again we are limited to surmising these craft.

EVIDENCE FOR MESOLITHIC BOATS

There is one possible Mesolithic dug-out boat from Ireland, from Brookend, Co. Tyrone on the shores of Lough Neagh, itself a huge inland lake. This was a fragment of a heavy, curved oak plank with toolmarks from a flint axe, dated to 5490-5246 BC. However, there is also good archaeological evidence for Mesolithic canoes from northern Europe, particularly Scandinavia, The Netherlands and France. In particular, archaeological excavations – both underwater and in coastal environments – in Denmark have recovered several distinctive Mesolithic canoes.

These Mesolithic Scandinavian craft are dugout boats, hollowed out by stone axe and fire, from large lime, poplar or oak tree trunks. These are often narrow, light craft hewn down to a thin, delicate shape (enabling them to be easily portaged or carried through woods, from waterway to waterway). They usually have a rounded bow and a flat stern, occasionally the latter being made by a separate plank that is inserted into a groove. These craft may have been used for fishing, as burnt clay and charring in the interior suggests that small fires may have been lit within them – this is a technique used while fishing at night; the light of the fire attracts fish to the surface where they can be speared.

These Late Mesolithic canoes would have been propelled by wooden paddles. The Danish site of Tybrind Vig produced finely carved paddles where the heart-shaped blades were decorated with incised, geometric patterns that had probably been originally coloured with plant dyes. It is apparent that these craft were understood in more than functional terms, as some were used as burials for the dead. It has been suggested that corpses may have been laid in the craft and deposited in shallow water, suggesting again that these people saw themselves as closely linked to waterways and that the sea was a symbolically important space.

PILOTAGE AND PADDLING IN THE MESOLITHIC

We can know little about pilotage – the craft and skill in navigating small boats – in early prehistory, but we can come to some conclusions. It seems obvious that people had the ability and knowledge to move along coastlines, to travel between islands and to cross the seaways between Ireland, Britain and perhaps ultimately to Atlantic Europe. We can see this from the inhabitation of small islands immediately off the Irish coastline.

Dalkey Island, situated a few hundred metres off the Dublin coastline, was the location for a Mesolithic and Neolithic occupation site. The island is separated from land by a narrow stretch of water, but it is deep, with strong, tidal currents and piloting a small boat across it would take some skill and care. Lambay Island, situated at much more distance off the Dublin coastline was the location of a late Neolithic stone axe quarry, and presumably judging by Mesolithic lithics found around the island, it was also settled at this earlier time. Rathlin Island, off the north-east coast was also a source of porcellanite and it was also settled during the Mesolithic and Neolithic – despite the fact that tide and current conditions make it difficult to approach. This evidence probably indicates relatively regular journeys back and forth across stretches of sea that appear short but still take some time to traverse in a small boat.

It is clear then that people were moving back and forth along the coast and across the sea, at various times transporting animals, people, stone axes, porphyry, porcellanite, pitchstone and other exotic materials. Undoubtedly, people travelled across the sea for other reasons too, to exchange news, to visit, to meet marriage partners or to explore. Mesolithic and Neolithic peoples probably chose their time carefully when they set out to sea, particularly when any long distance journey was intended. A good knowledge of weather patterns, tidal cycles and offshore currents would have been an obvious requirement; while monitoring of the movement of the sun, moon, stars, birds and marine life provided more information when travelling on the seaways. In later times, people preferred to set out on the surface of the ocean only at suitable times in the sailing season

– between April and November – and this must have been even more important in early prehistory.

Indeed, Graeme Warren has suggested that travelling on the sea would have been another rhythm of life for Mesolithic hunter-gatherers; that people's social world (and the distances they intended to travel) would have expanded and contracted according to the seasons, from the long days and distances of safe navigation in the summer to the reluctance to set out on the wave-tossed seas of stormy, dark winter. In any case, we need to move towards an understanding of how people may have moved along the sea in everyday life.

Archaeologists investigating a Mesolithic occupation site at Bay Farm, Co. Antrim carried out an interesting experimental archaeology project on the potential of sea travel along the north-east coast (*17*). Seeking to understand the territory that could have been exploited from the Mesolithic site, they journeyed out from it in various directions. Archaeologists walked up the glen, into the hills and along the coastal beaches, travelling a few kilometres in a couple of hours. However, they also set out exploring along the coast in a Canadian open canoe. Using paddles and working in tandem with the tides and currents, they discovered that they could move much more swiftly along the coastline, travelling up to five kilometres in only thirty minutes. In other words, when travelling by sea in a canoe one can easily move four to five times the distance than one can on land. In the Mesolithic, people may well have regarded their hunting territories and social worlds very much in terms of elongated zones along the coast.

17 Digital Terrain Model of NE coast of Ireland and SW coast of Scotland (Rory Quinn, UU)

Did people cross the sea often during the Mesolithic? Perhaps they did for specific tasks and events, rather than routinely. Although there is some evidence for long-distance connections (e.g. the cattle bone from Ferriter's Cove) and technological indicators of movement between the Isle of Man and the east Irish coastline, it does seem from lithic analyses of stone artifacts from Irish sites that late Mesolithic communities were developing a distinctively insular technology quite different from that found in Scotland, Wales and England. But undoubtedly there was knowledge of the seaways, not least because it is possible to see Ireland from high points along the coast of Britain. In any case, the ensuing centuries with the onset of the Neolithic were to bring people, ideas, animals and goods from across the sea.

3

Neolithic farmers, landscapes and seascapes, 4000-2500 BC

INTRODUCTION

The Neolithic period (4000-2500 BC) brought significant social, economic and ideological changes to the island of Ireland, and ultimately transformed its landscapes. It is certain that some of the people, animals, crops and ideas that underpinned these social and landscape changes came to this island by boat. Cattle and cereal crops not native to this island were certainly brought here from across the sea, and perhaps there was also some immigrant farming groups. Indeed, it is also possible that red deer were first introduced onto this island at this time – perhaps through human action too. It is believed that cattle were the most important domesticated animal, followed by pig and sheep, but it seems likely that cereal growing (using emmer wheat and barley) was at least as important as stock raising.

Most archaeological evidence for Neolithic settlement and economy has led scholars to interpret the period in terms of the establishment of a farming lifestyle, of houses, enclosures and field-systems in a bounded, pastoral landscape. Neolithic houses are now a common archaeological discovery, and are interpreted as the permanent domestic residences of extended families situated within wider managed agricultural landscapes. At the Neolithic field-systems at Céide in north Mayo, these settlement enclosures and megalithic tombs were set amongst such fields by about 3500 BC (*18, 19*). It can be seen then that this is a significantly different society and way of ordering the land than that of Mesolithic hunter-gatherers.

This interpretation of a Neolithic sedentary society in Ireland contrasts with most recent archaeological interpretations in Britain, where it is believed that early Neolithic societies continued to be largely mobile communities, with cattle herding and occasional farmed clearances in an otherwise wooded landscape.

18 The Ceide coastline of north Mayo, location of an extensive Neolithic landscape of enclosures, field systems and megalithic tombs (Aidan O'Sullivan)

This fits with an idea that there was a slow transition from hunter-gatherer to farming ways. Irish archaeologists preferring to investigate the origins of farming and the uses of megalithic tombs have shown little interest in maritime life ways. However, it is important to recognise that some localities and regions may have seen a degree of settlement mobility, seasonal or otherwise, and perhaps also a broad spectrum of forager-farmer economies based largely on maritime resources. Certainly, we have archaeological evidence for Neolithic people living by the seashore. This includes Neolithic houses and field systems in coastal regions, Neolithic shell middens, as well as Neolithic megalithic tombs overlooking bays and inlets. There is also interesting evidence for Neolithic occupation of marine islands, such as at Lambay, Co. Dublin – where Neolithic communities used porphyry quarries on the island's summit as the focus of stone axe production. In this chapter, we will tack between the Mesolithic and Neolithic, exploring how people lived beside, moved along and buried their dead by the sea.

LIVING BY THE SEA IN THE NEOLITHIC

Neolithic farmers and their seascapes after 4000 BC
Moving from the Mesolithic into the Neolithic period (4000-2500 BC), we are faced with some different challenges and issues in thinking about how people lived by the sea. Archaeological and palaeoenvironmental evidence indicates that

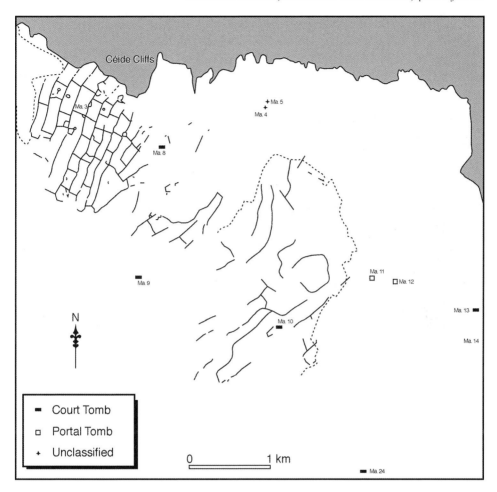

19 Map of Ceide Neolithic field systems (after Caulfield 1992)

Neolithic farming practices were introduced on to this island shortly after 4000 BC, probably by at least some immigrant groups who brought with them new types of cereal crops and animals (e.g. cattle). Traditionally, Neolithic landscapes, settlement and society in Ireland have been understood in terms of a shift towards a farming lifestyle and economy.

Neolithic settlements and houses have produced hearths, pottery, occasional evidence for lithic production and use, animal bones, saddle querns for grinding grain, as well as the actual remains of cereals, nuts and fruits. It is believed that cattle were the most important domesticated animal, followed by pig and sheep, but it seems likely that cereal growing (using emmer wheat and barley) was at least as important as stock raising. In other words, most Neolithic landscape studies envisage a settled, farming population who directed their energies towards livestock raising and the tending of arable crops within a land that was now being cleared of woodlands.

Obviously, this image is of a people with a significantly different society and lifestyle to that of hunter-gatherers. It also contrasts with most recent archaeological interpretations of the early Neolithic in Britain, where it is still believed that people continued to be largely mobile, with cattle herding and occasional farmed clearances in an otherwise wooded landscape. However, the archaeological evidence from Ireland (and indeed Scotland) is better explained in terms of a settled, sedentary life.

Nevertheless, it is important to remember that some farmers may have continued to use wild resources from both woodlands and the seashore. It is certainly the case that foraged, wild resources are often found on permanent settlements. At a Neolithic house excavated at Tankardstown, Co. Limerick, gathered wild foods such as hazelnuts and crab apples were found inside the house along with cattle, sheep, goat and pig bones and charred wheat grain; indicating the continued importance of some wild foods at the same time as arable crops. It is also clear that there is also archaeological evidence for movement through the wider Neolithic landscape, both in terms of local activities around dwellings as well as transitory, seasonal or specialised occupation sites at more remote locations in the landscape (uplands, woodlands, low-lying lakeshores and rivers). There are various questions then. How did Neolithic farming groups live by and work the seashore? Did they gather shellfish; did they trap and fish; did they collect raw materials from beaches and coastal cliffs? In other words, how did Neolithic people use, perceive and understand the seascapes that they lived in?

NEOLITHIC COASTAL SETTLEMENT AT CÉIDE, NORTH MAYO

The most spectacular evidence for a Neolithic community living in a coastal landscape is found at Céide in north Mayo, situated on hills sloping down to the edge of high cliffs on the Atlantic coastline (*18, 19*). It is now known that late Mesolithic communities also inhabited this coast. Graeme Warren's recent excavations of a late Mesolithic site eroding into the sea at Belderrig have uncovered an intriguing occupation site. It seems that hunter-gatherers were living beside this small bay, working quartz into distinctive late Mesolithic tools. It is also thought that they were fishing the bay itself, as fish bones have been recovered from organic deposits. The late Mesolithic site was subsequently buried under blanket bog. Indeed, not far from the site there are traces of some Neolithic field walls, built by communities that succeeded the hunter-gatherers at Belderrig.

The better-known Neolithic landscape at Céide, situated several kilometres to the east, is spectacularly preserved underneath metres of blanket bog that formed during later prehistory. Archaeological research by Seamus Caulfield over the years has led to the discovery of an intact Neolithic field-system, consisting of kilometres of stonewalls gridding the hills into a ladder-like system of long rectangular fields. Within this extensive field-system, survey and excavation has also revealed the existence of several settlement enclosures, presumably the dwelling places and farmyards of local farmers. This was a community who did not separate their dwelling and ritual landscapes, and Neolithic court tombs are also buried under the bogs. Radiocarbon dating and palynological studies have also recently revealed that the Neolithic landscape of Céide, north Mayo was in use during the early Neolithic, and perhaps was abandoned by c.3500 BC.

It is certainly interesting that these early Neolithic settlements, fields and tombs are situated within what is essentially a maritime landscape. Strolling amongst the fields today, it is evident that it is the ocean that dominates the view. It stretches across the entire northern horizon; one can see the ocean swell with its wind-tossed wave crests; storm clouds approaching; the islands out to sea, as well as the headlands, small bays and inlets situated along the otherwise daunting cliffs. Despite this maritime setting, the Céide Neolithic landscapes are usually interpreted as evidence for a permanently settled, sedentary farming society and cattle grazing on a grand scale, with little need for the exploitation of wild resources. This seems likely, especially considering the fact that the sea is mostly inaccessible beyond the high, precipitous cliffs situated only a few hundred metres away. The sea is near but it is inaccessible. However, it is also possible that these Neolithic communities occasionally fished the sea from the cliffs or from small boats harboured in the inlets and bays further along this coastline, or that they gathered shellfish and bird's eggs along the rocky shorelines and in the cliff nests. On the other hand, just because these resources were there does not mean that they were exploited.

NEOLITHIC DWELLINGS ALONG THE ANTRIM COASTAL LANDSCAPE

In fact, we probably should imagine Neolithic communities as making use of coastal and maritime resources in ways that were both socially and economically complex. For example, within the Antrim glens of north-east Ireland, there is evidence that Neolithic communities ranged across the entire landscape, from the uplands down to the foreshore. At Glencoy, Neolithic people placed their megalithic tombs in the uplands, while they themselves lived in settlements back from the coast in strategic, low-lying locations in the valleys. They also visited the beaches at the ends of the valleys for the exploitation of flint, as is indicated by specialised hunting or lithic production sites in the glens (20).

At Mad Man's Window, in Antrim, Neolithic chipping floors and stone axe rough outs were found with Neolithic pottery, flakes, scrapers and leaf-shaped arrowheads. At Bay Farm II, a Neolithic occupation site near marshlands produced occupation debris, postholes, charcoal, flint cores, axes and Neolithic pottery. It is probable that people made regular visits to the beaches at the ends of the glens seeking the abundant supplies of flint pebbles and nodules that can still be seen within the chalk.

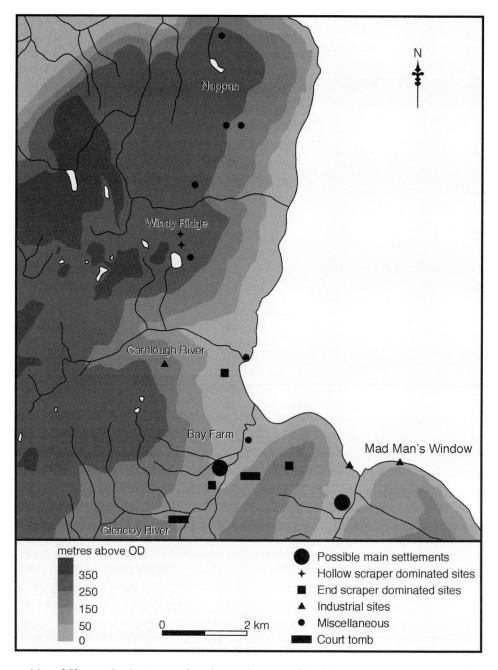

20 Map of Glencoy, Co. Antrim coastline showing location of Neolithic settlements and tombs (after Cooney 2000)

It is also likely that different social groups, in terms of age, rank or gender, within the community, might have been responsible for these various work activities along the shoreline – echoing what may have been practiced during the Mesolithic.

On the other hand, other Neolithic dwellings in coastal landscapes have been investigated and have produced little evidence for the use of wild maritime resources. Neolithic houses have been recently excavated by Dermot Moore at Ballyharry, on the Islandmagee Peninsula between Larne Lough and the Irish Sea. These were coastal sites, located overlooking Larne Lough. However, there is little sense of maritime resource exploitation.

Similarly, Neolithic houses at Ballygalley, Co. Antrim were located in a maritime setting, on low ground some 500m from the shore of Ballygalley Bay – on the north-east coast of the Irish Sea. Ballygalley House 1 was a large, sub-rectangular structure dating from 3776-3386 BC, probably with a pitched roof and an external annex. This was a dwelling of a farming community, as indicated by the presence of Einkorn wheat and cattle bone. Towards the end of the period of occupation, living conditions may have been wet, as suggested by liver-fluke snail shells and caddis fly cases. At the end, the house may have been deliberately deconstructed, and its wall slots filled with water-rolled stones and flint nodules taken from the seashore.

However, despite this interesting detail, the Ballygalley Neolithic community were not fishing, fowling or gathering shellfish. Indeed, even the beads used for personal adornment were of stone rather than of marine shells. On the other hand, they were using raw materials that imply local and long-distance maritime connections. Flint nodules may have been gathered from the local beach, while porcellanite was brought from Tievebulliagh and by boat from Rathlin Island. However, there were also items on the site that had to be brought from further across the sea. Stone axes were found that came from Great Langdale, in Cumbria in north-east England and from Cornwall. There were also many pieces of pitchstone that would have been brought to Ballygalley from the island of Arran, in the Firth of Clyde. Indeed, it seems likely that Ballygalley may have been some type of redistribution place, a feasting house or a ritual, public structure. It was in this sense, a place on the Neolithic seaways.

NEOLITHIC COASTAL SANDHILL OCCUPATION SITES AND SHELL MIDDENS

Neolithic occupation sites are known from sandhills and coastal dunes, particularly along the north coast of the island. Few of these 'sandhill' settlements have been excavated, and there are also problems of stratigraphy. On occasion, archaeologists and antiquarians searching in the nineteenth and twentieth century have found Neolithic stone axes and flint, along with later prehistoric brooches, early medieval pottery and medieval coins on the same ancient ground surface. This is because of the naturally dynamic nature of these coastal deposits. Winds and coastal erosion may remove original deposits, resort them and drop them down together so that objects of different periods are found beside each other.

However, there are some Neolithic coastal occupation sites that are relatively well understood. Archaeological excavations on the Murlough Peninsula, at Dundrum, Co. Down, have investigated some of these. At Dundrum Site 6, an occupation site had fireplaces, possible shelters, pottery and crude flint. At Dundrum Site 12, a Neolithic pebble-floored hearth produced worked flints, along as well as what archaeologists term Western Neolithic pottery and Grooved Ware. Radiocarbon dates from this latter site place it at about 3940-3100 BC. These seem to have been short-term occupation sites, associated with some unknown activity on this Irish Sea coastline.

There are also some shell middens that have produced diagnostic Neolithic flint tools, pottery and an array of evidence for the seasonal exploitation of shellfish during the fourth millennium BC. Perhaps the best example of this is in the Carrowmore landscape, Co. Sligo. This is a region rich in Neolithic megalithic tombs, including the passage tomb of Maeve's Cairn situated on the hill-top of Knocknarea. This mountain is situated right on the coastline, providing extensive views across the estuaries and sand flats of Sligo and Ballysodare Bay. At the base of the steep slopes of Knocknarea mountain, there are extensive shell middens amongst the sand dunes at Strand Hill – and Göran Burenhult's excavations indicated activities there in the Neolithic, Bronze Age and Iron Age.

At Culleenamore, a shell midden contained a hearth which produced a radiocarbon date of 3770-3110 BC (*21*). Shells found were mainly of oysters, with some cockles, mussels, periwinkles, scallops and limpets. It has been suggested that these shell middens were used by Neolithic communities who moved seasonally around the Knocknarea peninsula. During the summer time they may have moved with their cattle to upland summer pastures on the mountain itself, where they may have lived in small hut structures. Some people from the community may have moved down to the shoreline for fishing, fowling and seal hunting. The Culleenamore shell middens are mostly composed of oyster shells, and these could have been used for food and for bait for fishing or sealing. Although no seal bone was recovered from the middens, there are sandbanks out in Ballysodare Bay reputed today to be the best seal-hunting waters of the west coast of Ireland. This model of seasonal movement is obviously one that draws inspiration from the Mesolithic. However, the distances involved at Knocknarea are so small and so localised that these trips along the coastline could easily have been made on a daily or periodic basis. Neolithic farming communities could easily have exploited the seashore for their own purposes, while at the same time herding cattle and growing crops on the lands around Ballysodare Bay.

21 Prehistoric shell middens at Culleenamore, showing Knocknarea in background (Aidan O'Sullivan)

FROM SEAFOOD TO STEAK: DIETARY CHANGES FROM THE MESOLITHIC TO THE NEOLITHIC

In other words, there is some evidence for Neolithic coastal occupation and for various things done by the seashore, including both gathering of shellfish and working of flint. However, there does seem to be a significant shift in diet and subsistence from the Mesolithic to the Neolithic.

Rick Schulting's (and others) recent scientific studies of early prehistoric human skeletal material from coastal contexts around Britain and Ireland have focused on stable isotope analysis of the collagen remaining in the bones. This form of analysis enables a reconstruction of the origins and nature of the protein consumed by a person in the 10-15 years before his or her death. So, for example, people who live predominantly on a 'marine' diet of fish, shellfish and other marine foods will have distinctive traces of this in their bones. Similarly, people who eat cattle meat, milk and cereal foods – a 'terrestrial' diet – will also have a unique isotopic composition in their bones and teeth. Schulting's studies have revealed a surprising but fairly consistent pattern across the Mesolithic-Neolithic transition in north-west Europe, as well as Britain and Ireland. Almost all Mesolithic bones from coastal locations (for example, the human bone from Ferriter's Cove) reveal evidence that the people in the Mesolithic had a predominantly, although not overwhelmingly, marine diet. In contrast, early Neolithic bones (such as the human bone from Carrigdirty Rock, Co.

Limerick; bones from Kilgreaney Cave, Co. Waterford; from the Neolithic portal tomb at Poulnabrone, Co. Clare and from a Neolithic megalithic tomb in the Phoenix Park, on the banks of the River Liffey) indicate that there was an almost complete shift to a terrestrial diet. All these sites are located in broadly coastal landscapes (estuarine and otherwise), but all show the people had a land-based diet.

This is striking evidence for dietary change. It seems that one of the first things that happened at the beginning of the Neolithic was that people stopped eating seafood, in fact avoiding it almost totally. Did Neolithic communities 'turn their backs' on the sea, for some unknown cultural and social reasons? This may have been something that was both cultural and symbolic – people started to eat foods provided by domesticated animals and plants because they wanted to live in a new way, to enjoy different foods, to express new forms of social identity. Perhaps a diet of meat and bread was something that was associated with proper, appropriate behaviour. They may have regarded 'fish-eaters' as people to be scorned, people who betrayed through their practices and diet the fact that they were uncultured or even not fully human (populations worldwide have a depressing tendency to see 'others' as not really people). Schulting has pointed out that the ethnographic record shows that amongst pastoralists around the world in historical and recent times, there is a strikingly consistent prejudice against the eating of fish – sometimes for sound dietary reasons (it may rot and sicken people more easily). Other observers have noted that amongst some modern Canadian Indian communities, such as the Cree who themselves depend to a large degree on hunting and trapping, that riverine fish-eaters from nearby territories are seen as somehow impoverished and not as cultured as the Cree. In any case, it does argue that Neolithic coastal dwellers no longer depended upon shellfish, fish and seaweed, although they may occasionally have eaten these foods or done other things on the seashore.

It is important to emphasise that the sea was still a space resonant with social and symbolic meanings, but that these were different from what had gone before. The sea may no longer have been seen as a place of toil and source of food, where one gathered with one's community and kin for social occasions. Neolithic people may have associated the sea more with local and long-distance communications, with trading, raiding, alliances and objects that came across the ocean. Perhaps, Neolithic communities may have had myths and stories about the animals (i.e. deer, cattle, sheep) and plants (cereals) that had once come across the sea, so for these reasons the sea may have still been seen as a source of benefit, but not directly of food itself.

DEATH AND THE SEA IN THE NEOLITHIC

Neolithic megalithic tombs and seascapes

Recognising that the ocean may have been seen as a liminal space during the Neolithic, a zone at the edge of the world to be associated with ancestors, exotic animals, plants and objects from afar, it is worth looking at how seascapes impacted on people's ritual activities. When archaeologists have thought about the distribution and context of Neolithic human remains in the Irish landscape, they have usually focused on megalithic tombs and cemeteries. These burial monuments include court tombs, portal tombs, passage tombs and wedge tombs; they vary in form, location and depositional practices, ranging in date across the Neolithic and (in the case of wedge tombs) well into the later Bronze Age. It is also true that they represent an Irish expression of a 'megalithic culture' that is found along the Atlantic coastline of Europe and debate has long gone on about how ideas and beliefs were transmitted along the Neolithic seaways. It is certainly striking that Neolithic megalithic tombs often face the sea, or are precisely located at particular places in coastal landscapes that provide striking views across bays, inlets and the open ocean itself.

At an island-wide or regional scale, it is also evident from the distribution of megalithic tombs that Neolithic communities lived along the coastal regions. Neolithic court tombs are scattered across the northern part of the island, with distinctive concentrations along the north-west Irish coastline of Donegal, Sligo, Mayo and Galway in particular. Indeed, at Céide, there are court tombs amongst the Neolithic field-systems and enclosures that lie along this coastline, indicating that this monument type was used within a living landscape. On the east coast of the island, there are also court tombs in the mountains overlooking Carlingford Lough, Co. Louth. Similarly, Neolithic portal tombs show dense distributions along the coastline of Donegal – often sited along the bays and inlets of its indented Atlantic coastline.

Indeed, Eamon Cody's recent archaeological studies of all the megalithic tombs of Donegal show that the location of that county's tombs is markedly coastal in character. All but 25 of its 114 megalithic tombs are within 3km of the coast, while 38 sites are less than 1km from the coast. The distribution of Neolithic passage tombs in Ireland also shows an occasional coastal focus – particularly with the passage tomb cemetery of Carrowmore, Co. Sligo. Indeed, the most prominent passage tomb here – Maeve's cairn on the summit of Knocknarea – is dramatically sited with extensive views across Sligo and Ballysodare Bays, and down to the beaches of Strand Hill and beyond. Knocknarea can also be seen from along the Sligo and May coastline – rising almost like an island above the sea. Similarly, in Waterford in south-east Ireland, Neolithic tombs have a predominantly marine or riverine distribution. Indeed, the small passage tombs around Tramore, while being coastal sites, have also long been seen as similar to those found on the Scilly Isles, off south-west England. While more recent studies suggest that the Tramore passage tombs are actually not unlike other Irish sites, it is certainly possible that there were strong cultural connections across the sea between these two regions.

In the late Neolithic and Bronze Age, wedge tombs were also often placed close to the sea – particularly in the north-west and along the peninsulas of Cork and Kerry in the south-west. On the edge of Toormore Bay, Co. Cork, Billy O'Brien excavated a wedge tomb at Altar that produced cremated human bone, an unburnt human tooth, charcoal and some periwinkles and limpets. However, radiocarbon dating revealed that these deposits were separately placed in the tomb over millennia – across the Early Bronze Age and the later Bronze Age, while towards the end of the Iron Age, a pit in the centre of the burial chamber contained periwinkle and limpets, with some fishbones of wrasse and eel. Here was an ancient burial place at the edge of the ocean that was a focus of ritual activity across the generations.

Indeed, at a local scale, it is possible to suggest that particular Neolithic communities placed their tombs in intensely coastal locations – perhaps suggesting that some people saw themselves as being connected to the waters of particular sheltered bays and inlets. The Neolithic court tomb at Audleystown, Co. Down – which was used for the burial of at least thirty men, women and children, along with pottery, flint objects and bones of cattle, horse, sheep and pig in two opposing galleries – was placed right on the shores of Strangford Lough, directly overlooking its islands and the estuary of the River Quoile. At Ballinran, Co. Down, a Neolithic court tomb is sited within a stone's throw of the beach of a small sheltered bay on Carlingford Lough. The Neolithic court tomb of Millin Bay, Co. Down is also sited only a few metres from the intertidal zone of this enclosed bay on the Ards coastline, Co. Down (22). We may be looking here at people's identification with the local topographical features of the coast. Indeed, on occasion Neolithic court tombs seem to mirror in their enclosed courts, the maritime bays and inlets that they overlook. Future archaeological studies might aim to explore how Neolithic communities constructed monuments in ways that were inspired by such coastal physical features.

On occasion, some Neolithic tombs may have been built close to or even on top of ancient shell middens, such as may have happened at Rush, Co. Dublin. At this site, investigated in the early nineteenth century, a tomb appeared to have been placed on an earlier shell midden. The excavator describes finding to the north of the burial chamber 'a bed of periwinkle shells some eight inches thick, and some limpet and mussel shells intermixed'. One of the intriguing things about Neolithic tombs is that marine shells have also often been found in the burial chambers of the monuments, or occasionally as later deposits in and around the grave. At Newgrange passage tomb, it is possible that the nine fragments of marine shells recovered from the site excavation was the result of beach sands being brought in for packing between the stones of the chambers.

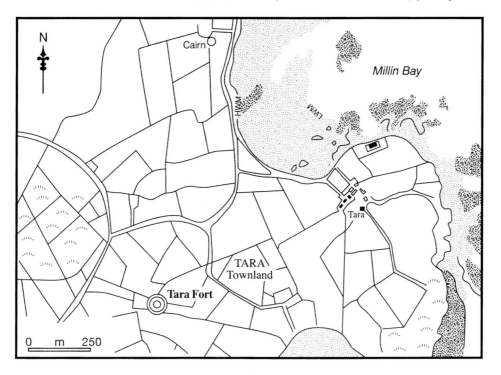

22 Map showing coastal location of Neolithic court tomb at Millin Bay, Co. Down in the top right hand corner

At sites like Lough Crew (where a passage tomb had two hundred limpet and cockle shells, as well as the bone of a whale possibly dating from a later, Iron Age occupation phase) and Fourknocks, Co. Meath (where a perforated sea shell used as personal jewellery, as well as unperforated scallop and oyster shells were recovered), it is clear that shell fish (or shells) were being brought large distances from the sea.

The discovery of marine shells is not limited to passage tombs, as they have also been found in court tombs such as Clontygora, Co. Armagh and Ballinran, Co. Down (where a 'nest' of winkle shells were placed in a pit as a secondary deposit in the grave), at wedge tombs at Drum and Screedagh, Co. Sligo and at the 'Linkardstown' type burial at Poulawack. Co. Clare (where there was a large oyster shell in the chamber). Marion Dowd has recently shown that amongst the materials possibly associated with a Neolithic cave burial at Kilgreany, Co. Waterford were six perforated Flat periwinkle shells (Littorina) and a bead made from a fish vertebra. Obviously, these deposits may not be related to the 'economic' exploitation of marine resources, but hint at the symbolic role of shells in people's cosmologies or religious beliefs, or the ways that they were used in personal ornament and dress.

NEOLITHIC HUMAN BONE AT DALKEY ISLAND SHELL MIDDEN

When archaeologists have thought about the distribution and context of Neolithic human remains in the Irish landscape, they have of course focused on megalithic tombs; the passage tombs, portal tombs and court tombs that seem to have been built as formal places for human burial. However, Neolithic skeletal remains have occasionally been found in coastal shell middens.

Perhaps the most striking example of a human burial in a marine context is the Neolithic human skeleton of a young male found buried below or within early prehistoric shell middens on Dalkey Island, Co. Dublin. It has already been discussed how these Dalkey Site II and V middens represented periodic or episodic activities there across thousands of years in the late Mesolithic and the Neolithic, as the island's occasional occupants trapped seals, pig, birds and fish and gathered limpets, worked stone and deposited objects in pits. The early Neolithic human burial found in the shell midden at Site II was radiocarbon dated to 3350-2700 BC. The body was disarticulated, but the cranium was filled with periwinkles – despite the fact that the surrounding midden was mostly of limpets. Intriguingly, this suggests that the skull had deliberately been packed full of winkle (*Littorina*) shells before it was placed in the ground, implying some link between people and sea life. Dalkey Island is situated directly off the coast and had been occupied in the Mesolithic and Neolithic, with the occurrence of stone axes and pottery implying that this was a fairly conventional coastal occupation site. However, Barbara Leon's recent re-analysis of the Dalkey midden deposits and of the Neolithic stone axes and associated material indicate that these were deliberate deposits of objects that had been placed into pits dug into the midden. We might interpret the Neolithic skull and stone axes as ritual deposits in a liminal space on the seashore.

NEOLITHIC HUMAN BONE AT CARRIGDIRTY ROCK, SHANNON ESTUARY

Neolithic human remains have also been found on a coastal site at Carrigdirty Rock, Co. Limerick (*23*). This site was identified in an intertidal archaeological survey of the Shannon estuary, when Neolithic, Bronze Age and medieval structures and environmental deposits could be seen in the mudflats. The Neolithic Carrigdirty Rock site was located in environmental deposits that indicated that it had originally been located in an estuarine landscape of reeds, marshland and mudflats. Subsequent changes in relative sea levels means that this site is now submerged and is only visible at very low tides.

It may have originally been an estuarine wetlands occupation site, as amongst the objects recovered from the foreshore were a tiny stone axe, chert fragments, water-rolled stones, charcoal, burnt hazelnut shells and chopped and charred round

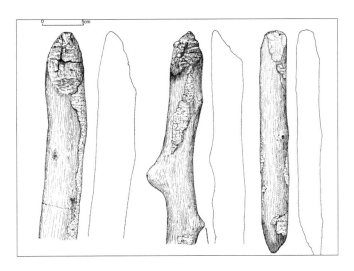

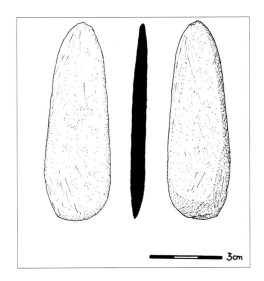

This page: 23 Reconstruction drawing of Neolithic site at Carrigdirty Rock, Co. Limerick with associated artefacts (Aidan O'Sullivan)

wood of hazel and apply branches. In this region of the Shannon estuary, there is actually little other Neolithic settlement evidence. On the hills overlooking the estuary, there are a few megalithic tombs dated to the late Neolithic, while stone axes have been found from both the river itself and the lands around it. Indeed, some recent palaeoenvironmental studies in the locality suggest that there is no significant clearance of woodlands here until later prehistory. Was the Shannon estuary region not really settled by farmers until the late Neolithic? In any case, the Neolithic Carrigdirty Rock material poses interesting questions as to how we interpret coastal sites after the Mesolithic. Was this the occupation site of a Neolithic group who were essentially living a hunter-gatherer lifestyle in the wetlands? Was it instead, as seems more likely, a seasonal wetland occupation site of a Neolithic community who drove their livestock down into the wetlands during the summertime?

However, the site may be more intriguing still. Amongst the finds recovered at the site were a large fragment of a human skull (radiocarbon dated to c.3700-3500 BC). The skull fragment was from the top of the cranium and the upper forehead and it was apparently broken off post-mortem. There was also a human clavicle (shoulder bone), which may have been gnawed by dogs or other predators. The occurrence of human bone on occupation sites is known in the Neolithic, although it has not been the subject of close study. It is interesting that the deposition of human remains in coastal environments recalls what occurred during the Mesolithic. It is possible that on the upper Shannon estuary, instead of burying their dead in megalithic tombs, that people placed fragments of human remains in particular places.

MOVING ACROSS THE WATER: BOATS AND NAVIGATION IN THE NEOLITHIC

Neolithic boats: the archaeological evidence

Boats, pilotage and the ability to travel by water would have been the same in the Neolithic as it was in the Mesolithic. There is certainly no technological reason why the basic form of craft would have changed, although no doubt the occasional movement of people and larger animals might have required larger vessels. In any case, Neolithic dugout boats are known from Ireland. Although most Irish dugouts have been recovered from the inland waterways, some have also been found in coastal salt marshes and sea-loughs, with a handful of examples from open coastal waters.

At Ballylig, Larne Lough, Co. Antrim two dugout boats were found in peats that were overlain by marine mud and were radiocarbon dated 3641-3378 BC and 3700-3382 BC. Both boats were found close to a sea lough into which there are no navigable rivers, so it seems more likely that they were for moving around the sea, albeit close to the shore.

24 Strangford Lough Neolithic dugout (Wes Forsythe, UU)

On Strangford Lough, a well-preserved dugout was identified lying in peats on the intertidal foreshore of Grey Abbey Bay and investigated by Wes Forsythe of the University of Ulster. This was a large, well-made vessel carved of oak, with a rounded bow, and thick, strong sides. It has been radiocarbon dated to 3499-3032 BC. Sea level rise since early prehistory implies that this vessel may have been originally deposited in a salt marsh set back from the lough (*24*).

Recently a possible prehistoric dugout boat was recovered from the Irish Sea off Gormonston, Co. Meath (*25*). The boat was discovered by the Archaeological Diving Company during the excavation of Bórd Gais Éireann's Irish Sea interconnector pipeline in 2002. Lying in the sands, an intact portion of the dugout survived, along with a range of broken fragments. The vessel was of a simple construction, but was quite substantial and was hewn from a single trunk of oak whose original girth was in excess of 1.1m in diameter. The intact portion represents the stern of the vessel. It is in excess of 30cm thick and rises above the body of the vessel, whose sides and base are less than 10cm thick. Overall, the profile tapers gently from the stern section forward. The dugout has a flattened hull. Its sides are curving, and its gunwales are low. The gunwales retain a series of small transverse holes that are rectangular in shape, and are spaced equidistantly down the sides. They also occur on several of the timbers that were dredged. These perforations represent the most distinguishing characteristic of the woodworking on this vessel. It is probable that they served a role in securing additional features to the sides of the boat; planks perhaps that raised the sides of

25 Gormonston dugout boat (Niall Brady, Archaeological Diving Company)

the vessel or possibly some outriggers that would have made it more stable. The splintered pieces that were recovered during the dredging suggest that the vessel was in the order of 7m in length. This was a substantial craft, recovered from maritime contexts on an open ocean coastline.

In general, archaeologists have tended to regard dugout boats as inherently unstable and unsafe to use in waters away from rivers and lakes. However, this may be more reflective of archaeologists' fears than of the reality of the use of craft in the past. From the Amazon, Africa, south-east Asia there is plenty of ethnographic video footage showing children playing around in dugouts, balancing on the edges while fishing or skillfully guiding them through rapids and small waterfalls. It may well have been that early hunter-gatherers and farmers around this island chose to only go out on the ocean on flat, calm seas, but they may still have done it in dugout boats.

During the Neolithic it is certain that people were moving back and forth across the Irish Sea regularly, as people, goods, animals and ideas about monuments moved back, forth and along the Atlantic seaways. Gabriel Cooney has suggested that during the Neolithic, we should envisage the Irish Sea (and perhaps too the Atlantic coast) in terms of islandscapes, spaces along which there was much movement and communications. Indeed for travelers across the Irish Sea, the mountains around the coastline – the Wicklow mountains, The Mournes, the Lake District fells and Snowdonia would have appeared to be islands. Both these and the real islands were important places to aim for while travelling in a low-slung boat.

Gabriel Cooney's excavations on Lambay Island, off the Dublin coast, has revealed extensive and fascinating evidence for Neolithic quarrying of porphyry and ritualized deposition of objects at the Eagle's Nest close to the island's highest point. There is also extensive stray lithic evidence for Neolithic occupation elsewhere around the island. Clearly, Lambay Island was a significant location on the Irish Sea coast – and may have been marked by a cairn at Knockbane. Similarly, on other Irish Sea islands, such as Caldey, Arran and Anglesea, high points of the island were marked with prehistoric tombs or cairns. In this way, Neolithic tomb builders were both monumentalizing these sea islands, while also placing their ancestors in places with significant views across the seaways. It might be because these islands were seen – as islands often are – as places for meeting and encounter.

Indeed, standing either at the Neolithic passage tombs at Gormonston, Co. Meath or at the Neolithic tomb of Barclodiad-y-gawres on Anglesea, both overlooking the sea, one gains a sense of maritime-oriented commmunities and the proximity that Ireland and Wales have to each other across the sea – Fernand Braudel's 'liquid plains of the ocean'. This is perhaps why the Isle of Man – located midway across the Irish Sea and at a point where both northern and southern tidal regimes circulate – has an early prehistoric material culture that shares much with its different neighbours around it. The Isle of Man, Wales and the Irish east coast were spaces where peoples, ideas and cultural traits could encounter each other. The ocean explains why there are so many similarities between the megalithic monument traditions of Ireland, Scotland and Wales.

The isles of the north: Bronze Age
and Iron Age maritime traditions in Ireland

INTRODUCTION

The Bronze Age (2500-600 BC) brings various social, economic and technological changes to the island of Ireland. Although Early Bronze Age (2500-1700 BC) settlement evidence remains sparse, the archaeological evidence for Middle (1700-1200 BC) and Late Bronze Age (1200-600 BC) settlement activity has been greatly enhanced in recent years. It seems likely that later Bronze Age communities in Ireland witnessed several important changes, particularly the emergence of a stratified, hierarchical society increasingly focused on warfare and tribal identities towards the end of the period. Bronze Age burial practices seem to indicate an emerging social ranking, perhaps based on kin-group, social role, age, gender and latterly prowess in combat. Recent landscape archaeological studies have suggested that regional or political territories were starting to form in the Late Bronze Age and that the location and boundaries of these can be identified through distinctive and variable island-wide patterns of hoard deposition, barrow and monument construction and other activities.

Bronze Age hillforts – particularly large enclosures at the summits of hills – have been identified at several locations. Archaeological excavations of some of these at Haughey's Fort, Co. Armagh; at Mooghaun, Co. Clare; at the cliff-fort at Dun Aonghusa and at Rathgall, Co. Wicklow indicate that they were predominantly constructed c.1200 BC in the Middle Bronze Age – perhaps relating to significant climatic and social changes about this time. These hillforts may have been central to these emerging tribal territories, perhaps serving as community political or ceremonial centres, or perhaps as the occasional dwelling places of social elites.

Smaller Bronze Age settlements are also increasingly known, particularly through the discovery of enclosures during recent roadway schemes. These enclosed settlements may have been farmsteads and are occasionally associated with field-systems, fulachta fiadh and ritual monuments such as standing stones and barrows. It is likely that Bronze Age dwelling enclosures were one element in local landscapes that were organized so as to express local and community ideas of ancestry, kinship and land-tenure. These small settlements, typically enclosed and situated on well-drained, thin soils well suited to arable agriculture typically contain one or more circular houses, but there were some settlements containing larger clusters of such houses. The inhabitants of these Bronze Age farmsteads and dwellings were typically engaged in intensive mixed-farming on light, well-drained soils, with cattle, pigs, sheep and goats herded in the locality, and wheat, barley and other arable crops probably cultivated within field-systems.

It is becoming clear that Bronze Age settlement landscapes were structured to enable the exploitation of various different raw materials and food resources. Early Bronze Age sites associated with the extraction of copper ores have been identified at Mount Gabriel, Co Cork and Ross Island, Co. Kerry. These sites were also undoubtedly the locations for specialist or metalworkers occupations. Coastal wetland occupations have also been found, such as the Middle Bronze Age houses, pits and features by estuarine marshlands at Meadowlands, Co. Down and the Middle Bronze Age wooden hut structure associated with cattle bone at Carrigdirty Rock, Co. Limerick on the Shannon estuary. These coastal sites may have been associated with seasonal cattle grazing on the summer marshes. Bronze Age coastal shell middens have also been recorded in sand dunes. It seems likely that occasional use was being made of such littoral resources as shellfish and cattle grazing on the thin machair grasslands. Other common indicators of Bronze Age activity in coastal wetlands are fulachta fiadh (burnt mounds or fire-cracked stone, clay and ash, associated with troughs for boiling water and typically dated to c.600-900 BC), probably the most numerous type of archaeological site that has been identified in the Irish landscape. They may indicate short-term or seasonal activities in river valleys, lakeshores and coastal lands and may have been used repeatedly as cooking places, saunas and baths, places for treating leather or human remains. Occasionally found in association with standing stones and barrows, they may also represent communal gathering places at the boundaries of social territories, where people congregated to eat, wash, celebrate the multitude of festivals that farming societies have or perhaps perform rituals associated with the dead or with watery spirits.

This Bronze Age settlement activity in wetland landscapes could be taken as evidence for population pressure, social instability, increasing growth of blanket bog and perhaps even climatic deterioration caused by deforestation and volcanic eruptions. Certainly, these various factors, allied to increased social stratification and competition for land, may have lead to wetlands being included in a wider social and economic use of the landscape. However, it is more likely that Bronze Age communities were making use of various localities in the landscape simply as part of a flexible economic strategy established since early prehistory. In other words, while permanently occupied, dispersed farmsteads were of key importance in society, and there may also have been at least some members of the community involved in wetland habitation, settlement mobility and the seasonal movement of cattle or sheep herds.

In contrast, our archaeological evidence for settlement and landscape in the Iron Age (500 BC-AD 500) is extremely scarce. The Iron Age remains an enigma in many ways, with little known about its people, settlement and economy. There is little archaeological evidence for an invasion of 'Celtic' peoples. If anything the record testifies to many social and ritual continuities with the Late Bronze Age. Most archaeological evidence for the Iron Age is limited to ceremonial sites and stray finds of spectacular bronze and gold metalwork. Iron Age ceremonial sites, and linear earthworks (such as Navan, Co. Armagh, at Dun Aillinne, Co. Kildare, Rathcroghan, Co. Roscommon and Raffin, Co, Meath) were certainly used during the Iron Age, but we remain largely in the dark as to questions whom and how. There is some, and growing, evidence regarding Iron Age dwelling places, most recently revealed by major motorway developments. The evidence for Iron Age burial, while scarce, is relatively well known, usually involving the insertion of cremated deposits or inhumation burials into Neolithic or Bronze Age barrows, tumuli or cairns.

Iron Age agriculture, as indicated from faunal studies from excavated ceremonial sites does seem to indicate the herding of cattle, pigs, sheep and goat. Cereal cultivation, as indicated by beehive querns and recently discovered wooden ard-heads, may have been of some importance. However, a striking feature of Iron Age palaeoenvironmental studies is the constant identification of an 'agricultural lull' in the pollen record between about 100 BC and AD 340, when there is widespread evidence for large-scale woodland regeneration and a fall in cultivated land plant indicators. What are the reasons for this lack of Iron Age settlement evidence in Ireland? Did some major catastrophe (climate change, a disease epidemic) have a malign effect on Iron Age population levels? Is it possible that Iron Age societies in Ireland focused on power and warfare to such an extent that virtually all energy and wealth was invested in high-status ceremonial structures and high-status metalwork? Towards the end of the Iron Age, Ireland becomes increasingly drawn into the Roman world, with both trade evidence and burial practices reflecting trends there.

Across this vast period, there is obviously much archaeological evidence for coastal activities. In recent years, some of the most exciting evidence for coastal landscape and settlement in the Late Bronze Age and Iron Age in Britain and Ireland has been produced by coastal archaeological surveys. Late Bronze Age and Iron Age houses, trackways, fishing structures and plank boats discovered on the Severn estuary, the Somerset Levels and the Essex marshes all indicate the importance of the coast in a social, economic and symbolic sense. Somewhat similar evidence has been investigated in Ireland, particularly on the Shannon estuary. These sites indicate the role of seasonal settlement and occupation on coastal marshes, activity that may have been mostly oriented towards cattle herding, hunting, fishing, fowling, but that it also included the ritual deposition of later prehistoric metalwork in coastal wetlands. Another area of enquiry is the archaeological evidence for Late Bronze Age and Iron Age boats, thus enabling archaeologists to explore the role of movement in coastal waters and sea-going trade and communications. In this chapter, we will explore two main themes: coastal settlement and economy and the emergence of boats and sea-going vessels in Late Bronze Age and Iron Age Ireland.

LIVING BY THE SEA IN THE BRONZE AGE AND IRON AGE

Promontory forts are a distinctive archaeological feature on the Irish coastline, usually consisting of a narrow headland or promontory, cut off from its hinterland by a stone wall, or series of banks and ditches (26). As with other coastal locations, these sites often show evidence for long-term occupation, not always contemporary with the enclosing features. It is probably the case that some of these promontories were occupied in later prehistory. At Dunbeg, Co. Kerry, an early medieval promontory fort was preceded by a probable Bronze Age site.

26 Promontory fort at Cahercarberymore on Kerry coastline. Bronze Age standing stones, barrows and fulacht fiadh have been found close to such promontories, suggesting some liminal role in later prehistory (Aidan O'Sullivan)

The larger defences of the early medieval fort covered an earlier ditch radiocarbon dated to 802–536 BC. It is also interesting that promontory forts down the west coast, particularly in west Clare and north Kerry, are often associated with barrows, standing stones and fulachta fiadh. Tom Condit's aerial photographic surveys around Kilkee, Co. Clare have demonstrated that promontories were often the location for ring barrows, occasionally situated beside or even within promontory fort defences. It is possible that during the Bronze Age such headlands were seen as liminal spaces and potentially of supernatural importance, thus attracting such monumental activity.

BRONZE AGE CLIFF–TOP FORT AND MARITIME LIVING AT DÚN AONGHUSA, CO. GALWAY

Amongst the most striking evidence for Bronze Age coastal settlement in Ireland is the well-known cliff-top stone fort at Dún Aonghusa, in the Aran Islands (*27, 28*). This site is almost iconic of the rich archaeological evidence of the west coast of Ireland. Its stone ramparts stand two hundred metres above the sea, on a high, precipitous cliff exposed to the gales of the Atlantic Ocean. Although seemingly situated in an isolated location, out on the Aran Islands in Galway Bay; as ever this is a question of perception. Dún Aonghusa is located on a useful height, providing extraordinary views down the west coast of Ireland. On a good day, Mount Brandon is visible way off to the south at the end of the Dingle Peninsula, Co. Kerry. Indeed, when fishing from a boat recently under the cliffs, we noticed that Dún Aonghusa is the only clearly identifiable monument on the entire southern cliff line of the island and it dominates the sea approaches (as it was undoubtedly meant to in the Bronze Age and early medieval period).

Dún Aonghusa was surveyed and excavated in recent years by Claire Cotter as director of the Discovery Programme's Western Stone Forts Project. As a cliff-top settlement, the site was probably first occupied in the Middle Bronze Age with a sequence of activity stretching into the medieval period. The well-known ramparts are not so easily dated, and may well have been built or augmented in the early medieval period. In any case, at Dún Aonghusa, there is particularly good evidence for occupation in the later Bronze Age, between 1000–800 BC. The evidence for settlement on the clifftop includes a number of circular houses, open area hearths and metalworking debris (e.g. clay moulds for the production of bronze axes and swords). There is also evidence for wealth and long-distance contacts, such as sunflower pins and amber beads (which would ultimately have been brought from Scandinavia). The site seems to have been the dwelling place of a community who combined maritime and island resources. Finbar McCormick's studies of the faunal evidence indicate that cattle and sheep were herded on the island, and were possibly fed on seaweed.

27 Bronze Age cliff-top fort at Dún Aonghusa, Aran Islands, Co. Galway (Bank of Ireland)

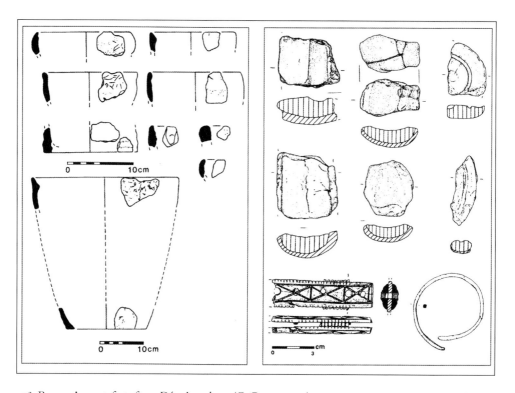

28 Bronze Age artefacts from Dún Aonghusa (C. Cotter, 1993)

However, there is very good evidence from Margaret McCarthy's studies – of the more than five thousand fishbones recovered – that there was inshore fishing for ballan wrasse (in some people's opinion, an ugly, gluey fish), and smaller amounts of conger eel, scad, ling, pollock and the occasional cod. These were probably caught in rock pools on the lower, northern shore of the island, or potentially using long lines from the clifftop (which stands 80m above the water level). This is an excellent area for fishing today, where feeding grounds at the base of the cliff encourage the presence of shoals of fish. Fish were probably caught from spring to autumn, the advantage of the latter season being that the oily fish could be more easily dried and salted for storage. Fish caught in April-May would also have been useful for an over-wintering farming community. Indeed, it has also been suggested that the environmental limits of the island led the site's occupants to also depend on wild resources of birds and fish.

The Bronze Age cliff-top dwellers at Dún Aonghusa were also fowling, as is revealed by Tanya O'Sullivan's studies of at least 1000 bird bones recovered from the site. Guillemot were the most common, with smaller amounts of razorbill, puffin, shag, cormorant, kittiwake and herring gull. Shellfish (including periwinkles, limpets) were also gathered on the rocky foreshores. Interestingly, the range of shellfish present on the site implies a very localized gathering strategy (not including shellfish that could have been obtained only a few kilometres away). There are hints that the community were also eating seaweed and sea vegetables, as is indicated by the tiny mussels found on-site that cling today to strands of dilsc. This seaweed was probably boiled, as may yet be indicated by residue analysis of the coarse ware pottery recovered during the excavations. Claire Cotter sees the site in terms of the maritime landscapes of western Ireland, with fishing, farming and its location on a sea-route all significant aspects of this settlement on the Atlantic coast.

BRONZE AGE AND IRON AGE SETTLEMENTS ON COASTAL AND ISLAND LANDSCAPES

Some Bronze Age settlement sites have been investigated in coastal landscapes, and occasionally they have evidence for the use of maritime foods and raw materials. At Carrigillihy, Co. Cork, a Bronze Age enclosed settlement was investigated by Michael O'Kelly (*29*). The site was located on a gentle slope by the coast on the west side of Glandore Harbour, close to a promontory fort (of unknown date). The Bronze Age enclosure had a fairly substantial oval-shaped house (10m by 6.7m), built of stone walls, located centrally within a small stone enclosure (24m across). A gateway into the enclosure, situated on the east, faced out towards the sea. Although there was little animal bone, the recovery of periwinkle shells indicates some usage of local marine life. A dark, charcoal-rich occupation layer produced coarse ware pottery, a bronze awl, and radiocarbon dates of 1510-1220

29 Reconstruction of Bronze Age enclosure at Carrigillihy, Co. Cork (after O'Kelly, 1951)

BC and 1130-850 BC, perhaps suggesting two phases of occupation. Indeed, the site was also subsequently occupied for a third phase in the Middle Ages, when a rectangular house was built on the earlier site.

At Aughinish Island, Co. Limerick on the banks of the Shannon estuary, several stone enclosures were investigated prior to the building of an industrial plant there. This was a low-lying island on the estuary mudflats, overlooking an extensive intertidal zone today and facing up towards the mouth of the Fergus estuary, itself a focus of significant Bronze Age activity. Eamonn Kelly's excavations revealed that the enclosures were built of low, stone walls or banks with a single entrance way. Within the enclosures there was a single roundhouse. At site 1, the occupation was situated on exposed bedrock and little survived of the houses. However, the site did produce several pits that were filled with marine shells, some coarse pottery, saddle querns for grinding grain, as well as a bronze tanged chisel and pin. Aughinish site 2 located a few hundred metres to the south-east also produced circular round house, coarse ware pottery and some pits filled with shells. These were the dwelling enclosures of a small Late Bronze Age community, who dwelled within these circular houses, and as well as tending the lands around them, gathered shellfish from the rocks along the coast. Other marine islands that saw occupation in the Bronze Age included Dalkey Island, Co. Dublin – where there is evidence in the form of clay moulds and crucibles for metal-working activity during the period. The Bronze Age inhabitation of offshore Atlantic islands is also attested to by the presence of fulachta fiadh, enclosures and field-systems such as Inishark and Clare Island, Co. Galway.

BRONZE AGE ESTUARINE SETTLEMENT, MOVEMENT AND RITUAL ACTIVITIES ON THE SHANNON ESTUARY

It is also clear that Bronze Age settlement activities extended down into wetland or coastal landscapes. Bronze Age coastal wetland settlements or metalworking sites are known from the edges of estuarine marshlands. A Middle Bronze Age coastal fen-edge occupation near Strangford Lough was excavated at Meadowlands, Co. Down. This produced two circular houses with hearths and possible cooking pits with burnt stone, with finds including cordoned urn pottery, a stone axe and several flint scrapers. The Meadowlands occupation was situated at the edge of the former estuarine marshes of the River Quoile, possibly indicating that its inhabitants were engaged in cattle herding, hunting and fowling in the wetlands.

Regional landscape studies are one way of investigating later prehistoric societies and providing a broader context for understanding the role of coastal and estuarine landscapes. In recent years, the Discovery Programme's North Munster Project investigated this region on the lower Shannon for later prehistory. Eoin Grogan's landscape and excavation research revealed that the region saw the emergence of a socially complex, politically powerful and well-connected community. From the Middle Bronze Age onwards, we see the emergence of the use of major hillforts and small hilltop enclosures – presumably as power centres for local and regional social groups. Palaeoenvironmental evidence also indicates that during the Middle to Late Bronze Age, there was population growth and a clearance of woodland for the first time in south-east Clare. The deposition of large hoards of Late Bronze Age bronze objects and gold ornaments in the region's wetlands indicates the growing economic and political power of some of these social groups by c.900 BC. Archaeological surveys have also revealed the presence of numerous small stone enclosures, situated on rockland soils and often associated with small field-systems, standing stones and fulachta fiadh and the occasional metalwork hoard or stray find. These enclosures are very similar to known Bronze Age sites (e.g. Carrigillihy and Aughinish, above) and it is likely that these were the homesteads of small social groups belonging to these Bronze Age populations.

Archaeological survey has also revealed that many of these probable Bronze Age settlements are located along the hills fringing the upper Shannon estuary and Fergus estuary. The North Munster Project's intertidal archaeological surveys of the Shannon estuary's mudflats have also lead to the discovery of a number of unique Middle and Late Bronze Age dwellings and other structures (30).

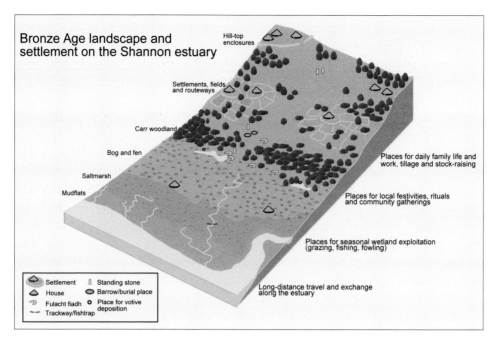

30 Hypothetical model of Bronze Age inhabitation and use of Shannon estuary (O'Sullivan 2001)

31 Carrigdirty Rock Bronze Age reconstruction drawing, Shannon estuary (from O'Sullivan 2001)

A Middle Bronze Age hut found at Carrigdirty Rock 1, Co. Limerick on the Shannon estuary, consisted of a circular wooden structure preserved on a shelf of submerged organic peats exposed at low tide. The site was probably originally constructed in a fen or carr woodland located at some distance back from a previous estuary channel.

The hut was constructed of an inner ring of light alder wood poles that had been carefully sharpened so that they could be driven down into the peat and these have been radiocarbon dated to 1681-1529 cal. BC. Small outlying stakes may represent a light fence or wall. The site has not been excavated yet, but it produced a single piece of immature calf-bone. The Carrigdirty Rock structure could be interpreted as the remains of a small roundhouse, perhaps between 4.6-6m in diameter, constructed with posts holding up a low roof thatched with reeds. It certainly could have provided adequate shelter for herders living with their cattle on the marshes, or for people hunting or fishing on the wetlands during the drier, warmer months of the summer (31).

Other undated (but probably Bronze Age) features from this archaeological complex in the Carrigdirty Rock intertidal peats included isolated groups of posts and two very large cleft oak planks, laid horizontally and at irregular orientations in the peat. These oak planks may have served as trackways or creek bridges in the wetlands. At Carrigdirty Rock 3, a shallow, oval pit located amongst the trunks and roots of a fen-carr woodland produced disarticulated red deer bone and pink footed goose bone, while chopped pig bone and mature deer antler had been recovered from the immediately adjacent peat surface. These various features may indicate a range of later prehistoric activities in these estuarine environments. It is possible that the contemporary settlements of these wetland communities are located amongst the stone enclosures, fulachta fiadh and standing stones that are found on the low hills and terraces that overlook the Carrigdirty Rock estuarine marshlands. Although occurring some centuries later, it is also interesting that a Late Bronze Age hoard from Carrigogunnell, Co. Limerick and the Shannongrove, Co. Limerick Late Bronze Age gold gorget were recovered from wetland contexts at the edge of these estuarine marshlands. It reminds one that Bronze Age activity in these estuarine wetlands could have involved complex social, economic and ideological perceptions of a landscape that is essentially liminal and located at the edge of the 'normal' world. These estuarine wetlands, dominated by seasonal and other temporal environmental rhythms, may have been more than just sources of economic benefit.

On the Fergus estuary, to the north, there is also archaeological evidence for Bronze Age enclosed settlements on the drylands overlooking the estuarine marshes. Indeed, recent excavations in advance of motorway development at Newmarket-on-Fergus, Co. Clare uncovered Middle Bronze Age fulachta fiadh and burials right down at the edge of marshlands. The North Munster Project's intertidal surveys in the 1990s identified an unusual Late Bronze Age wooden structure at Islandmagrath, Co. Clare, where the estuary channel meanders

32 Islandmagrath, Co. Clare Late Bronze Age structure, Fergus estuary, Co. Clare (from O'Sullivan 2001)

between some lowlying drumlin hills. This wooden structure was built of two parallel rows of post-and-wattle fences, hurdle panels, brushwood and branches (*32*). A range of radiocarbon dates have indicated that it was built between 800–550 BC. The structure, probably originally constructed in intertidal estuarine clays with reed swamps in the vicinity, could be interpreted as either an unusual fish trap, a 'hard' or complex wooden jetty for beaching and unloading boats, or perhaps as a well-built trackway providing access across the mudflats and reed swamp. It is certainly located on a potential route way for people and animals crossing a narrow point of the upper Fergus estuary, moving between islands and drylands. Certainly, the landscape to the east is known to have been intensively settled from *c.*200 BC, when Mooghaun hillfort, hilltop enclosures and smaller farmsteads were occupied by a wealthy, socially stratified and regionally powerful community.

It is possible that Bronze Age evidence from the estuarine mudflats suggests that these local communities made use of the estuary's resources by means of a mixed farming strategy with cattle and sheep herded on the coastal marshes for the spring and summer pastures with perhaps livestock and crops also tended on the dryland terraces and hills, while no doubt fishing and hunting was also important. On the other hand, there are other interesting explanations. By the Late Bronze Age especially, these local communities were depositing gold dress fasteners, bracelets and gorgets, bronze axes and weapons into the estuary's marshes, creeks and bogs. For example, a Late Bronze Age gold bracelet and a gold dress-fastener were recovered in the past during estuarine reclamation works on the upper Fergus estuary, Co. Clare. Again, these are hints that the sacred and secular were intertwined in these coastal wetlands – that people were both inhabiting these marshes and also using them during ritual practices. The estuarine wetlands may have been seen as a sacred space, within which there were particular places where otherworldly spirits and entities could have been encountered and contacted.

BRONZE AGE AND IRON AGE COASTAL SHELL MIDDENS

Bronze Age and Iron Age shell middens are also known from sandhills and coastal dunes, particularly on the west coast of Ireland. These sites consist of spreads of shell, burnt stone, bone, pottery and other finds. They have in the past been investigated by antiquarians as well as more recently by archaeologists in advance of golf courses or other developments. They are also particularly prone to erosion by waves and wind, located as they are in sand dunes or under the thin sod of coastal machair soils. Indeed, at Omey Island, Co. Galway, Tadhg O'Keeffe's archaeological excavations of an early medieval cemetery eroding into the sea revealed that there was also a Bronze Age shell midden under the site. Agricultural overstocking today can often lead to a destruction of the sod cover, thus exposing the archaeological features within the dunes and bluffs to serious erosion and collapse. Bronze Age and Iron Age shell middens are known from Beginish, Co. Kerry; Culleenamore, Co. Sligo and from False Bay and Doonloughan, near Ballyconneelly, Co. Galway on the Connemara coastline.

In recent years, a particularly rich and complex series of Bronze Age and early medieval middens near Ballyconneelly – namely at Doonloughan Bay, False Bay and Mannin Bay, Co. Galway were exposed by such erosion and investigated by Finbar McCormick, Michael Gibbons, Emily Murray and others (33). An Early Bronze Age shell midden at Doonloughan 1 was situated above the high water mark at the edge of a tiny inlet known as False Bay. The midden survived as a 30m spread of oyster shells and burnt stone. It also had a small pit that had been filled with shells, burnt stone and sherds of up to four or five food vessel pots (a distinctive Early Bronze Age type). Other finds from the vicinity included chert scrapers.

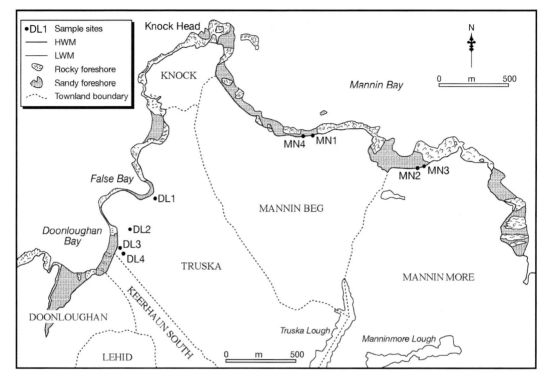

33 Bronze Age and early medieval middens at Doonloughan, Co. Galway (after McCormick *et al.* 1996)

Palaeoenvironmental studies of the deposits also revealed the presence of burnt grains of barley (*Hordeum*) and large numbers of limpets, winkles, oysters and a small amount of cattle bone. Otherwise, Emily Murray has shown that no fish bones were recovered and that analysis of food residues adhering to the pottery indicates a generally land-based diet. The False Bay midden was radiocarbon dated to 2094-1880 BC.

It is tempting to interpret a site like this as some kind of an occupation site – given the presence of burnt stone (used for cooking?), shells, barley and burnt bone. However, it could also be pointed out that an archaeological site like Doonloughan 1 reasonably closely resembles an Early Bronze Age burial site – although no human bone was recovered. In Early Bronze Age burial practice, fragments of bone, burnt stone, broken pottery and food offerings may be placed together in a pit. In recent years, it has been suggested that 'fragmentation' is a common theme in Bronze Age ritual – representing complex ideas about society, identity and ritual practice. In other words, it may well be that the ritual use of middens and the liminal perception of the ocean that we have already discussed in early prehistory continued into the Bronze Age.

Late Bronze Age and Iron Age middens were also located immediately further to the north. At Mannin 2, a long stretch of midden with at least three phases of occupation or burning was exposed in the eroding sandy bluffs. Excavation revealed the presence of stake holes, pits and possible hearths. The shells were mostly of limpets, with small amounts of sheep/goat and cattle. There was also a rich palaeoenvironmental deposit of burnt grains of barley and oats, with weeds including fat hen, knot grass, docks and charlock – which was probably growing in cultivated arable crops growing in fields in the locality. The precise date of the midden is unclear, but radiocarbon dating of the shells suggests activity in the last few centuries BC. It might be suggested from these deposits that again people were either carrying out ritual activities at the edge of the sea, or that arable crops were being grown in fields overlooking the seashore.

The Neolithic shell midden sites at Culleenamore, on Ballysodare Bay, Co. Sligo also saw re-activation and renewed activity throughout the Middle Bronze Age, the Late Bronze Age and into the Iron Age. The upper levels of the midden produced bronze, pottery, glass and other objects. The shoreline was still being used by people who were gathering oysters, cockles, mussels, periwinkles, scallops and limpets. A hearth was radiocarbon dated to 770-600 BC. Most intriguingly, the ancient shell midden was also dug into during the Iron Age (c.200 BC) for the burial of a child, and the site subsequently accumulated more shells from occupation activity. The burial of a person in a shell midden both recalls early prehistoric practices, as well as a phenomenon that continued through the Medieval period into modern times. While, such recent burials often signified the burial of unknown outsiders, of unbaptised children, or of drowned sailors – in the Iron Age, it may be yet another example of people reaching back into the past at a time of grief and social disruption.

Iron Age shell middens, dating to c.385-176 BC, from Ballymulholland, Co. Derry also provide intriguing evidence for later prehistoric occupation in sand dunes, as well as potential craft or production activity. This site was located in eroding sand cliffs on Magilligan Foreland fronting onto the Foyle estuary, Co. Derry and was excavated by Jim Mallory and Finbar McCormick (34). At Ballymullholland 1 (the largest of three middens discovered) a thin band (some 36cm thick) of charcoal, shell, bones and some metal slag was exposed over a 25m length of the sand cliff. However, the site's stratigraphy was complex with lenses of natural wind blown sand, as well as several cultural horizons. The shells were mostly of the species *Arctica islandica*, with smaller amounts of cockles, winkles (some small shells possibly had been adering to bladder wrack seaweed which was brought to the site). Small amounts of animal bone were recovered from cattle, red deer, pig mandible, sheep/goat and cetacean (possibly of the size of a pilot whale). Bird bones found included gannet and probably common gull. Interestingly, there was no fish bone. Palaeobotanical studies indicate that the site was located in a landscape that was largely treeless, dominated by grasses, sedges and plantain that may have been used for rough grazing.

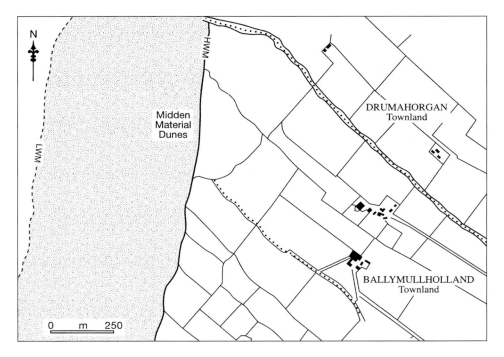

34 Location map of Ballymullholland, Co. Derry

Some threads of seasonal evidence from the animal bone (e.g. the pig bone) suggest occupation in the late winter/early spring time. Within the cultural layers, there were also a few archaeological features including two postholes and a pit. Amongst the few finds was some iron slag – nodular aggregates of rust coloured material with black pools of vitrification in the interior – from the blooming process. The Ballymullholland site might be interpreted as an occupation site of people who were eking out their scarce food resources after a long winter, but the presence of iron working suggests interesting things too.

It should also be noted that, as with Neolithic megalithic tombs, marine shells are often recovered from Bronze Age burials. A necklace of sea shells was found with a Bronze Age burial at Chapelizod, Co. Dublin, while unperforated sea shells have also been found with several other burials in pits and cists with Food Vessel and Urn burials. Most probably they represent some element of personal clothing, but the deposition of whole and fragmentary marine shells may also be some representation of the person's identity.

BOATS AND NAVIGATION IN THE BRONZE AGE AND IRON AGE

Peoples of the Atlantic shore

It is clear from a range of archaeological evidence that during the Bronze Age and Iron Age, there were strong cultural and economic connections between the various peoples inhabiting the shoreline of the Atlantic coast – leading to the movement of technologies, ideas and cargoes of objects (e.g. amber, bronze and gold objects). The presence of Bronze Age and Iron Age metalwork, amber and other imported items from western and central Europe, Scandinavia and even the Mediterranean, is itself an indicator of some measure of maritime trade and communications between Ireland, Britain and the continent. It goes without saying that such objects were brought by boats, across the seaways between these islands and the continent. Indeed, underwater archaeologists diving on the seabed off Langdon Bay and Morecombe Sands in Britain have found accumulations of bronze axes and tools suggesting that they were lost when ships had sunk during a storm.

Indeed, it has been suggested that the cultural similarities and even the languages spoken by the early historic peoples of Ireland, Scotland, Wales and Brittany result not from the migrations of populations in the Iron Age, but from the older connections between these maritime populations that stretch back into the later Bronze Age. Long-term traditions of maritime trade and communications along the Atlantic seaways may have enabled the evolution of so-called 'Celtic' languages during later prehistory. Although situated at the frontiers of the Roman empire during the late Iron Age, it is also evident that Ireland participated in the Roman world – as can be seen by even the small amount of Mediterranean or Roman silver, coins, objects and even burial practices on this island.

Recognising this, archaeologists are still faced with a lack of evidence for what the vessels were like that enabled the movement of people across the Irish Sea and along the Atlantic shore. In recent years, Early and Middle Bronze Age wooden boats capable of navigating along the Atlantic seaways have been discovered on the estuaries and coastline of Britain. In particular, Middle Bronze Age sewn-plank boats, of sophisticated and complex design, have been recorded at Brigg and North Ferriby (on the Humber estuary, in north-east England), at Caldicot, in the Gwent Levels of the Severn estuary, at Dover (on the south coast of England). These are interesting discoveries, particularly the plank boats that were found on the Welsh shore of the Severn estuary – in waters that fringed the Irish Sea.

Unfortunately, the archaeological evidence for late Bronze Age and Iron Age boats in Ireland is poor. Irish archaeologists have yet to find a clearly confirmed prehistoric ocean-going craft. Several dugout boats in Ireland have been dated to the Late Bronze Age and Iron Age, but they are rarely found on the coast – mostly deriving from lakes and rivers. A spectacularly large Bronze Age dugout boat was found at Lurgan, Co. Galway – this may well have been a war canoe or other significantly high-status vessel. By the Iron Age, we do have the evidence for larger sea-going boats, particularly in the form of a golden model of a boat found in the Broighter hoard, Co. Derry. It is likely that by the Iron Age there were various boat-building traditions in northern Europe, from Scandinavia, to the North Sea and down to the Mediterranean. From the Irish midlands, we have an unusual smaller plank-built craft that is unmistakeably built in the form of the Roman style boat. This Iron Age boat from Lough Lene, Co. Westmeath certainly implies the presence of knowledge of Mediterranean or northern European boat-building traditions in Ireland. Although no Roman military or cargo carrying vessel has been found in Irish waters, we should probably assume that various types of ocean going craft were moving up and down the Irish Sea, and indeed around the west coast of Ireland.

BRONZE AGE BOATS

So, we have to turn to British archaeology to understand what types of craft might have been used by Irish later prehistoric mariners. What boats could have been used in maritime travel during the Bronze Age? It is less likely that prehistoric log-boats were used as coastal craft. They are unstable and their low freeboard (i.e. the height of the sides above the waterline) mean that they would have been too easily swamped by waves. In fact the earliest craft that we know of that could have been used for easy ocean voyages are the Bronze Age sewn plank boats from England and Wales. All these craft were built of large oak planks, fastened together using yew or willow twisted ropes. The boats were flat bottomed, were fairly long and had no evidence for masts or sails. Most probably they were propelled by a crew of paddlers, using long slender paddles. Although large and heavy, they would have moved fairly fast across calm waters. It is estimated that the English Channel, between Dover and France, could have been crossed using one of these Bronze Age plank boats in five or six hours, while the Humber boats would have been placed to make a journey across the North Sea to the Dutch coast in 24 hours.

BRONZE AGE BOATS FROM THE HUMBER ESTUARY AND SEVERN ESTUARY

The earliest known Bronze Age boat fragments are the planks from three or four different craft found at North Ferriby, on the Humber estuary of north-east England (35). These planks were recovered in the decades after 1938 by E.V. Wright, who explored for years the intertidal mudflats of the Humber. It is probable that up to three boats are represented by the remains at North Ferriby, dating to about 2030-1780 BC. All of these planks derive from deliberately

35 Reconstruction of the North Ferriby Bronze Age boat (from Wright 1991)

dismantled craft, the largest of which measured 14.35m in length by 2.6m in beam. The planks were sewn to a keel plank with yew withies, the holes caulked with moss. Transverse bars of ash stiffened the craft and side strakes were skillfully joined to the lower timbers. The Early Bronze Age Ferriby boats with their absence of sails and the lack of a distinctive keel would have been paddled, to be used for moving along creeks or for navigating the estuary itself – and occasionally for crossing the North Sea. Another Middle Bronze Age boat is known from a single oak plank recovered in the 1990s from the ancient silts of a river now known as the Nedern, that once flowed through the estuarine levels of the Severn estuary. This plank dated to about 1600 BC was evidently also taken from a large vessel.

BRONZE AGE DOVER BOAT

Amongst the most spectacular archaeological discoveries of recent decades was the identification of a Middle Bronze Age boat, dated to 1575-1520 BC, by the Canterbury Archaeological Trust at Dover in 1992 (36). The discovery is a story in itself. It was made by professional archaeologists engaged in excavations prior to the construction of a major roadway by-passing Dover town to the Ferry port. This involved the digging of a hole six metres deep below the street level

36 Reconstruction drawing of Dover Bronze Age boat (from Clark 2004)

of the modern town. The excavations had dealt with the stratigraphy and finds of the site's medieval archaeology and had gone down into the natural sands of the original prehistoric coastal environment. Indeed, it was a stroke of luck that it was found at all, as the archaeologists recognised the presence of planks in these deep levels during a lunch break, and had to race to excavate it before developers moved in to complete the road's construction. Although the sides and south end of the boat were found, the north end of the boat remains unexcavated under the buildings and streets of the modern town of Dover.

The Dover boat was quite large, measuring up to 2.3m in width, with a possible length of up to 15m (i.e. it was potentially longer than a modern, double-decker bus). The boat was built entirely of oak planks and yew wood ropes. It was shaped like a modern punt, with a flat bottom, vertical sides and a flat sloping south end. Each side curved upward from the bottom by a specially shaped 'ile' plank resembling half a split dugout. The two broad bottom planks were held together by wedges and transverse timbers slotted through holes in rails and cleats were left standing inboard. The planks were sewn together using yew withies and the plank seams were made watertight with a caulking of moss and beeswax laid on the inboard face of each seam. Tool marks show that the boat was fashioned by axes with curved blades, probably palstaves. The boat has much evidence for use and wear. A number of natural splits in both curving lower planks had been repaired by stitches and laths. There is no evidence of the method of propulsion or steering, leading archaeologists to suspect that it was moved by paddles.

The boat was buried in silt 6m below ground level. Palaeoenvironmental studies show that it formerly lay in a fresh-water river, where it had been partly dismantled before it was abandoned. Although it was found in silts of a freshwater environment the vessel is thought to have been too small for the river that it was abandoned in. Moreover, there was some marine shell, quartz sand and glauconite grains ('foreign' to the Dover area) adhering to the underside of the boat – possibly resulting from a previous period when it lay on an ocean beach. This suggests that the Dover boat was probably used for coasting and for cross-channel journeys. The navigation across the 11km wide English Channel to France, although dangerous, could probably have been made by experienced paddlers well inside a day.

PRESTIGE SEAFARING IN THE BRONZE AGE

It is clear that the Dover boat was a prestige artefact, accomplished using the best raw materials, and assembled with skill and a lot of physical labour. It probably carried a crew of up to sixteen people and could have held a large cargo of hides, bronze objects, ingots or scrap. Indeed, the Dover boat should be regarded as the product of a wider kin-group or even the population of a political territory, rather than of a family or household. Building a plank boat may have been as much a community event as building a barrow or a hillfort. Some archaeologists have thought that these boats were mostly used as local ferries or river-craft, designed for inshore travel or for crossing narrow and relatively calm estuarine channels.

However, if a Bronze Age boat as complex and superbly made as this one is not to be considered as an occasionally ocean-going craft, it has to be wondered what spectacular type of ancient boat scholars are waiting for? Indeed, given the fact that the perception of risk is culturally specific (i.e. Bronze Age people may have easily accepted the significant dangers of seafaring because of the potential rewards) and allowing for a coastal community's knowledge of their craft and the opportunities provided by weather, currents and tides, it seems reasonable that some of these boats were indeed the craft that plied the ocean waters between these islands and the continent. In Bronze Age Ireland (as in Britain) men and women (perhaps chosen members of ruling social elites) going on a sea-going voyage to carry 'Irish' tin, bronze axes, swords or gold to Britain, or to collect Scandinavian amber beads, jet and other exotic or prestige objects from distant lands, may have been participating in an event with strong ideological and social overtones for the community. Participating in an ocean voyage may have bestowed some people with a much-desired reputation for courage, seafaring ability, social connections and a knowledge of distant places, much as pilgrimage to distant places was seen as a personally transformative experience in the Middle Ages.

IRON AGE BOATS

While there is a gap of knowledge in the Late Bronze Age, by the Roman Iron Age there re-emerges some historical and archaeological evidence for seafaring craft in north-west Europe. Most famously, there is Caesar's description of the plank boats of the Veneti at about 50 BC – a tribe who controlled the maritime trade routes of the Armorican coast to the mouth of the River Loire. These boats had hulls constructed of oak planks fastened to internal frame timbers using iron nails. They had a high stem and stern, apparently to enable them to withstand Atlantic waves, and were rigged for sails of hides or soft leather. Caesar describes how these craft could run before the wind and with their flat keels, they could sail through shallow water and safely run aground on rocks. The writer Strabo also suggests that they were caulked with 'seaweed' – probably moss or reeds. Although there is little archaeological evidence for these craft, a large iron anchor with chain found in the Iron Age Bulbury hillfort, not far from Poole harbour probably represents equipment from one of these ocean-going craft. Also from the first century BC are those Iron Age coins that show depictions of large, deep-hulled sailing ships with a mast set amidships. It is unknown from whence sails were introduced, but it is probable that some debt is owed to Mediterranean craft that would have been moving up the Atlantic coastline.

In the early centuries AD, there is plentiful archaeological evidence for seagoing ships along the northern coast of Europe, as various Romano-Celtic boat traditions emerged amongst the countries along the North Sea. It is also likely that both Roman warships and Mediterranean style trading ships were seen regularly in the waters around these islands.

IRON AGE BROIGHTER GOLD BOAT MODEL

What types of boats were in use in Iron Age or Roman-era Ireland? It seems likely that they were a combination of wicker-built currachs and latterly the oak plank boats that would have been sailing up the edge of the Roman Empire on the other side of the Irish Sea. While no large Iron Age wooden vessel survive in Ireland, we do have the evidence for such craft in the early Iron Age Broighter hoard, from Co. Derry (37). The Broighter hoard of gold objects was found on the south shore of Lough Foyle, close to its entrance, at the end of the nineteenth century. In 1896, two local ploughmen, James Morrow and Thomas Nickle discovered it while working a field in the reclaimed coastal levels. The hoard was probably a deliberate votive deposit in coastal marshlands, possibly as an offering or gift to the Celtic sea god, Mannanán Mac Lir. The hoard consisted of a gold boat, a gold model cauldron, a tubular torc, two gold chains and two looped terminal twisted torcs, all of which can be dated to the first century BC on account of the La Téne decoration on the tubular torc.

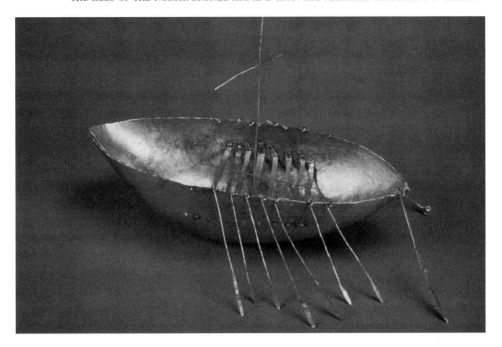

37 Iron Age Broighter boat model (National Museum of Ireland)

The Broighter boat model is of particular importance as it is the earliest representation of a boat in Ireland. It was made from a single, beaten sheet of gold, 18.4 cm long, which was split and rejoined at the prow and stern. The model clearly represents what must have been a large sailing craft with one central mast and nine oar ports. The boat had nine original thwarts or seats, one of which is now missing (having been sold to a jeweller). Each thwart is associated with an oar port on both its starboard and port side, and is secured to the hull by small gold rivets or pins that pass through the hull of the vessel.

The central thwart placed amidships is slightly wider than the others and has a centrally placed perforation which holds a mast. The mast is hook shaped, but this may not be an original feature and may have occurred as a result of damage. The hook was not straightened by the goldsmith in Dublin, to whom the find was taken to for 'fixing', as this piece was originally interpreted as a boat hook and not a mast.

The yard has also subsequently been attached to the mast which would have held a single small square sail. The oars are fastened to the vessel through row locks made up of wire rings at the gunwale. Originally the oars were found unconnected to the vessel but later tied to it for display purposes after the model was recovered. A large steering oar was also recovered and is attached on the port side of the vessel by a similar method of bindings as the oars. There is also a tiny corresponding hole on the starboard stern which has been interpreted as a fastening position for the steering oar suggesting that the helmsman had an option of where to mount the oar. In addition to these accessories other pieces which have been interpreted as a grappling iron and three forked poles used for punting were also found.

There has been much scholarly debate as to whether the Broighter Iron Age gold model represents a hide-covered or a wooden boat. It has been suggested that the 'straight rim of the gunwale and the short curved stem' of the Broighter boat were indicative of a skin-covered craft. One antiquarian in 1902 saw faint marks on the sides of the vessel as indicating wooden ribs and the framework of a wooden skeleton of a vessel covered with hides. Others have suggested that the lack of any internal framing, the unusual tub shaped hull of the vessel and its large size are unlike any known skin-covered craft. They also note that the pinning of the thwarts through a skin-covered hull would also have caused problems in keeping the boat dry – although of course it is a boat model, not a boat.

It is certainly possible that the Broighter model represents the earliest depiction of a skin-covered boat in Ireland, as it is a type of vessel frequently mentioned in the writings of Roman historians around the time the hoard was made. Pliny in his *Natural History*, written in the first century AD, records that the Britons sailed in boats of osier covered with sewn hides, and later that boats in British waters were made of wickerwork covered with hides. A third-century historian also recorded that 'the sea which separates Ireland from Britain is rough and stormy throughout the year; it is navigable for a few days only, they voyage in small boats of pliant twigs, covered with skins of oxen. During the time they are at sea, the voyagers abstain from food'. So, it is certainly likely that 'Iron Age' voyagers set sail in hide-covered craft.

LOUGH LENE IRON AGE BOAT

Although it was not discovered in a maritime context, an Iron Age boat found in the Irish midlands is interesting because of the intriguing details of its construction. The boat was found in 1968 in the waters of Lough Lene in County Westmeath by divers from the Mullingar Sub Aqua Club. The planks, which had been known to local people for many years, lay in 4-5m depth of water, at a location about 70m from the shore.

The boat (*38, 39*) remains consisted of one long oak plank and one short oak piece skilfully scarfed together (using pegs and stitching), which formed the bottom as well as one oak plank from the side. The boat was broken at the prow and stern, so its length cannot be reconstructed, but it was certainly in excess of 7.9m. At the time of its discovery, two carved willow oars were found underneath the planks. A single side strake, 6.5m long was found associated with the bottom planking and would have been secured to it by mortise and tenon joints. Eighteen mortises were visible on the plank after initial recovery with

Right: 38 Lough Lene Iron Age boat being removed from water (Aidan O'Sullivan)

Below: 39 Lough Lene Iron Age boat drawings (after Waddell 2000)

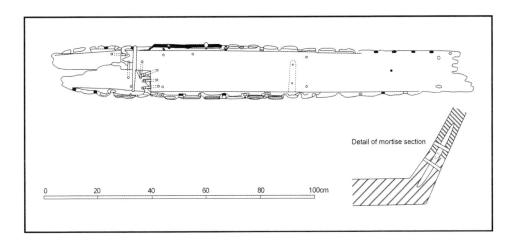

Detail of mortise section

0   20   40   60   80   100cm

seven tenons surviving. There was also evidence that the strake had been stitched to the lower timbers. A single rowlock survived on the strake when the divers first recovered the boat but this was subsequently lost and its form cannot be fully attested.

The surviving portion of the hull indicated that it was a flat-bottomed vessel with straight sides and that the oak planks were assembled using yew wood free-tenons in mortises and yew wood treenails. The scarf joints also utilised dovetails, withy stitching and were possibly luted with wood resin or linseed oil. The plank was radiocarbon dated to between 400-100 BC. However, the radiocarbon sample was taken from slow-grown yew wood, so it is possible the boat could date to the first century AD.

Most remarkably then, the boat was carvel built in the manner of Mediterranean boats, using mortise and free-tenon techniques which had died out in Europe by the seventh century AD. This method was probably originally developed well before 2000 BC and had been used by the Egyptians. It is the only boat of its kind found in Ireland and is one of less than ten such craft found in north-west Europe which date to the Roman period. It has been suggested that this narrow, low vessel was carried by a merchant or group of merchants from Roman-occupied territory travelling through the country. The annals are littered with references to travelling groups carrying their transport with them over rough ground. Certainly, other Iron Age monuments are known from the vicinity of the lake. A barrow situated on a hill overlooking the lake was excavated and produced an imported Iron Age bronze Somerset bowl with cremation deposits dating to the last few centuries BC. This raises intriguing possibilities for the presence of Iron Age settlement in the region. However, the Lough Lene boat does not have to indicate the presence of Roman shipwrights or traders. The presence of such an exotic item in an Irish midlands lake could be explained by the presence of a local shipwright versed in European shipbuilding skills. However, this still leaves open the question of why local groups would demand such an unusual craft – perhaps it was part of the attractive package of goods that the Roman world represented.

NAVIGATION AND SAILING BOATS BETWEEN IRELAND, BRITAIN AND WESTERN EUROPE

Our understanding of navigation methods and sea routes in later prehistory basically have to be constructed from diverse evidence; the distribution of artifacts, the occasional discovery of boats and through some scraps of written evidence. Firstly, it is worth noting that in recent years some archaeologists have called into question the idea that there were ever long-distance route ways during the Bronze Age, whatever about the later Iron Age. It has been suggested that in fact, there would have been many shorter journeys in small sea-going craft that were moving along the North Sea and around the coast of Britain and Ireland. These sea voyages may have taken months, not weeks.

Indeed, some Bronze Age archaeologists have interpreted such later prehistoric sea routes as networks of localised communications hugging the coast, with mariners going ashore for the night, travelling only at times of long daylight (April to September), using paddles, breezes, tides and currents to move slowly and safely from point-to-point and always within sight of land. Overnight voyages that had to be made across the open sea (such as across the English Channel or across the Irish Sea) may have been made overnight, to arrive at dawn. Bronze Age and Iron Age navigation, as in later periods, would have involved moving between known places, which were marked by landmarks (mountains, cliffs, headlands), or by seamarks (shoals, reefs, tidal races). Out at sea, sailors would have navigated through their knowledge of winds, moon, North Star, some star constellations, as well as experience of speeds, sailing conditions, etc. – using dead reckoning (moving in lines from point-to-point).

Sean MacGrail through his study of the archaeological distributions of imported objects and his knowledge of the seas has suggested that the principal sea lanes in later prehistory between Europe and the British Isles were firstly from the Rhine to Thames estuary; across the straits between Dover and Calais (where France is clearly visible from the English coast) and from Western Brittany to south-west Britain and south-east Ireland, with boats moving back and forth from Loire and Garonne estuaries. It must also have been the case that Ireland was linked via seaways to western Scotland and ultimately Scandinavia. These sea lanes would have then been linked into more local sea lanes along the coast, estuaries and river mouths.

However, by the Iron Age, longer sea routes do seem to have emerged and were also linked into local trading networks. For example, it has been proposed that Mediterranean traders sailed the Atlantic route to Brittany, and then goods were moved by local peoples, using native sailing routes. Certainly, by about 500 BC, Ireland begins to appear in the writings of early Mediterranean/Classical histories and geographies. According to the Roman texts of the sixth century BC, the Atlantic sea lanes ran from Britain/Ireland to Brittany, to Tartessus in southern Portugal, through the Straits of Gibraltar to the northern shore of the Mediterranean. On the basis of such sixth-century BC descriptions, it is thought that voyages between Brittany and Ireland took two days. One classical text states that Ireland is a 'two-day voyage from Oestrymnides islands to the *sacra insula*, rich in turf, near Albion, and thickly populated by the Hierni'. Covering this distance in two days would require a boat to travel at a speed of five knots, so this is indirect evidence in itself that sail boats were in use.

Roman contacts with Ireland is attested to in both historical and archaeological sources. Pliny the Elder writing in *c*.AD 77 records that 'Hibernia (is the) same width as Britain but less in length; with the shortest crossing from Silures tribe in Britain. In the second century AD, Tacitus recorded that Hibernia was in the

Gallic Sea between Britain and Spain, and that it was smaller than Britain but had a similar climate. He also wrote that its approaches and harbours are well known to merchants. In an intriguing reference dating to *c*.AD 116, Juvenal wrote that 'Roman arms [were] carried beyond the shores of Iuverna' suggesting (if its truth were accepted) that some form of military force – a legion or at least an exploratory party – had entered the country. Other Roman authors also give us a sense of that imperial perception of Ireland. Solinus writing in *c*.AD 200 records that Ireland is a 'stormy sea passage from Britain navigable only a few days a year'. In fact, it seems probable that at least one Roman vessel fell victim to the stormy conditions off western Ireland. A fragment of Roman amphora was trawled up in fishermen's nets on the Porcupine Bank that is well off the west coast of Ireland. This must have either been lost overboard from a vessel or trawled up from a wreck lying on the deep seabed. One might imagine that the merchant's or military vessel was blown out into the western ocean by a gale and had never returned.

So, it is clear then that by the second century AD, the Irish coastline was well known to Roman writers. The earliest accounts of the ports, headlands and river mouths of the Irish coast are provided in the geographer Ptolemy's second-century AD *Guide to Geography* (published as a map in AD 1477) with its map projections, tables of latitude and longitude and brief descriptions of places in different parts of the world. They record tribal names, significant settlements, river mouths, headlands and harbours. Ptolemy's knowledge of the location and importance of these different ports would have derived from contacts with the soldiers, sailors and merchants who would have plied the seas between Ireland and mainland Europe at this time.

Indeed, it is likely that throughout the early centuries AD, there were strong maritime trading and other cultural connections between the Irish coast and Roman naval forts and the Romano-British populations along the west coast of Britain. There is evidence that Roman coins, silver spiral rings and disc brooches and other objects were deposited at various Irish pagan cult sites, such as at Newgrange, Co. Meath. It is possible that such deposits were made by Romano-British immigrants, merchants or by Irish mercenary soldiers returning from the empire with new beliefs.

It is also possible that Romano-British merchants or traders established a trading and manufacturing base on the coastal promontory at Drumanagh, beside the modern village of Loughshinny, in north Dublin (*40, 41*). This dramatically situated site has closely-spaced ramparts enclosing a massive promontory, overlooking a fine natural harbour and possible copper mines to the north. It is known that Roman-era objects have been recovered by treasure hunters from within this site, although these are not yet published. Michael Ryan has suggested that Drumanagh was an emporium of some sort, where the manufacture of high status objects occurred – including the production of native Irish Iron Age snaffle-bits of bronze and iron.

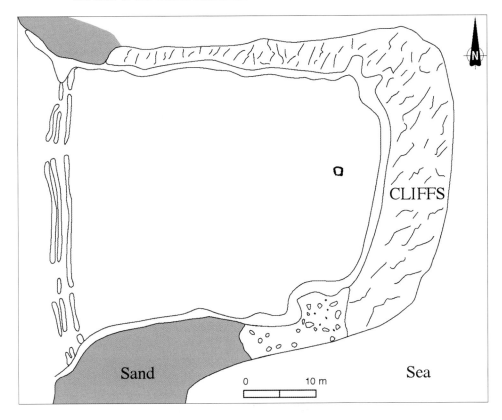

40 Loughshinney/Drumanagh promontory fort (after Raftery 1997)

41 View across sea between Lambay Island and Drumanagh (Aidan O'Sullivan)

The recovered objects also included large copper ingots in the form of cakes that are typically found in the Roman Empire. These were either imported from abroad or were made locally in the Roman fashion from the copper ores found along the coast. Roman coins and Romano-British brooches found on the site also provide evidence for overseas trade and the movement of goods. Ploughing during the 1970s exposed some possible hut sites and a sherd of late Roman two-handled wine storage vessel, suggesting both settlement and wine importation, as might be expected on a high-status residence and emporium. Although Drumanagh was described some years ago in the media as a major Roman military site, this seems unlikely. One thing that it is — is an impressive maritime archaeological site. Drumanagh provides an excellent view across the sea to Lambay Island, situated about 8km to the south-east, where there is also a similar promontory fort. Probable first-century Romano-British human burials were discovered on Lambay Island in the early twentieth century. Drumanagh is located directly across the ocean from the Roman naval fort at Holyhead on the other side of the Irish Sea — the location of the modern ferry port that connects Britain to Ireland today.

Saints, ships and seaways: early medieval coastal landscapes and traditions, AD 400-1200

INTRODUCTION

The collapse of the Roman Empire in the fifth century AD saw profound social, ideological and economic changes across Europe, and Ireland was as influenced as any other region by these developments. Indeed, the weakening and ultimate collapse of Roman power in Britain was to lead to Irish pirates raiding western British villas and towns, taking slaves and loot back to Ireland in the fourth and fifth centuries AD. It is also possible that early Irish colonies were established in Wales and Scotland, although this remains a subject of debate – but maritime connections were to lead to the introduction of Christianity amongst other things.

Through the early medieval period, population and demographic changes in Ireland saw the expansion and intensification of settlement landscapes in tandem with innovations in agricultural technology and crop production, in livestock management (e.g. dairying), and in craft and industry. Society changed too, as political power and territorial organisation saw a transition from one based on tribal chiefdoms and kin-based social groups to one that was based, by the ninth and tenth century, on dynastic lordships. As elsewhere in western Europe, a socio-economic system that was based on reciprocity and clientship was gradually transformed into one that was based on feudal labour services to a lord, urban markets and international trade and exchange. In Ireland, the introduction of Christianity also shifted belief systems and practices and probably lead to significant developments in the landscape (e.g. the growth of monastic centres and church estates).

There is abundant archaeological and historical evidence for coastal living and maritime traditions throughout the early medieval period (AD 400-1200). Early Irish laws of the seventh to eighth century AD indicate the ownership and exploitation of coastal and estuarine fisheries, and the flotsam and jetsam of the seashore. Early medieval saints' lives provide a sense of people's perception of the ocean and particularly their sense that its islands were spiritually rewarding places at the edge of the world, but they also provide anecdotal detail on shipbuilding, fishing and other coastal activities. Annalistic entries mention sea battles, fleets of ships and natural coastal phenomena. However, archaeology is particularly important and has provided evidence for coastal landscapes, economic practices, and also indicates the scope of maritime trade and communications between Ireland, western Europe and beyond to the Mediterranean.

By the end of the early Middle Ages (i.e. between AD 800-1100), we see a significant shift in aspects of maritime life on this island, as Ireland gets increasingly drawn into the northern Atlantic world. Viking and Hiberno-Norse coastal settlements were established at places like Dublin, Waterford, Cork and Limerick, the wealth of which was primarily based on maritime trade and communications. We also get new traditions of boat building as Nordic-style vessels start to be used in Irish waters. At the same time, native Irish historical sources continue to describe the coastal zone as a space of teeming activity – both in terms of exploitation and the movement of marine fleets and the battles of Irish, Anglo-Saxon and Viking fleets. Indeed, by the ninth and tenth centuries, Irish dynasties had their own fleets of ships sailing the seaways and imposing a sea-derived power on their neighbours.

Although the early medieval period brings radical changes to the Irish landscape, one of the striking things of maritime archaeology is the sense of continuity to be found on many coastal sites. From the beginning of the early Middle Ages, many coastal communities lived and worked at the same places that had previously been inhabited by older generations. Some coastal promontory forts, unenclosed dwellings and coastal shell middens that had previously been occupied in the Neolithic, Bronze Age and Iron Age also see reactivated and increased activity through this period. The early Middle Ages also sees a reiteration of the sea as a liminal zone between this world and the otherworld, as early Christian monks, inspired by a new religious ideology brought from the Mediterranean and Gaulish world, occupied the distant islands of the western seaboard. It might also be suggested that there are strong continuities in aspects of coastal trade, from second to third-century connections across the Irish Sea, to sixth- to seventh-century seaways from Gaul, up to the tenth- to eleventh-century North Atlantic trading routes developed by the Vikings. On the face of it, this seems to simply represent the long-lived traditions and underlying structures of coastal life, work and travel; that people still lived and worked to the rhythms of the ocean, its currents, tides and seasonal cycles. However, there are also strong themes of innovation and change, and some of these places were used in new and interesting ways, reflecting dynamically changing social and political conditions.

EARLY MEDIEVAL SETTLEMENT AND LANDSCAPES ON THE COAST

Early medieval coastal promontory forts

Perhaps the most enigmatic early medieval coastal settlements are promontory forts, typically defined by earthen banks and ditches or stone walls cutting off a headland or clifftop (*42*). It has already been shown that some promontory forts were occupied in the Bronze Age and Iron Age. However, there is also good archaeological evidence for their occupation in the early medieval period, including the sites at Larrybane, Co. Antrim, Dunbeg, Co. Kerry and Dalkey Island, Co. Dublin. Indeed, Drumanagh, Co. Dublin, the promontory fort mentioned in the previous chapter, may also have been occupied in the early medieval period, as amongst the Iron Age objects recovered there was a dome-headed bronze pin dated to the tenth to eleventh century AD. Promontory forts have traditionally been interpreted as refuges or strongholds although this seems unlikely or at least over-simplistic and is probably largely based on our traditional perception of coastal sites as being 'at the edge'. However, if we shift our perspective around to consider these promontory forts as places within seascapes, other interesting insights emerge. It is possible that some promontory forts were deliberately placed in prominent positions along coastlines and were intended to be seen from the sea, while they also provided their inhabitants with views across sailing routes. In particular, with the development of fleets and trading routes around the island, promontory forts established by local kingdoms could have both monitored and controlled aspects of sea traffic.

At Dunseverick, Co. Antrim, there is an impressive promontory fort that is known to have been an early medieval royal site of the Dál Riada, an extended tribal grouping with strong maritime connections between north-east Ireland and south-west Scotland (*43*). There are annalistic references to both *Dun Sobhairce* itself and to the maritime fleets of the Dál Riada throughout the seventh and eighth centuries AD. Dunseverick is located on a headland on high clifftops. Although there would have been few landing places in the vicinity, it provides excellent views across the sea towards Rathlin Island and the south-west coast of Scotland in the distance. The tides, currents and winds along the north coast also mean that it was sited on a significant maritime route way across the sea. In Adomnán's seventh-century *Vita sancti Columbae* (hereafter *Life of Columba*) there is a mention of a dangerous whirlpool at a place known as *Coire Breccáin*, off Rathlin Island, understood to be on the sea route between Ireland and Scotland. In Cormac's Glossary, dated to *c*.AD 900, there is a description of this eponymous Breccán, a merchant of the Uí Néill who used to trade with fifty currachs between Ireland and Scotland and whose fleet was lost in these dangerous seas. The clifftop also was fortified at later stages. It was used as a manorial centre by the earls of Ulster in the thirteenth and fourteenth centuries, and was taken from the O'Cahans by McDonnells in the sixteenth century.

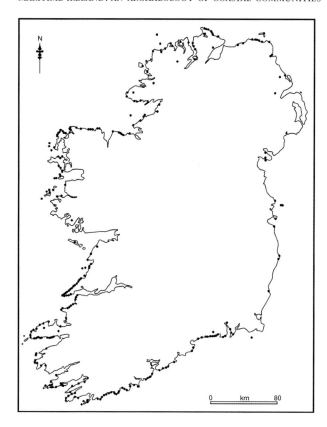

Left: 42 Distribution map of promontary forts in Ireland (by Markus Redmond from Ashe Fitzgerald 2000)

Below: 43 Dunseverick, Co. Antrim (Rosemary McConkey, UU)

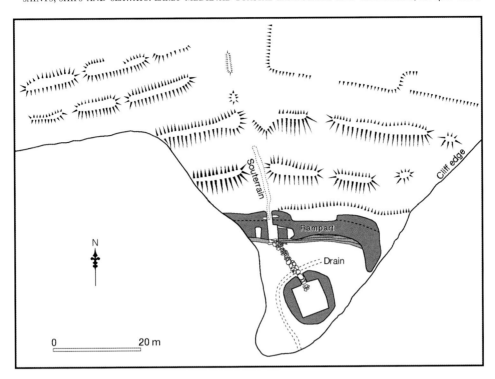

44 Plan of early medieval promontory fort at Dunbeg, Co. Kerry (after Barry 1981)

At Dunbeg, Co. Kerry, a promontory fort is dramatically situated on a cliff top on the steeply sloping, south side of the Dingle Peninsula (44). The site was clearly occupied over several phases, perhaps as early as the Bronze Age. It is defined by four closely-spaced banks and ditches, with a stone house and souterrain in the small, enclosed interior. Radiocarbon dates from the occupation deposits suggest that the site was inhabited from the ninth to the thirteenth century AD. Interestingly, most of the animal bone from the site was identified as cattle, sheep, pig, with small amounts of goose and cod. Dunbeg is placed at a location providing extensive views across Dingle Bay, and its inhabitants could have watched any coastal traffic moving around the Kerry coast. The site would also have been highly visible to maritime travellers, dominating entry into the bay itself. That the Dingle Peninsula had long seen coastal traders from far flung ports can be seen by the fact that the early medieval monastic site of Reask at the end of the peninsula has produced imported E-ware pottery, probably brought by Gaulish wine-traders. Dunbeg promontory fort, occupied slightly later than that, also probably observed the sailing routes between Viking Cork and Limerick in the tenth and eleventh centuries AD.

In any case, despite their coastal location, these promontory forts often produce relatively little evidence for the exploitation of coastal resources. At Larrybane, Co. Antrim, an early medieval promontory fort was situated at the edge of good agricultural land and its economy was mostly devoted to sheep-rearing in particular, as well as cattle herding. Here was some evidence for hearths and large amounts of souterrain ware. However, there were also bones of cormorant, shag, puffin, curlew and merlin, fishbones of cod, saithe, pollock, whiting and wrasse, along with limpets, winkles and oysters. The impression gained is of an essentially agricultural community, who occasionally may have trapped birds and collected eggs on the cliffs, and caught fish in the sea below. The presence of cod might also suggest that use of ocean-going craft fishing offshore.

EARLY MEDIEVAL COASTAL RINGFORTS AND UNENCLOSED DWELLINGS

Apart from coastal promontory forts, there is a wide range of early medieval settlement types (i.e. ringforts, crannogs, unenclosed dwellings) that can be found in coastal regions. Emily Murray has noted that at early medieval ringforts like Deer Park Farms, Cahercommaun, Ballyfounder Rath, Rathgurreen and Rathmullan, there is evidence of the eating of seabirds and shellfish, the latter undoubtedly transported several miles inland to these sites from the coast. At the early medieval platform ringfort at Rathmullan, Co. Down (situated about 1.2km from the sea on the Lecale Peninsula) there were significant amounts of mussels, smaller amounts of oysters and limpets and fish bones from cod. The early medieval site at Ballynarry, Co. Down, although 3km from the sea, produced quantities of winkles and limpet shells. At Deer Park Farms, Co. Antrim a raised ringfort situated at the head of one of the Antrim glens that sweep down to the sea, there was also evidence that seaweed was being brought from the shore some miles away, either for use as animal fodder or perhaps for producing dyes for clothing manufacture. Again, these were early medieval farming communities, largely producing their wealth and food from pastoral farming, but who made occasional use of coastal raw materials and foods.

In recent years, the archaeologist Alan Hayden has been excavating an intriguing early medieval farmstead at Bray Head, on Valentia Island, Co. Kerry. The archaeological evidence from the site includes several houses, an eighth-century corn-drying mill, rotary querns, carbonised oats and wheat and small amounts of fishbone. While the early medieval site is known to have been occupied between the seventh and the ninth century AD, it was also occupied through the late Middle Ages. By the fifteenth century, there was a small, nucleated settlement or clachan of rectangular houses surrounded by field-systems. The early medieval site was located on the south-facing slopes of the island, overlooking the sea channel between the island and the mainland. Down below it, out on the sea itself is the tiny, rocky island of Illaunloughan (see below), a known early medieval hermitage island. The Bray Head early medieval farmstead may have been the place that provisioned the hermits living on Illaunloughan Island.

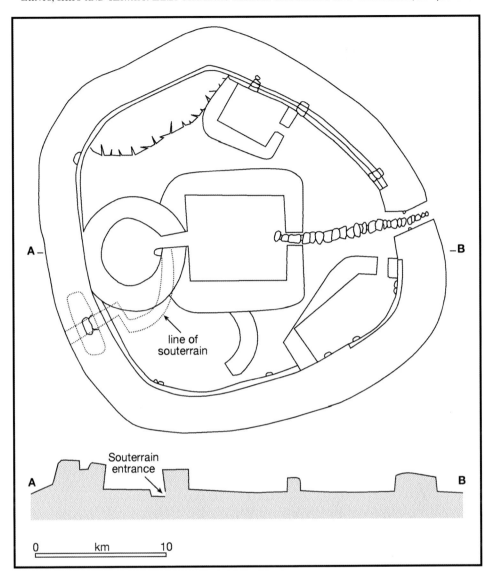

line of
souterrain

Souterrain
entrance

45 Early medieval caher at Leacanabuaile, Co. Kerry (after O'Sullivan and Sheehan 1996)

Other early medieval settlements often produce intriguing evidence for various activities directly associated with the sea. On the early medieval ringfort at Leacanabuaile, Co. Kerry, amongst the various domestic objects and agricultural tools found was an iron nail with a rove attached, quite similar to the ship's nails used within the Nordic shipbuilding tradition (45). It is certainly possible that the site's inhabitants had contacts with Viking seafarers, as sites in the region have been associated with Norse activity – not least the early medieval settlement at Beginish that may well be an actual Hiberno-Norse maritime haven. On the other hand, this ship's nail (if such it is – it could also be a fastening from a door) may imply the use of small ocean-going plank-built craft amongst native communities.

EARLY MEDIEVAL COASTAL SHELL MIDDENS: PLACES OF THE POOR OR SPECIALIST METALWORKING SITES?

Along the coastal littoral of the west coast, there is archaeological evidence for early medieval unenclosed dwellings and field-systems situated on the sandy, machair soils between the boglands and the open sea. Some of these early medieval sites are also to be linked to coastal shell middens situated in the dunes at the edge of the seashore. These early medieval middens remain enigmatic and poorly understood; not least because they were used by people 'outside history'. Early medieval documentary sources provide some evidence for the role of the seashore as a source of food, raw materials and fertilizer and the ownership of flotsam and jetsam, the detritus thrown up by the tides, was clearly defined in early Irish law as belonging to the local landowner. By and large, however, these early Irish historical sources typically ignore those who worked on the seashore gathering shellfish and eggs, hauling up seaweed for fertiliser or food, hunting seabirds, or dispatching stranded whales and seals.

However, archaeological evidence is clear that early medieval coastal communities gathered shellfish on rocky foreshores, either for food, bait or dye production. Indeed, early medieval coastal shell middens have been found all around the Irish coastline, but particularly in the west and north, from Kerry, up to Connemara and around Donegal to the Antrim coast. We have already seen that shell middens were used throughout prehistory, but many have also produced early medieval objects. Generally, early medieval shell middens have produced scanty evidence for structures (mostly postholes and hearths), along with large deposits of shells, as against small amounts of animal bone and finds.

At Minnis North, Co. Antrim, excavations of a shell midden produced early medieval pottery, flint debitage, a bone pin as well as winkles, limpets and small amounts of cattle, dog, horse and red deer. Intriguingly, it also produced human remains which were radiocarbon dated to AD 681-826. At Doonloughan, Co.

46 Early medieval shell middens at Doonlaughan, Co. Galway (Aidan O'Sullivan)

Galway, archaeological investigations have explored the Bronze Age oyster middens along the sandy coastline of Connemara (46). At Doonloughan 3, a dune-top midden of limpets and winkles had evidence for some occupation activity and burnt wooden structures, radiocarbon dated to AD 723-889 (possibly contemporary with a dwelling further along the dunes, described below). An early medieval plain, pennanular brooch is associated with this midden.

At Oughtymore, Co. Derry, at the edge of the Magilligan Foreland sandy plain overlooking the Foyle estuary, an early medieval midden site was dated to AD 630-880 (47). It produced early medieval souterrain ware, and a blue glass bracelet and lignite bracelet. Animal bones recovered included cattle, pig, sheep/goat and horse, as well as some gathered red deer antler. Fish bones identified included eel, cod, plaice/flounder, haddock, salmon/sea trout, while shellfish included winkles, cockles, mussels, oysters and whelks. There was also some carbonised rye and barley. Palaeobotanical studies were carried out subsequently (at the time of investigation of an Iron Age midden at Ballymulholland situated directly to the south). These suggested that Oughtmore midden was located in an open landscape, where trees and bushes had been gradually cleared back, and which may have been used for rough grazing and for growing arable crops. There were also some seasonal markers in the animal bone; pig were slaughtered in March-April, salmon caught in April to August, eel trapped in late summer/early autumn, while the rye was grown in April to August. In other words, the evidence suggests occupation or activity from early Spring well into the Autumn months.

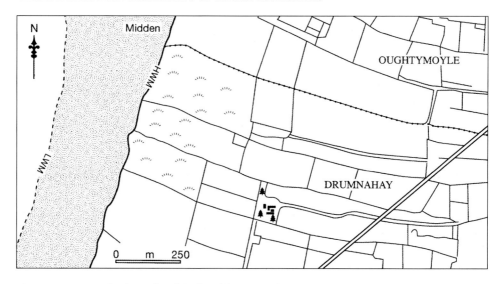

47 Location map of early medieval shell midden at Oughtymore, Co. Derry

    Shell middens are places (as we have seen for prehistory) that are seemingly situated at the edge of the world, exposed to storms and inclement weather. There is a temptation then to interpret these sites as also socially places at the edge, where the poor and landless people gathered food. It is also tempting to explain them as places where labourers and tenants of both secular and monastic estates gathered food or worked on dye production. It is also possible that this work was done by women and children as part of their wider contribution to the household and farm economy. In any case, medieval coastal communities were gathering scallops, limpets, oysters, dogwhelks, perhaps in the spring and summer time but potentially also through the autumn too. This might suggest that instead of being seasonal dwellings for mobile communities, these could have been more permanent residences. Certainly shell middens are often associated with unenclosed hut sites and field systems (i.e. at Doonloughan, on the Aran Islands and at various other locations along the sandy machair plains of the Connemara mainland and islands). Emily Murray has suggested that such shell middens were increasingly occupied from the seventh century AD, at the same time as peaks in ringfort and crannog occupation, suggested a rise in population and encouraged or forced some communities to live on the margins by the coast. It is possible that these coastal sites were occupied by people who were tending cattle, sheep and goats that would have been grazing on the comparatively rich grasslands on the machair soils.

    However, there are other ways to interpret these early medieval shell middens, not least because they have evidently produced diverse evidence for food production, as well as crafts and industrial production, and also the burial of human remains. The occasional presence of early medieval human skeletons in middens, such as at Truska and Minnis North, might suggest the burial of strangers, social outcasts or outlaws in places away from normal burial grounds – in the manner of later medieval burials in cillíns on coastal headlands. It is also possible that some of these are burials of people who were holding on to their ancestral pagan beliefs well into the Christian period (high sand dunes would certainly look like *ferta* – the ancestral burial mounds that were used during the Pagan/Christian transition).

On the other hand, some of these midden sites were high-status or industrial in function. Some of the shell middens on the Donegal coast, such as those at Ballyness Bay, Maghera and Dooey, are amongst the richest early medieval settlements in north-west Ireland. At Dooey, Co. Donegal, an early medieval midden complex (which was used as a burial place in its later phases) was situated on a peninsula and under a sand dune at the edge of a machair plain. There were several phases of occupation amongst the dunes. An early phase, possibly dating to the sixth century AD, saw habitation and fireplaces used over a large area. In Phase 2, the centre of the site was defined by a shallow, arcing ditch. By Phase 3, this ditch started to infill with windblown sand and refuse. This seems to have been the dwelling place of people who spent their time forging iron objects, casting bronze brooches and pins and working bone and antler. In Phase 4, probably during the eleventh century AD, the abandoned midden settlement was reused as a burial ground. Excavations of the site's midden deposits produced oyster, mussel, clam, periwinkle and limpets, as well as piles of broken dogwhelks. The latter might indicate that they had been used to produce purple dyes from the rotting shellfish meat. There was also extensive evidence for on-site craft production and industry, including iron slag, and the debris of bronze, bone and antler working. The presence of moulds, crucibles and lead models for at least fifty distinctive early medieval brooches and pins suggests that some objects were being cast on-site.

The Dooey site was probably the work place of high-status smiths producing objects along the dunes, perhaps for distribution. It is possible that Dooey was an early medieval beach market, situated on the North Atlantic seaways between north-west Ireland and Scotland. The early medieval kingdoms of Donegal were certainly oriented to the sea, so this should be seen as an element of the maritime traditions of the north-west. It has already been mentioned that early medieval shell middens and occupation sites also produce dog whelk, periwinkle and limpets.

Dog whelk (*Nucella lapillus*) is often thought of today as being unpalatable to human taste (in fact they are poisonous). However, dog whelk shells have been found at various shell middens along the west coast. At Iniskea North, Co. Mayo, Francoise Henry excavated an early medieval occupation site of rectangular in the lofty sand dunes of the island where the most common shellfish remains found were dog whelk. When exposed to the sun, dog whelk meat produces a liquid that turns variously green, blueish-purple and purplish-red (depending on how long it is exposed), so it is possible that it represents dye production.

However, it requires a great deal of labour (i.e. thousands of shells) to produce small amounts of purple dye, so much so that it could only have been used for dyeing threads, hems or the ends of garments, as befits a colour with royal or imperial connotations, or perhaps for purple ink for manuscript decoration.

THE IMPACT OF THE SCANDINAVIAN PEOPLES ON THE COASTAL LANDSCAPE

It has long been thought that the initial Viking impact on Ireland between between AD 795 and *c*.830 was largely one of lightning raids that should have left little or no archaeological trace. The first recorded Viking raid on Ireland took place in AD 795. Between AD 800 – 820, most raids were sporadic and were mainly concentrated on the north-west coast. However, by the 830s, Viking tactics had changed and raiding camps were established to allow crews and warring parties to over-winter in Ireland. Annalistic references suggest that the earliest camps were on the coast at Annagassan, Co. Louth and Dublin, both established in AD 841. Several raiding bases were established in subsequent decades also on the coast, such as at Narrowwater, Co. Down and Lough Swilly, Co. Donegal, or inland such as at Rossnaree, Co. Meath. The term used to describe these rapidly fortified camps in the annals was *longphort*, literally meaning ship-enclosure. The annals also indicate that these longphorts were mostly temporary sites, and that many were destroyed ten or twenty years after their construction.

The archaeological identification of longphorts remains controversial. Eamonn Kelly has suggested that they may have looked like a site at Athlunkard, Co. Limerick (on the Shannon estuary), where a D-shaped enclosure fronting on the river is associated with ninth- and tenth-century objects. More recently, much excitement was caused by major archaeological discoveries on a site on the banks of the River Suir at Woodstown, Co. Waterford, where it seemed that discoveries of a Viking burial – weapons, decorated weights, silver ingots and other objects – implied that this was indeed a longphort of the mid-ninth century AD. However, other scholars have previously suggested that the raiding Viking fleets would simply have taken over native Irish fortifications or monastic sites, thus making use of their pre-existing enclosures, buildings and food-stores. At Woodstown, recent archaeological evidence suggests that the site was initially an early medieval monastic enclosed site, probably occupied in the seventh century AD. This site was then taken over by Vikings in the ninth century AD.

There are other intriguing early medieval coastal sites that imply some Scandinavian activity or influences along the west and south-west coast. One of the problems of interpreting this evidence is that we are not sure how securely we can identify ethnic groups in the past (i.e. Irish, Anglo-Saxon, Viking, Hiberno-Norse) through architecture, dress, objects and lifestyle. The term 'Norse' itself might be taken to variously refer to language, genetics, ethnicity and material culture. However, it does not follow that people lived within distinct ethnic communities, using only a limited range of material culture. In other words, does the discovery of a Hiberno-Norse ringed pin or a distinctive house in a coastal sand-dune signify the presence of a population group of Norse origins – or does it simply indicate the far-flung, maritime connections of 'Irish' populations living on the western seaways during the 'Viking Age'?

There is certainly at least some evidence for the burial of Norse people on the Irish west coast. At Eyrephort, Co. Galway, a small bay on the Connemara coastline provides an ideal ship harbour for vessels sailing down the west coast of Ireland. One of the few Norse furnished burials (i.e. a burial with gravegoods) from the west coast was found at a site overlooking the bay. It was the grave of a strongly built, young man who had been buried with a Viking sword, shield and dagger in the sandy machair soils. This Viking burial may represent nothing more than the burial of a fatally injured raider, who had died on board his ship while returning from a raid down the west coast. On the other hand, it might represent the burial of a significant member of a community of Norse settlers living beside their Irish neighbours on the Connemara coast. It is likely that this young man was of some status and it may well be that only he would be buried in such a distinctive way, leaving others to be less easily identifiable. There is certainly a range of archaeological and historical evidence from the west coast that suggests at least frequent Viking raids in the ninth century, while place-names and stray finds of Viking silver are also suggestive, but not conclusive.

An interesting site in this regard is the early medieval occupation site and human burials recently found in sand dunes at Truska, Co. Galway (within a few hundred metres of the Doonloughan Bronze Age and early medieval middens mentioned above). The site overlooked False Bay, a narrow, naturally enclosed bay facing into the Atlantic (much used by surfers today). The site was exposed and partly destroyed through sand dune erosion and it was investigated as a rescue excavation by Erin Gibbons and Eamonn Kelly. A sunken, rectangular, stone-built house with a defined entrance ramp had been constructed in a pit in the sandy, machair soils. In the primary phase of occupation, a compact floor of white sand had a hearth from which were recovered shells, fish bone, cattle, sheep, pig and horse bone, as well as a probable tenth-century double-sided antler comb, that is certainly arguably of a Hiberno-Norse style. The second phase of site occupation saw the deposition of a clean floor of sand, in which there was charcoal. In the third phase of activity, the house was abandoned, the door blocked with stones (one of which was a fragment of a rotary quern). Soon after the site's abandonment, probably during the ninth century AD, two bodies were buried outside the end of the house (laid out in a way with the head to the west that is not normal of Christian burial tradition). The Truska site certainly represents an early medieval occupation site. It might be argued from the rectangular house, the bone comb and the burials, that this was a Norse dwelling.

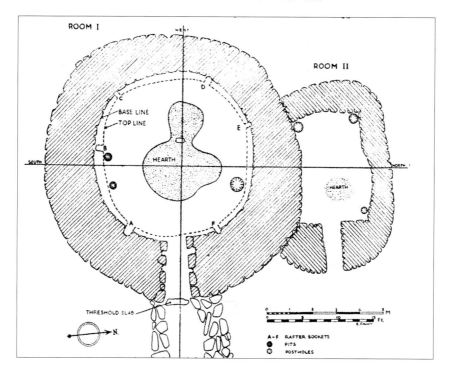

48 Plan of House 1, Beginish, Co. Kerry (after O'Kelly 1956)

The early medieval coastal settlement of Beginish, Co. Kerry is also another good example of one of these potential Norse coastal sites (48). This is a small, low, sandy island to the east of Valentia Island. The site was an unenclosed early medieval settlement, with at least eight stone houses used over two phases and a field-system. House 1 (belonging to phase 2) was a sunken, round house constructed around a pit. The door entrance was approached by a stone-lined passageway and a lintel was found to have runes inscribed on it, suggesting that it dated to sometime towards the end of the early Middle Ages. Finds from the excavations included bronze, bone and iron implements and dress ornaments, saddle and rotary querns, as well as stone line and net sinkers indicating inshore and offshore fishing for ballan wrasse. There was also evidence for the gathering of scallops, oysters, periwinkles and limpets. Amongst the finds that have recently inspired a re-interpretation of the site were a steatite (soapstone) bowl, distinctive Hiberno-Norse ringed-pins and the rune-inscribed lintel stone. John Sheehan has recently suggested that Beginish may have been a tenth-century Scandinavian settlement on the south-west coast, used as a way-station for mariners sailing from the Hiberno-Norse town of Cork around the south-west coast (and past Beginish) to the Hiberno-Norse town of Limerick. Like the early medieval Bray Head and Illaunloughan sites discussed elsewhere, the Beginish site may at other times also have been linked to a small early medieval hermitage on Church Island, to which it is connected by a sandbar.

VIKING AND HIBERNO–NORSE TOWNS ON THE COAST

By AD 914, Viking towns were being established around the coast that served as trading and settlement centres – Dublin, Wexford, Waterford, Cork and Limerick all owe their origins to this period. In the tenth and eleventh century, Dublin became the centre of their activity and developed as the primary Viking town in the Irish Sea region. By this stage, Hiberno-Norse were increasingly assimilated into Irish society, and the Ostmen (as they called themselves) were very much part of the Irish political scene. The archaeology of Scandinavian and Hiberno-Norse settlement in the tenth and eleventh century is still largely understood in terms of the development of these towns, as might be expected given the quality of archaeological information being produced by recent excavations in Waterford, Wexford, Cork and Dublin.

Traditionally, it is believed that the Vikings founded the town of Dublin (although there were almost certainly native Irish church settlements already there). The Irish annals state that in AD 841, a Viking fleet was still present at Duiblinn and a longphort was established to raid Leinster and Meath. This longphort was probably a defended enclosure on the river bank, used as a permanent trading base. It was either located on the River Liffey near Islandbridge-Kilmainham (e.g. Viking burials found there in the nineteenth century and the 1930s imply at least the use of native Irish cemeteries) or was somewhere north of the present location of Dublin castle. Recent archaeological excavations in Dublin have uncovered burials of probable Viking raiders, perhaps even dating to well before the historically attested longphort. Other excavations in Temple Bar have also located Viking type dwellings dated to ninth century that may represent the longphort settlement itself. In any case, in AD 902, that earliest Viking settlement was apparently sacked by the Irish kings of Brega and Leinster and its inhabitants (or at least the political elite of the settlement) expelled, whence they went to northern England and the Isle of Man.

In AD 917, these Norse settlers returned and established the town of Dublin proper, probably at *Dubhlinn*, somewhere at the confluence of the River Liffey and the Poddle, near Temple Bar. This was an ideal location for a settlement, on high ground overlooking the River Liffey, protected from the south-east by Poddle. It also had access to the river for boats. Although initially located at the east, the town gradually expanded westwards along High Street, so that by the eleventh century it was a large thriving urban settlement, with streets and houses inhabited by a large, ethnically mixed population of traders, craftsmen and slaves.

What was the Hiberno-Norse town on the Liffey estuary like? We know it was enclosed within a large earthen bank, topped with post and wattle fence. We have good archaeological evidence for houses, streets and plot boundaries, that suggest that the town was laid out in an organised if cramped fashion, following the contours of the hill. At Fishamble Street, twelve tenement plots can be traced more or less constantly across time, with the occupation of at least 150 different houses over 150 years. These houses were probably owned by individuals, but the evidence suggests that the town was laid out according to the instructions of a central regulating authority. Hiberno-Norse Dublin's houses were entered from the street, each had vegetable plots, gardens and midden spaces out the back. Other structures included pig pens, workshops and storehouses. The town was a major centre for craft production, with such raw materials as wood, leather, bone, antler, amber and metals used for domestic equipment and high-status goods. In terms of economy, it is likely that the townspeople were largely self-sufficient, raising pigs and goats, while beef cattle, agricultural produce and raw materials were brought in from the surrounding countryside.

There is also evidence that the people of Hiberno-Norse Dublin, Cork and Waterford consumed a lot of fish and shellfish – perhaps more than the native Irish. Indeed, recent stable isotope analyses of some early medieval human skeletons hints at an increased marine diet in Ireland in the Viking Age and Anglo-Norman periods. This is also suggested by the archaeological evidence for the increase in use of early medieval wooden fish traps on the Shannon estuary and Strangford Lough (and elsewhere around the coastline of Britain) after about AD 1000. At Hiberno-Norse Dublin, fishing was clearly important, as lead line-weights, wooden net-floats and stone sinkers found in excavations indicate fishing using lines and nets from both the shoreline and offshore in boats. Margaret McCarthy's archaeozoological studies of deposits from Dublin, Waterford and Cork confirms this focus on marine species, with bones from hake, cod, ling, plaice and herring all known from these towns. Undoubtedly too, there were wooden fish traps situated along the banks of the river. It is also likely that the Vikings were involved in hunting marine mammals, such as porpoise, whales and seals. Indeed, an iron harpoon head found at Fishamble Street was probably used for this purpose. Wildfowl such as teal, duck and mallard were also trapped in the estuarine marshlands.

Hiberno-Norse Dublin was a town located on an estuary, and the river frontage provided access to boats bringing in people and goods from distant lands. Burials were also placed in barrows on the edge of the marshes, particularly along the southern bank. Indeed, one of the earliest cemeteries was located upstream at Kilmainham-Islandbridge, where during the ninth century, some of the inhabitants of the original longphort were buried.

THE EARLY MEDIEVAL CHURCH AND SEEKING THE 'DESERT IN THE PATHLESS SEA'

The sea and its islands in the early medieval imagination
In the early medieval Irish imagination, the sea was an awesome place at the edge of the world. In early Irish mythology, the dead were thought to travel across its waters to the otherworld. Early Irish saint's lives and voyage tales also depict the

sea as a place of transformation and spiritual danger. Indeed, the sea is depicted as a space between this world and the abyss of Hell, a frontier zone where monks battled the forces of the devil.

In the sixth and seventh century, Irish Christian monks were inspired by the writings of St Anthony, and by the well-known tradition of desert monasticism of Egypt, began to establish hermitages and monasteries of their own in isolated places. In early medieval texts, this was the *pergrinatio pro amore dei*, 'pilgrimage or exile for the love of God', and there is historical evidence for the pilgrimage of Irish monks into Anglo-Saxon England, Merovingian France, and Italy, establishing monasteries abroad. But Irish monks were also setting out on pilgrimages into the Atlantic ocean, establishing monasteries on islands off the west coast. Thousands of Irish monks also sailed off the western coast of Ireland into the North Atlantic, looking for a 'desert in the pathless sea'.

By the late sixth century, when St Columba left Ireland to go to Iona, early medieval monasticism was firmly established on the islands of Ireland and western Britain. Most of the islands off the western coast of Ireland, Wales, Scotland, the Orkneys and Shetlands, and perhaps the Faroes and Iceland saw monastic activity by the eighth century. Thence, most of the western islands of Irish Atlantic shoreline also have early monastic sites (particularly well-known examples such as the Skelligs, High Island and Aran Islands almost dominate the popular image of early Irish Christianity).

Why were islands settled by early Irish monks between the seventh and the eleventh centuries AD? We can partly answer this by reference to descriptions, motifs and incidents in the early medieval saints' lives and voyage tales. These historical sources reveal that early medieval people often understood islands as distant and isolated places, bounded by water, to which access could be controlled. Islands were also often seen as places of symbolic and ideological potential, being liminal places close to the supernatural otherworld, where fantastic monsters, otherworldly people, experiences and phenomena could be expected. Early medieval Christian ideology saw the sea as a place of potential symbolic and religious potential, a liminal space between this world and the abyss of hell.

Furthermore, in early Irish mythology, the dead were said to go to Tech Donn, to the house of Donn, an otherworldly figure associated with death. Tech Donn itself was reckoned to an island off the south-west coast of Ireland, a place known today as Bull Rock, off Dursey Island, Co. Cork. Another common theme in the saints' lives and the voyage tales was the association between islands, moral restraint and redemption. In several of the voyage tales, the hero goes sailing out on the ocean and finds himself on an island where there are women who provide sex and comfort. Ultimately, the hero has to escape from the temptations of these women to become a proper person. Evidently we are looking again at the misogynistic beliefs of monastic scribes, but there may also have been an idea that islands were places for personal, spiritual regeneration.

Over the years, numerous Irish scholars (such as Francoise Henry and Michael Herity) have looked at the archaeological remains of early Christian communities on the islands of the Atlantic seaboard. There remains a popular belief that these island monasteries remained isolated from the rest of the world, thus promoting the notion of the early Irish church as one that was dominated by ascetic hermits, around whose cells or tombs the pious gathered to form monastic communities. In recent years, Sharon Greene has been exploring the early medieval archaeology of the islands of the Connacht and has argued that these island monasteries were not entirely remote. Indeed, some may have been deliberately situated on significant long-standing maritime route ways and were very much integral to the history and politics of the territories of the neighbouring mainland. Some monastic islands of the west coast, such as Inishmurray, Skellig Michael and Church Island, have to be imagined then in terms of wider regional maritime landscapes, as is implied by the hagiographical references to saints sailing back and forth on their voyages. Tomás Ó Carragáin has suggested that Skellig Michael, the archetypal 'remote island hermitage' was sustained by extensive termon lands on the mainland, that later became the estates of the late medieval priory of Ballinskelligs. Viewed in this way, Skellig Michael was not a peripheral island monastery, but a significant outpost of mainland church territories, situated on important west coast seaways.

EARLY MEDIEVAL MONASTIC ISLANDS AND PILGRIMAGE TO INISHMURRAY

Through the early Middle Ages, some of these monastic islands, if they were ever remote, were drawn into the wider world by the huge numbers of pilgrims that travelled out to them. Jerry O'Sullivan has recently carried out archaeological excavations of the early medieval monastic remains on the island of Inishmurray, Co. Sligo (*49*). This monastery was founded on this island in the sixth century, reputedly by St. Molaise. It was raided by Vikings in 795 AD, suggesting it was well known and perhaps well-off by that time.

The archaeological remains of the monastery include a massive stone enclosure, churches and beehive cells. The earliest church, Tech Molaise, has been radiocarbon dated to eighth century AD. An early medieval cemetery has also produced burials between the tenth to twelfth century AD. Other archaeological features on the island include huge collections of carved stones, cross-slabs, as well as leachta – cairns of stone erected at the churches and at intervals around the island's periphery, used as penitential stations by pilgrims. Recent excavations elsewhere (on Omey Island, Co. Galway) suggest that such leachta were erected in ninth and tenth century AD, and it may have been the same at Inishmurray.

In any case, Inishmurray is often thought of as representing the classic features of an early Irish monastery. However, Jerry O'Sullivan's alternative explanation

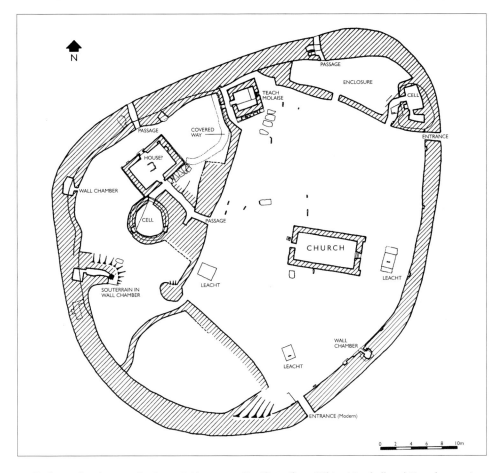

49 Early medieval monastic site at Inishmurray, Co. Sligo (from White Marshall and Rourke 2001)

is that the churches, beehive cells and leachta represent a destination for early medieval pilgrims, with hostels, public churches and an important focal point at the saint's tomb. In other words, some early medieval island monasteries became significant foci for popular pilgrimage towards the end of the early Middle Ages, suggesting again that these were not remote, isolated islands.

THE EARLY MEDIEVAL MONASTIC ISLAND OF HIGH ISLAND, CO. GALWAY

High Island (*Ard Oileáin*), Co. Galway is one of the best preserved early medieval island monasteries, largely because of the island's inaccessibility and remoteness (*50*). It was occupied for a period in the nineteenth century, by miners, but otherwise has been abandoned since the Middle Ages. The island is named after its cliffs, which rise precipitously to a height of 200ft out of the sea, making the island highly visible from all along the Connemara coast. The island is

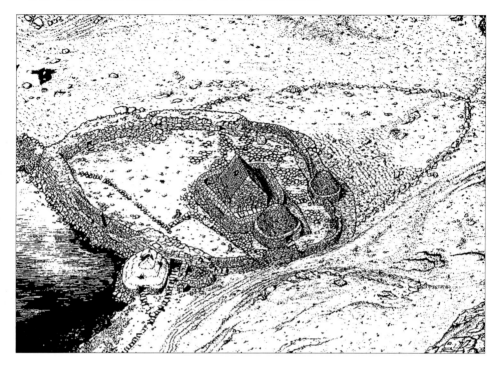

50 Reconstruction drawing of early medieval monastic enclosure on High Island, Co. Galway (from White Marshall and Rourke 2001)

uninhabited today, and lies 3km from mainland, although it should be viewed as being surrounded by other islands (Inishark and Inisbofin being the most prominent). During winter and during storms it can be very difficult to land on the island, presumably it was also so in the early Middle Ages.

It is thought that a monastery was founded on the island by a Saint Féchín in the sixth century AD. The monastery seems to have been occupied from the seventh to the eleventh century AD, and was then abandoned. Although most of the early medieval monasteries in Connacht are fairly obscure, there is mention of at least one of the abbots of the monastery, for example in the annalistic reference to the death of 'Gormgal of Árd Óilean' in AD 1014. However, because the early medieval monastic site was abandoned in the eleventh century, there was no further development on the site to destroy it.

The early medieval monastery was located in a sheltered valley at the south-west of the island. A quadrangular stone enclosure or cashel was located adjacent to a small freshwater lake. Within the cashel, there was a stone-walled church inside its own small enclosure. There were also at least four beehive cells. The cashel wall had a number of chambers within it, and there was also a rectangular building at the entrance to the enclosure. There are also other features around the island, including cross-slabs, leacht and hut sites.

An early medieval oratory was situated inside the small enclosing wall, and was probably built in ninth and tenth century AD. Several early medieval graves were

1 Achill Island south coast in a storm, Co. Mayo (Sharon Greene)

2 Rusheen, Iniskea Islands at low tide, Co. Sligo (Sharon Greene)

Top: 3 Dalkey Island, from Coliemore harbour, Co. Dublin (Aidan O'Sullivan)

Left: 4 Mesolithic site on Belderrig Bay, Co. Mayo (Graeme Warren)

Above: 5 Bushfoot enclosures, Co. Antrim (Nigel McDowell, UU)

6 Digital infrared aerial photograph of Ringneill shell midden, Strangford Lough, Co. Down

Above: 7 Late Bronze Age structure, Islandmagrath, Fergus estuary (Aidan O'Sullivan)

Left: 8 Dunseverick promontory fort, Co. Antrim (Nigel McDowell, UU)

9 Kerry Head promontory fort, Co. Kerry

10 Dunkilmore fort, Achillbeg, Co. Mayo

Above and below: *11* Doonloughan shell middens, Co. Galway (Aidan O'Sullivan)

Above: 12 Inishmurray, Co. Sligo (Photographic Section: Deptartment of Environment, Heritage and Local Government)

Below: 13 Inishmurray Leachtatemple, Co. Sligo (Jerry O'Sullivan)

14 Early medieval Bantry pillar stone, Co. Cork (Aidan O'Sullivan)

15 Viking Dublin children playing with a model boat (reconstruction painting by Jane Brayne)

16 Medieval fish trap reconstruction, Bunratty, Shannnon estuary (Painting by Simon Dick, from O'Sullivan 2001)

17 Digital Aerial Photograph of Dunboy castle and Puxley Manor (UU)

18 Medieval church and nineteenth-
century Martello tower, Dalkey Island,
Dublin Bay (Aidan O'Sullivan)

19 Carrickkildavnet
tower house, Achill
Island (Sharon Greene)

Above: 20 Beagh Castle tower house and nineteenth-century fishing village, Shannon estuary (Aidan O'Sullivan)

Below: 21 Dunluce Castle, Co. Antrim (Nigel McDowell, UU)

22 Donaghadee Harbour, Co. Down (Gail Pollock, EHS)

23 Simon Lover's nineteenth-century painting of kelp gathering in Connemara (Delargy Centre for Irish Folklore, UCD)

24 Twentieth-century Shannon estuary gandelow lying in boatbed in marsh (Aidan
O'Sullivan)

25 Bush Island post-medieval fish trap, Shannon Estuary, Co. Clare (Aidan O'Sullivan)

found beside and inside the church, and immediately surrounding it, burials that were marked by cross-slabs. It is likely that these were particularly important burials, perhaps of abbots of the island. The small early medieval beehive cells were essentially tiny houses, but could only have had one person living in them. One beehive was used as a kitchen and like the others had a paved floor, with successive layers of ash and soil indicating use across time. There were also several early medieval cross slabs, decorated in a distinctive High Island style that is quite different from those on Aran Islands, Caher Island, Inishmurray and on Iniskea island.

Interestingly, there is also striking environmental evidence for environmental change before and during the life of the monastery. Pollen analyses indicate that there was possibly some prehistoric settlement on the island. From about AD 650 onwards, there is an upsurge of arable farming, with grains of rye, barley and wheat identified in the pollen cores. The presence of wheat is surprising, given the prevailing windy conditions, as oats might have been expected to do better on the island's acid soils and the exposed, damp island. In any case, this increase in arable pollen is also matched by a decrease in arboreal pollen (a decline in scrubby woodland of hazel, elm, pine).

However, the clearest archaeological evidence for early medieval agriculture on the island was provided for by the discovery of an early medieval horizontal watermill. The watermill had a hillside reservoir constructed by building a stone and earthen dam across a small valley, with a feeder stream leading down to the main millpond. There was also a millpond – a natural lake that had been modified. Beyond the millpond, two channels were cut into the exposed bedrock, including a headrace to lead water to the mill and a second channel to release overflow during periods of heavy rainfall. There was also a stone mill-building located close to the cliff, historically known as Cuan a Mhuilin (harbour of the mill). In fact the horizontal watermill indicates that for a period, there may have been a substantial population on the island. Such mills would have been used for grinding large amounts of wheat, barley and rye, for making bread and porridge. It is probably also significant that the mill could have ground grain during winter, when access off the island might have been difficult.

AN EARLY MEDIEVAL ISLAND HERMITAGE AT ILLAUNLOUGHAN, CO. KERRY

It is also evident that quite dramatically small islands off the west coast of Ireland were occupied by early Irish monks. These were often bleak and inaccessible tiny pieces of land, that testify to the religious spirit of their occupants. However, it is also clear that these have to be seen as islands within broader maritime seascapes.

One of the most remarkable of these is the early medieval hermitage of Illaunloughan, Co. Kerry. Illaunloughan is a tiny, rocky island (0.1ha in size at high tide) lying about 400m off the coast at the modern village of Portmagee, between Valentia Island and the Kerry coastline (51). The island is lowlying and was always therefore an exposed location, regularly swept today by winter gales and storms. Illaunloughan island was recently excavated by Claire Walsh and Jenny White Marshal and its unusual early medieval settlement was shown to have been occupied by no more than five or six monks from the mid-seventh to the ninth century AD. However, the island's churches or oratories, reliquary shrine, and three round houses or cells mostly date to the eighth century AD, when there were two main periods of occupation.

A midden was located at the island's edge, adjacent to the hermits' cells. This has revealed the diet of early medieval monks. The midden, up to 1m deep, was largely composed of broken marine shells, butchered animal bone and stone. The monks made use of marine and land foods, with cereals, berries, cattle, sheep and pig, as well as shellfish, seal, fish and birds. Sheep and goat bones probably derive from animals herded on the neighbouring grassland slopes and brought to the island for meat. There were also bones of young cattle, which were probably also provisioned to the island from local dairy herds.

Unsurprisingly, maritime resources were being exploited by the island's inhabitants, with whale and seal bone found in the deposits. Emily Murray has shown that the shellfish assemblages were dominated by periwinkles (79 per cent) and limpets, both probably gathered from local rocky shorelines of the island and the mainland. Other shellfish collected included cockles, carpet shells, dog whelk, great scallop, topshells and oyster, amongst others. There was also extensive evidence for the trapping of seabirds and fish. Manx shearwater were the primary species of bird hunted, along with cormorant, kittiwake, puffin and others. Fish were also very important, with at least twenty species identified (e.g. bass, cod, conger, flatfish, gadidae, gurnard, hake, mullet, pollock, ray, saithe, salmon, scad, sea breams, shark, whiting and wrasse). Seabream, a summer migrant to the Irish coast, were taken in large numbers along with wrasse. Cod, hake and shark would have required offshore fishing from boats.

Charred plant remains found in the midden, huts and oratory included oats, naked barley and a small amount of wheat from the oratory (an offering?). Other plants, such as sheep's sorrel weed (unlikely to have grown on the island's shell-rich, calcareous soils) confirmed that these cereals were brought to this tiny island from elsewhere, They may, however, have been ground into flour using the quern stones found on the settlement. Other potential foods represented in seed assemblages included raspberries, rowan, hazelnut, vetch, docks, common chickweed, cabbages and common nettles, as well as mugworts and coriander that may have had medicinal uses.

This was not an ascetic diet, although it should be admitted that living on an Atlantic island in the winter would have been impossible without proper, nutritious food. On a tiny island like Illaunloghan, it is clear that there was insufficient space to grow such crops and vegetables in large amounts or to raise animals like cattle and sheep. Even with the exploitation of marine resources,

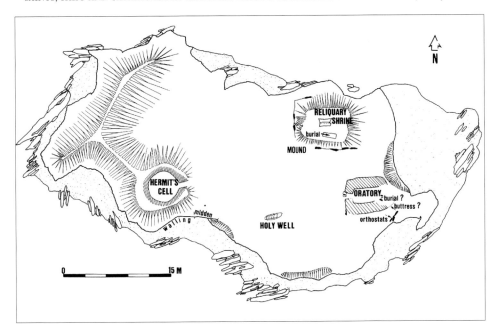

51 Early medieval site at Illaunloughan, Co. Kerry (OPW)

it would still have been necessary to have been provided with food by the people of the surrounding islands and mainland. It seems likely that the monks of Illaunloughan were being sustained by a mainland community, possibly the people living at the early medieval farmstead at Bray Head out on Valentia Island. Faunal analyses suggest that cattle, sheep and pig were all being transported onto the island, probably by people who were killing off their unwanted animals (either very young calves or cattle over 4 years age), as would have been the norm for a dairying community.

There was also evidence that the cattle were butchered on the island, and perhaps these were swum out to it. The midden was also inevitably the location of the domestic objects, which included whetstones, knives, rotary quern, glass and antler beads, combs and dress pins. The island was abandoned by the ninth century, although there is evidence that it was re-used or visited by pilgrims in the late Middle Ages

WORKING THE SEASHORE IN EARLY MEDIEVAL IRELAND

The sea's harvest

Early medieval historical sources indicate that the seashore was potentially a place of intense activity. Early Irish laws dating to the seventh and eighth century discuss rights to inshore and offshore sea fishing, the ownership of seaweed and driftwood, while the saints' lives describe the work of fishermen, the moving back and forth of boats and ships and occasionally the hunting of marine mammals. The seventh-century *Life of Columba* clearly states that the monks of Iona were trapping seals, and these were probably butchered for skins and meat. Their bones have been recovered from early medieval coastal sites at Church Island and Iniskea. Whalebone has been found on early medieval sites such as Raheens, Co. Cork, Rathmullan, Co. Down, Iniskea, Co. Mayo and Lough Faughaun crannog, Co. Down. Although it is possible that these were hunted, it seems more likely that they represent the use of accidentally stranded animals. Indeed, early Irish documentary sources claimed that during the reign of a just king unusually beneficial things occurred. It is probably for this reason that in AD 753, the *Annals of Ulster* notes a whale (with three gold teeth) was cast ashore at Bairche in Ulster during the reign of Fiachna son of Aed Rón, king of Ulster.

In contrast, for AD 827, there is a reference to a 'great pig-slaughter of sea-pigs [probably porpoises] by the foreigners' on the coast of Ard-Cianachta (in modern Co. Louth, on Ireland's east coast). This could again simply represent the opportunistic slaughter of a large group of stranded animals, but it may also imply hunting out at sea using boats and harpoons. Certainly, the fact that they refer to it at all and the use of the term 'foreigners' indicates that the Irish annalists found this to be a unique and extraordinary event, perhaps indicating too that whale and seal hunting was something that was more an activity practiced by Scandinavian peoples. By the eleventh century AD, the Muslim geographer al – 'Udrhi noted that the Irish hunted young whales between the months of October and January. Obviously, some of these activities on the seashore would leave little trace. On the other hand, recent intertidal archaeological surveys on the Shannon estuary and Strangford Lough have revealed physical traces (in the form of fish traps and mills) of what we might call maritime taskscapes, landscapes of marine-oriented labour that were intended to provide both food and income to local populations.

Perhaps amongst the most striking discoveries in Irish archaeology of recent years have been the early medieval coastal fish traps found on the Shannon estuary and Strangford Lough. Medieval fish traps were artificial barriers of stone or wood built in rivers or estuaries to deflect fish into an opening where they could be trapped in nets or baskets. In coastal and estuarine waters, fish tend to move up the shore with the flooding tide and drift back down with the ebbing tide, being attracted by feeding in the shallow water and by the nutrients in freshwater streams and rivers moving into the estuary. Thence, it is possible to trap them by erecting fish traps across these routes, with ebb-weirs catching fish moving down with the ebbing tide and flood-weirs catching fish moving up the shore with the flooding tide. Upon encountering these barriers, the fish would tend to move along the fences into the trapping mechanism, from which they could be removed later.

The fish traps typically consisted of two (or more) converging vertical fences or walls, thus forming a large V-shaped structure. At the apex or 'eye' of the two fences there would be a woven wicker basket supported on a framework, a net, or a rectangular or curvilinear enclosures of wooden posts or nets. However, medieval fish traps vary significantly in location, form, size, and style of trapping mechanism, depending on the relative size of the catch intended, the foreshore topography and current conditions and the customs and practices of local fishermen. Indeed, it is now clear that there is significant local and regional variations in the use of fish weirs around medieval Britain and Ireland.

EARLY MEDIEVAL FISH TRAPS ON STRANGFORD LOUGH

The Strangford Lough fish traps are located around the shores of this sea lough, but are mostly concentrated in Grey Abbey Bay and around Chapel Island in the north-east part of the Lough (52). At least fifteen wooden and stone-built fish traps have been recorded and the wooden traps in particular have been radiocarbon dated to between the eighth and thirteenth centuries AD. Strangford Lough would have had a range of fish species, including salmon, sea trout, plaice, flounder, mackerel, cod, grey mullet and skate with large numbers of eels in the abundant kelp growth. The Strangford Lough fish traps were ebb weirs, intended to catch fish drifting down with the falling tide. They usually have two long stone walls or wooden fences which converged in a V-shape to a point on the lower foreshore. This means that at every low tide they were exposed for about two to

52 Aerial photograph of Ogilby Island fishtrap (Environment and Heritage Service)

three hours, and while they enclosed a large area of foreshore, their owners and users had sufficient time to remove the fish and repair the structures.

The Strangford Lough wooden fish traps have fences measuring between 40m and 200m in length and are more or less V-shaped in plan. The fences were made both of single lines of posts and complex arrangements of paired posts thus creating an inner and outer fence. Post-and-wattle panels could have been carried out to the traps and slotted between these paired uprights and pinned in position using bracing props and horizontal pegs. Wooden fish traps at Cunningburn and Gregstown, near Newtownards also had stone walls along the base of the fence to protect them from erosion and undercutting. At the 'eye' of the converging fences, baskets or nets were probably hung on rectangular structures. The wooden fences would have deteriorated quickly and needed periodic repair. It is obvious that a significant amount of labour was required for their construction. Thousands of hazel, ash and oak poles and rods would have been felled, trimmed and hauled out from the neighbouring woodlands.

At Chapel Island, a large wooden fish trap has provided a radiocarbon date of AD 711-889. It has a lower, 'flood fence' 147m in length running parallel to the shore and a second, shorter fence running up towards the island. Archaeological excavations suggest that it was the subject of frequent repairs or that there was an attempt to make the fences 'fish-tight' through the use of hundreds of closely-spaced posts. Interestingly, there is archaeological evidence for settlement on the island, including a possible church structure within a promontory enclosure defined by a substantial bank and ditch. Traces of stone field walls can also be seen on the nearby slopes. The Chapel Island fish traps may have been linked to the regionally significant early medieval monastic centre of Nendrum, Co. Down which is located on an island across the lough.

In Grey Abbey Bay, 1.5km to the east, three wooden traps and four stone traps have been recorded. At South Island, a large V-shaped wooden trap crosses a tidal channel. This structure measures over 100m in length, was constructed of at least 500 posts and has a rectangular structure and possible basket at the eye. It has provided two separate radiocarbon dates of AD 1023-1161 and AD 1250-1273. Similar V-shaped wooden traps found elsewhere in the bay have produced radiocarbon dates of AD 1037-1188 and cal. AD 1046-1218. The traps may have used nets, baskets or rectangular pounds, post-and-wattle enclosures inside of which the fish remained until removed. The Strangford Lough fish traps were clearly in use in the bay throughout the Middle Ages. Some of the large wooden and stone fish traps may have been the property of the Cistercian community of Grey Abbey, which was founded in AD 1193. It is known that the early Cistercian communities were determinedly self-sufficient and the use of fisheries in the bay probably intensified after their arrival.

The Strangford Lough stone-built fish traps are broadly similar in size, form and orientation. They typically measure between 50m and 300m in length, 1.1m in width and probably stood between 0.5m to 1m in height. Fish could have swam over them on a flooding tide but would be trapped behind the wall during the last hours of the ebbing tide. The stone fish traps are variously V-shaped, sickle-shaped and tick-shaped in plan, mainly depending on the nature of the local foreshore. Large numbers of heavy beach boulders would have been collected from the foreshore for their construction. The stone-built fish traps would have needed repair after winter storms, no doubt a difficult task with barnacles on the rocks and only several hours available for work. The massive physical scale and form of the Strangford Lough fish traps probably indicates a local response to the broad, sandy beaches of the lough, although it is also clear that these were intended to literally harvest all of the fish out of this part of the lough.

EARLY MEDIEVAL FISH TRAPS ON THE SHANNON ESTUARY

On the Shannon estuary, in south-west Ireland, archaeological surveys have revealed evidence for several medieval wooden fish traps, dated to between the fifth and the thirteenth century AD. The Shannon estuary fish weirs tend to be small, V-shaped post-and-wattle structures (with fences 20-30m in length) with basket traps, hidden away within the narrow, deep creeks that dissect the estuary's vast expanses of soft, impenetrable muds. Despite being relatively small, they would have been undoubtedly effective as even a small barrier in these creeks could have literally sieved the water of all fish moving around with the tides. They were oriented to catch fish on the flooding or ebbing tide and could in season have taken large catches of salmon, sea trout, lampreys, shad, flounder and eels (the latter in October-November).

The earliest known fish trap is a small post-and-wattle fence (*c*.8m in length) on the Fergus estuary, Co. Clare (a tributary of the Shannon estuary), dated to AD 442-664 (one of the earliest in these islands). This was probably part of a fish trap that would have been used by the inhabitants of early medieval ringforts (enclosed settlements) on the low hills adjacent to the estuary. Early medieval fish traps have also been located on the mudflats of the Deel estuary, Co. Limerick (which flows into the upper Shannon estuary). Deel 1, dated to cal. AD 1037-1188 is a small V-shaped fish trap, oriented to catch fish on the flooding tide with two converging post-and-wattle alder wood fences measuring over 30m in length. A cluster of posts at the apex of the two fences probably represents the surviving remains of a trap. It may have been associated with nearby settlements on the neighbouring land, including early medieval ringforts and other earthworks. There are other, later medieval fish traps on this foreshore (see below), that provide intriguing evidence for local continuity of size, form and location, suggesting that they essentially replaced each other between the eleventh and the late fourteenth century AD.

Indeed, recent studies of early medieval fish weirs around the coastline of Britain and Ireland also indicates that there can be strong continuities of form over centuries. Anglo-Saxon fish traps on the estuaries of the Essex coastline were built, repaired and reactivated through the sixth to eighth centuries AD. Similarly Saxon and Norman fish traps on the Severn estuary indicate local continuities of form, so much so that it might be suspected that the fish traps themselves acted to preserve local memories of good fishing grounds. This broader perspective also reveals that early medieval fish traps were most in use in these islands in the seventh century AD, and also again in the thirteenth to fourteenth centuries AD, presumably relating to some social and cultural processes such as population growth and perception of fish as an economic resource.

EARLY MEDIEVAL COASTAL TIDE MILLS

In recent years, we also have the archaeological evidence for early medieval coastal water-mills at Little Island, Co. Cork and at Nendrum on Strangford Lough. Nendrum monastery on Mahee Island in Strangford Lough was one of the great maritime monasteries of Ireland between the seventh and tenth centuries AD. An eighth-century source, known as the *Litany of the Saints*, suggests that Nendrum had 'nine times fifty monks under the yoke of Mochoe of Noendruin', implying that it had a community of four hundred and fifty monks, to which number could probably be added a large lay population of labourers, craftsmen, servants and tenants. The monks, lacking any fresh water streams on their island environment, turned to tidal power to grind the corn to feed the large monastic population – building a succession of three tide mills on the intertidal zone adjoining the monastic complex. The site has been recently investigated by Tom McErlean and Norman Carruthers.

The monks built a large, enclosed mill pond on the upper foreshore, which filled naturally at every high tide and captured the water body that was then channeled during the low tide through a stone-built flume that provided a high-powered gush of water that turned the paddle wheels of the mills (53). The mill building itself survived largely intact and in and around the base of the mill were found broken millstones, wooden bucket staves, tool handles, lathe-turned wooden bowls and parts of the wooden paddles, hubs and axles of the mill's 'machinery'. Dendrochronology has revealed that the oak trees for the first tide mill were felled in AD 618 and AD 619 and so far it is the earliest tide mill in Europe. Two further tide mills on the same site of increasing sophistication later replaced it. The last mill has been dated to AD 787. These tide mills, driven by the renewable energy resource that is provided by Strangford Lough's prodigious tides, would have enabled the early medieval monks of Nendrum to process grain into flour for bread at almost an industrial scale – indicating the church's economic investment in arable agriculture around its own estates and elsewhere along the region's shoreline. Nendrum's inhabitants were probably also using the fish traps found elsewhere on the lough's intertidal zone.

53 Early medieval mill at Nendrum, Strangford Lough, Co. Down (courtesy of Thomas McErlean, UUC)

SHIPS AND BOATS IN EARLY MEDIEVAL IRELAND

Sources of evidence for early medieval boats

In contrast to elsewhere in northern Europe, the archaeological evidence for ships and boats in early medieval Ireland is very limited. Nonetheless, the early medieval annals and saints' lives frequently mention the marine fleets and battles of the Irish, the Anglo-Saxons and at a later stage the Vikings. In particular, we have a rich vein of evidence in the early Irish historical sources. These include the saints' lives (notably Adomnán's *Life of Columba*), the ninth- and tenth-century voyages tales (known as *immrama*), as well as the early Irish laws and annalistic references. These imply that there were different types of craft that were sailing the Celtic seas. There is also evidence from the depictions of ships on eighth-century cross-inscribed pillars, and latterly by the tenth and eleventh century, on high crosses. It has traditionally been thought that most of these accounts and depictions describe early types of curragh – simple hide covered craft. However, it is now thought likely that Irish seafarers would have been capable of making and using larger wooden ships and boats.

It is also likely that a wide range of different types of European craft would have been plying back and forth across the Irish Sea in particular, originating from a range of different cultural and ethnic traditions, such as Celtic, Anglo-Saxon and Frankish. It is even possible that Mediterranean craft, inspired by earlier Classical, Byzantine and Arabic shipbuilding traditions, were occasionally seen in Irish waters, particularly in the fifth and sixth centuries AD. There are accounts in one of the Iberian Lives of Greek merchants (negotiatores) sailing from the eastern Mediterranean to Meredia, in Galicia, but did they travel as far as Ireland? Tentative archaeological evidence for this is provided by the imported pottery (i.e. B-ware) found on some early medieval sites in Ireland originating from the eastern Mediterranean (i.e. the Greek islands, Anatolia and North Africa), although they could have been brought to Ireland by Gaulish or British craft. By the sixth and seventh century AD, the types of imported pottery found in early medieval sites are principally from western France, namely E-ware pottery. There are several historical references to the activities of Gaulish traders in Irish waters. For example, the medieval Life of St. Ciaran states that merchants from Gaul brought wine to the midlands monastery of Clonmacnoise (presumably sailing up the River Shannon), while the *Life of Columba* mentions Gaulish sailors arriving on the Scottish coastline of Dalriada.

Similarly, Frankish and Anglo-Saxon glass, weaponry and other objects also indicate other long-distance trading connections with lands across the sea. Presumably at least some of these objects arrived on foreign vessels and so would have been a common sight to Irish coastal dwellers, particularly along the east coast. Intriguingly, there is also a reference to a raid in AD 683 by a Saxon fleet on the Rivers Boyne and Liffey that carried off hostages and booty. Presumably Saxon ships were also involved in more peaceable interactions. Perhaps, archaeologists may someday discover a Gaulish, Saxon or even a Galician boat on an Irish east coast estuary. Although there are few Gaulish craft known, an early seventh-century, carvel-built wooden boat found at Port Berteau II, on the River Charente not far from the west coast of France probably gives a sense of what these craft looked like. On the other hand, Irish sea-goers would have been seen abroad too. The eighth-century *Life of Filibert* documents an Irish ship trading shoes and leather in the Loire region.

Ships and boats were also used in warfare. The Irish annals also occasionally refer to fleets of vessels involved in hostings, although these epigrammatic entries provide little detail on the form of craft used. They refer, famously, to an assembled fleet of the Dál Riada travelling to the islands of Coll and Islay, Scotland in AD 564. In AD 612, Tory Island was devastated by a marine fleet of unstated origins. Certainly, by the ninth and tenth centuries AD, Nordic-type ships were being used in Irish waters, by both Irish and Scandinavian fleets and were to profoundly influence Irish and Scottish maritime traditions. A recent remarkable archaeological discovery is the ship graffiti on what has become known as the 'hostage slab', found near an early medieval church site at Inchmarnock in Scotland. This ship graffiti stone appears to depict a Nordic-type longship with oars, steering rudder and a square sail. Most strikingly, a large, hairy warrior appears to be hauling towards the ship a recently captured and bound monk who is carrying what seems to be a book satchel.

SHIPS AND BOATS IN THE MONASTIC WORLD

So, what were Irish ships and boats like at the beginning of the Middle Ages? There has been a traditional tendency to only think in terms of hide-covered vessels, partly due to a too literal reading of classical and medieval texts. Certainly, early medieval sources do imply that hide-covered craft were common. However, there is also now an emerging sense that early medieval ships and boats may have been diverse in design and appearance. Early Irish laws depict boat-builders as skilled and socially significant craftsmen in contemporary society. For example, the legal tract *Uraicecht Becc* describes the legal position of 'a builder of *ler long*, and *bairca*, and *curach*. Various seventh- and eighth-century laws refer to hide-covered, wicker coracles (*clíab*) and larger boats (*náu*) used for fishing in inshore and estuarine waters.

Monastic writers, occasionally describing the worlds of maritime saints and ocean voyagers also provide useful evidence for the form of early craft. Adomnán's *Life of Columba*, written in the seventh-century describes the maritime life and traditions of the Scottish monastic island of Iona and it is a significant source of information on ships and seafaring. Jonathan Wooding's analyses of the terminology in the anecdotes referring to seafaring and sea-farers reveals that Adomnán uses different Latin and Gaelic (themselves based on Latin loan-words) names for different kinds of boats and ships. Some of these were clearly wooden plank-built craft, while others were made of wicker and animal hides. Adomnán seemingly uses the terms navis, longe navis and barca to refer to large sea-going vessels and presumably some of these were wooden craft. The construction of wooden craft is also implied in a reference to an incident where dressed timbers of pine and oak for building long ships were brought to Iona by fleets of currachs (curucis) and skiffs (scafís). Intriguingly, the word barca is used to describe a Gaulish trading ship implying that it was distinctively different, but not unfamiliar, to the monastic islanders.

In the early Middle Ages (and undoubtedly earlier), robust, ocean-going, hide-covered craft were also used in sailing along the western seaways, as well as for pilgrimage and penitential ocean voyaging. The lives refer to the *cimbul* and the small *curucus* that could be taken as names for early currachs, used both on inland waterways and inshore waters. However, it is also clear that these were capable of sailing on the open ocean. In the seventh-century *Life of Columba*, there is a description of how some monks voyaging on the ocean came under attack from sea creatures which struck the keel, sides, prow and stern of the vessel. Revealingly, the monks were anxious that the creature would pierce the 'leather covering' of the boat. It is clear that sails were used on both wooden and hide-covered craft, as is indicated by the descriptions of St. Columba's ability to miraculously change the course of the wind while seafaring or to raise a more favourable one. On other occasions, monastic voyagers haul in their sails to avoid colliding with whales, taking to their oars to row away.

In the ninth-century immram or voyage tale known as the Navigatio Sancti Brendani Abbatis (the voyages of Saint Brendan the abbot), there are various descriptions of methods of the construction of these hide-covered boats. The text describes the various voyages of Brendan around the waters of the North Atlantic (i.e. west coast of Ireland, the Faroes, Iceland, Greenland) during which time his crew experience many adventures including encounters with whales, and perhaps volcanoes and icebergs. These stories suggest that this and other voyage tales are an amalgamation of reports (and perhaps tall tales) told by secular and ecclesiastical sailors returning from dangerous voyages.

The voyage of Saint Brendan describes the boat used by the saint in some detail. It relates how Brendan gathered a crew of fourteen monks and built a light boat framed and ribbed with wood. Ox-hides tanned with oak bark covered this wooden framework and then the joints of the hides were smeared with fat to make them watertight. The boat was then equipped with a mast placed in the middle of the boat. As soon as the boat was launched the crew sailed westwards. They initially had no need to navigate apart from holding the sail with the wind and using a steering oar to guide the boat. Once they had become becalmed they took to the oars and rowed until their strength gave in. Brendan is mentioned as sitting and standing in the bow while praying, perhaps indicating the importance of this position in the vessel.

THE EARLY MEDIEVAL BOAT ON THE BANTRY PILLAR STONE

There is also some intriguing archaeological evidence for early medieval Irish boats on the Bantry pillar stone. This is an eighth-century, decorated stone slab situated within an early ecclesiastical site at Kilnaruane, Co. Cork, on a low hill overlooking Bantry Harbour, Co. Cork – one of the finest natural havens in south-west Ireland. The Bantry piller stone has long been seen as a realistic depiction of an early Irish wicker and hide currach – but it may be more complicated than that (54).

The Bantry pillar stone has on its surface the simple depiction of a boat crewed by five figures, who are apparently rowing their craft skywards into the heavens. Sitting at the stern is a helmsman, who is holding a steering oar on the port side of the vessel. In front of him, there are four figures that appear to be forcefully pulling on their oars in a realistic manner. There is also a possible sixth figure sitting forward in the bow, although hundreds of years of weathering of the stone make this detail impossible to establish. The iconography of the Bantry pillar stone has been interpreted in a number of ways. It has been suggested that the boat was a metaphorical image for the early Irish church as implied by the following passage from the Book of Homilies: 'The body of the church as a whole is like a great ship carrying men of many different origins through a violent storm.' Peter Harbison has suggested that figure with the raised hand may

54 Early medieval boat depiction on Bantry
pillar stone, Co. Cork (Wes Forsythe, UU)

be a depiction of the Christ stilling the tempest, so that it should be understood as
a biblical scene that is on view. Undoubtedly, this image inspired the descriptions
of saints calming storms by standing with a raised hand in the prow of his ship
that we read in the seventh-century *Life of Columba*. However the raised hand on
the Bantry pillar stone is indistinct and the figures in the boat certainly do not
seem to be engulfed in stormy water. It is also possible that the depiction is of a
peregrini or navigating saint such as Brendan setting sail onto the trackless ocean,
as is so often described in various voyage tales and saints lives.

But what of the boat itself? It has often been thought that the Bantry pillar
stone is a depiction of an early medieval currach. Certainly, the stone carving
clearly shows a smallish craft, with a distinct gunwale along the upper edge, a
blunt stern and a more rounded high-profile bow. It could be argued that this is
a craft with strong similarities with the modern naomhóg found along the coasts
of south-west Ireland. It is also true that the angled rowers with their oars are
evocative of men in a naomhóg, with the position and narrow form of the oars
showing that they were attached to the hull by thole pins. Indeed, a probable
seventh- or eighth-century wooden oar recovered during the Nendrum tide mill
excavations (see above) would be broadly of similar form. It is true that a vessel
built of wooden or wicker frames covered by animal skins would have excellent

sea-going capabilities, as they are tough, strong and flexible in the waves. More recent experiments, such as the one attempted by Tim Severin when he sailed a hide-covered boat to North America, suggest that they could also be fast, sailing distances of sixty to seventy miles a day. On the other hand, it is also true that Irish scholars have tended to be fixated on the currach, seeing the modern boat that is so familiar to us from stories and photographs from the Aran Islands and the Blaskets as the descendent of an age-old tradition. In actual fact, the modern currach has often been the result of quite significant social and demographic changes in the nineteenth century AD.

It has also been suggested that the Bantry pillar stone is depicting a wooden craft, with a distinct gunwhale and keel that may even be similar to contemporary Icelandic fishing boats. Certainly, as we have already seen, the early medieval Irish were indeed building and using wooden plank craft, along with other navigators along the Atlantic shore. On the other hand, other scholars have pointed out that this is an iconographic image, intended to convey a sense of either a biblical scene, the church or a navigating saint, so we should not be expecting it to represent all early medieval craft. Indeed, hide-covered craft may have been particularly associated with pilgrimage. The depiction of one type of boat on an early medieval cross does not mean that it was the only one existing in Ireland.

HIBERNO–SCANDINAVIAN SHIPBUILDING IN EARLY MEDIEVAL IRELAND

In the ninth and tenth century, Nordic type vessels began to be seen in Irish waters, inspiring both fear and admiration. The Irish chroniclers who recorded the Viking raids on the Irish coast from AD 795 onwards were obviously struck by the ferocity and speed of attacks on monastic coastal sites. It was a speed that was provided mainly by one thing – the versatile and impressive wooden seagoing ships that were developed by the Scandinavian peoples through the late Iron Age. These Nordic type ships were also to become the basis of Dublin's wealth in the tenth and eleventh century, providing the means by which merchants and traders made their way back and forth along the Atlantic sea lanes, to the Mediterranean, Baltic and the frozen islands of the North Atlantic. Indeed, archaeological excavations on the Norse colony at L'Anse aux Meadows, Newfoundland recovered a distinctive Dublin-type ringed pin that may have been worn by a Viking man or woman who had stopped at Dublin. In fact, one of the major contributions of the Scandinavian peoples to Irish culture was in terms of their influence on our maritime traditions, as can be seen both in boat-building terminology and the numerous coastal place names around the Irish coastline.

Scandinavian maritime archaeologists have established through the discovery and excavation of ships at Oseberg, Gokstad and Skuldelev much about the nature of these ships. Similarly, the types of boats and ships used by Norse raiders and settlers in Ireland were probably also double-ended, clinker-built vessels propelled by both sail and oar. The style of their construction gave them immense flexibility (i.e. they could flex with the waves) and made them very sea worthy, while their shallow draught (*c*.1m) enabled them to travel deep up into rivers, estuaries and shallow bays. The ships were light and sturdy and could be beached and hauled ashore if the weather turned or the crew were intent on attacking a nearby site. The raiding ships could carry a large complement of men with the largest warships able to carry in excess of a hundred men and experimental archaeology has shown that they could reach speeds of 20 knots in very favourable conditions, allowing them to outrun any enemies or suddenly arrive without warning. However, these Nordic ships were not only raiders. The Vikings also developed large, wider-beamed traders which could carry up to thirty tons of cargo with a crew of ten men and reach speeds in excess of ten knots. The crews onboard these vessels navigated by known landmarks on the coast and probably rarely travelled by night. Their ships are known to have crossed the Atlantic and to have reached, at the very least, the coast of Greenland.

There are numerous early medieval annalistic references to Viking ships sinking in coastal waters. In AD 919 the annals refer to a fleet of thirty-two Viking vessels arriving in Lough Foyle, Co. Donegal to a place where they met with 'straits and rocks'. In AD 922, the annals record the drowning of 1200 Vikings in their vessels at the mouth of the River Erne, Co. Donegal. Whatever the accuracy of these accounts, it must have been the case that such ships occasionally came to grief. Undoubtedly, somewhere around the Irish coast, lying in the sands of a sheltered bay or exposed by the tides on estuarine mudflats, there is the remains of a Viking ship. When it is found, it will be one of the most important discoveries made in Irish archaeology. However, for the moment there is no confirmed archaeological evidence for an intact Viking Age ship in Ireland.

What Irish archaeologists have found are large number of ships' timbers, including ships' planking, keels, stems, knees, stringers, bulkheads and other intricate floor timbers, as well as other elements from broken-up Nordic-type ships that have been excavated in medieval Dublin and Waterford (55). These timbers basically represent fragments of boats and ships dating from the tenth through to the thirteenth century AD (and although some are from late medieval structures, they date to decades earlier). These timbers are usually either recovered as articulated groups (i.e. boat planks still nailed together) or as individual pieces where they were often deliberately re-used in medieval waterfront revetments, drains and houses. Indeed, these stray timbers paint an evocative picture of the many old, rotting hulks of vessels that must have been lying on the River Liffey's mudflats, where they would have been hacked up as the townspeople required timber for other purposes. Virtually all these timbers came from vessels of the Nordic-type double-ended, clinker-built tradition. Interestingly, they indicate that there were various sizes of craft in use around Hiberno-Norse Dublin. Small boats (under 12m in length) similar to the ship's boat from Gokstad (2 and 3) would have been used for fishing, transport and perhaps as lighters for moving between larger ships and the shoreline. There were also larger boats and ships that would have been the warships, traders and ocean-going vessels.

Archaeological excavations in late Hiberno-Norse Waterford have also revealed some similar boat timbers. Nearly all of them were fashioned in the Nordic shipbuilding tradition. A single stem from the bow of a ship was found and dated to the late twelfth or early thirteenth century. Four or five strakes (boat planks) would have run into it and a small hole for a mooring rope was evident on it. The stem probably originally came from a small four-oared boat. Two floor timbers were found dating to the mid to late twelfth century, again probably coming from a small oared boat.

Some of the ships' timbers also give evidence for methods of propulsion, as there are twelfth-century century oars and paddles, which indicate the use of ship-going craft and a mast step was also found in Dublin, from a large boat used for transport and fishing. No complete vessel has survived so there is little evidence for methods of rigging on the craft (although some small wooden artefacts are interpreted as items used in tying ropes).

However, we can reconstruct ships' rigging and appearance from ship graffiti – simple depictions of ships scratched into wooden planks. Planking used in an eleventh-century drain cover at Winetavern Street, Dublin had sketches of two ships on it (56). The larger sketch shows the port side of a Nordic type craft. It has a high, curved stern with a steering oar on its starboard side. It has a single mast with a partially lowered yard with its sails furled. Three rigging lines run either side of the mast to the forward and aft while an arrow type feature on top of the mast head may represent a weather vane. A small double ended boat lies off the stern of the vessel and must be a tender either belonging to the boat or servicing it. A second boat was depicted on a smaller plank. This shows a double-ended ship with a high stem and stern with planking clearly shown. A large central mast has rigging lines running forward and aft.

A ship graffito from Christchurch Place depicts a clinker built vessel with only one end visible (57). The vessel has a short sturdy and blunt-ended post which is unlike the other more rounded depictions of Viking end timbers. The graffito shows a central mast with a yard and shows a little bearded man on top of the yard furling (tying up) the sail. Rigging shroud lines run from the yard to the gunwale of the vessel.

Small boat models have also been found during the course of the Hiberno-Norse Dublin excavations (58). Two were found in twelfth-century levels at Winetavern Street while a third was uncovered in a mid-tenth-century context at Fishamble Street. These little ships are again clearly Scandinavian in character. One is almost complete and is a double-ended boat with a rounded stem and stern. Both vessels have a hole on the amidships floor which would have held a mast while a number of small holes in the hull were for fixing rigging to. These models were probably used as children's toys and are paralleled elsewhere in Scandinavia.

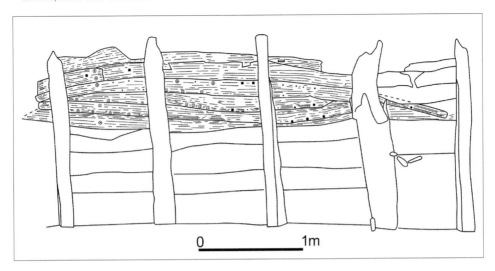

55 Early medieval ship re-used as part of waterfront structure, Winetavern Street, Dublin (from O'Sulllivan 2000)

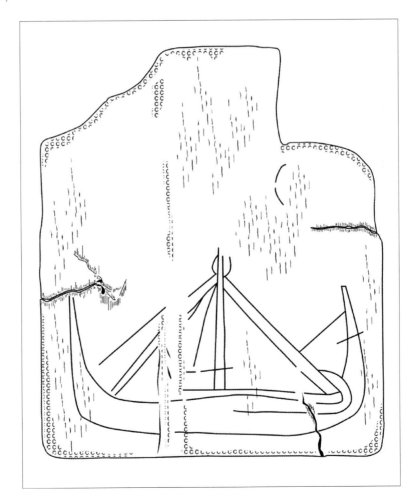

56 Viking ship graffiti on plank from Winetavern Street (after Christensen 1998)

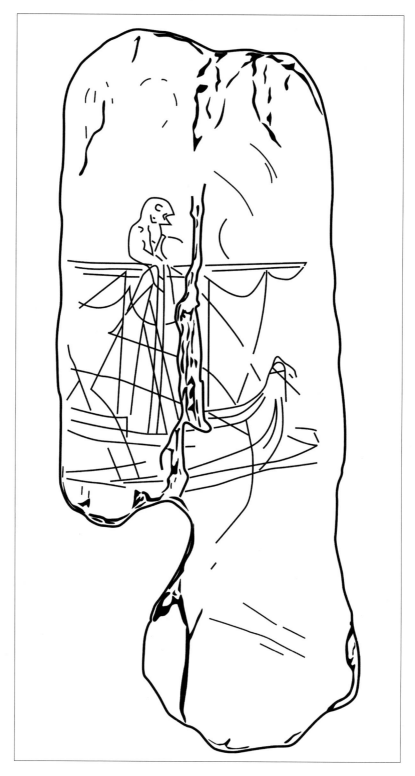

57 Viking ship graffiti on plank from Christchurch Place (after Christensen 1988)

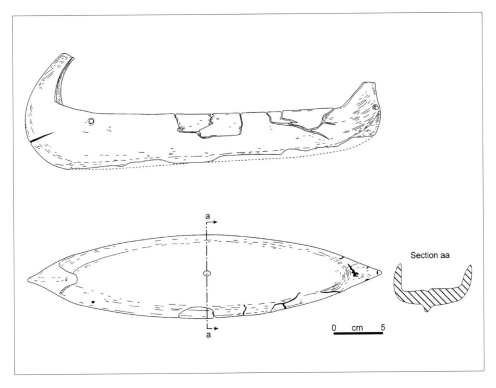

58 Viking ship model from Winetavern Street (after Christensen 1988)

It seems likely that Scandinavian craft would also have been adopted by the native Irish. Certainly, the form of these vessels impinged on the Irish imagination and consciousness in other ways. On several early medieval Irish high crosses, there are depictions of ships that are evidently Scandinavian in type. Amongst other things, these high crosses (usually dated to the tenth to eleventh century) that were situated within the monastic enclosure were probably used for educating the faithful, providing observers with illustrations of events and incidents in both the Old and New Testament. The diverse scenes depicted include Noah's Ark (59) and the occasion when Jesus saved Peter from drowning on the Sea of Galilee. The carvings themselves usually show a ship that is double-ended, with rounded hulls and high stems and sterns (i.e. a Scandinavian type vessel). Understandably, given that these are depictions on stone, only rarely are there details of masts, rigging or sails (although there are often paddles and steering oars). Despite the fact that these iconographic images are meant to symbolise ships, rather than rigorously record their nautical construction, it is evident that this was the contemporary image of a large, ocean-going vessel.

59 Noah's ark on east face of Killary Cross, Co. Meath (after Harbison 1992)

A HIBERNO-NORSE DUBLIN SHIP THAT SANK IN DENMARK

There is also archaeological evidence for Nordic-type ships built in Ireland that ended their days in Scandinavia. Dendrochronologists in the National Museum of Denmark in Copenhagen established in the 1990s that one of the famous Skuldelev ships was of Irish origin. The Skuldelev ships were excavated by Danish archaeologists between 1957 and 1962 in Roskilde Fjord in northern Zealand, one of the main islands of the Danish archipelago. The five Skuldelev Viking ships had been deliberately sunk in the late eleventh century to provide an underwater blockade in a channel leading towards the medieval town of Roskilde. The Skuldelev ships consisted of two merchant vessels, a fishing boat and two warships. One of the merchant ships (Skuldelev 1) was a large ocean-going trader, built of Larch wood that had been growing along the shores of the Baltic, probably in south of Norway. The second merchant ship would have been involved in inshore work. There was also a small ferry or fishing boat, as well as both a large and small warship.

The most impressive ship was Skuldelev 2 – a large warship or longship. Unfortunately, only *c.*10 per cent of the vessel had survived but careful reconstruction of the ship's lines and size suggest that it is the largest Viking ship yet found. Skuldelev 2 had an overall length of 30m and a width of 4.5m and a draught of just over 1m. The ship was propelled by between 50 and 60 oars and would have carried a crew of 60-100 men. It carried a large central mast with a sail area calculated at 150m². It could have attained an average speed of five knots and achieved better speeds in more favourable weather conditions. Recently, an experimental replica of the Skuldelev 2 ship was built and launched at Roskilde, Denmark and initial anecdotal reports suggest that it is startlingly fast. The weapon of mass destruction of its age, its arrival on an isolated shoreline with a complement of warriors would have struck terror into any heart.

Dendrochronological studies have shown that the ship was built between AD 1060-70. Statistical analyses known as dendroprovenancing also reveal that the ship was built not of oaks growing in the Baltic region, but of oak trees growing on the east coast of Ireland. Most probably, the Skuldelev 2 warship was built by Hiberno-Norse Dublin's shipbuilders, craftsmen who were working within the tradition of Scandinavian boat building that had been introduced into Ireland in the tenth and eleventh century AD. Ultimately one of the ships built in the Scandinavian tradition in a Dublin boatyard was to make its way to its ancestral home, ending up on the bed of a Danish fjord. No doubt, others lie on the floor of the ocean between Ireland, Europe and North America.

NAVIGATION AND SEA LORE: SAILING THE SEA LANES IN THE EARLY MIDDLE AGES

Most ocean voyages in the early Middle Ages would have been essentially local, as people moved back and forth along the coast for social and economic reasons, to trade, fish or travel between islands. However, the sea was also of key importance for long distance movement of people, goods and ideas, as it had been since prehistory. It has been suggested that in the period AD 400-800, most 'international' maritime traffic would have been up the Irish Sea, with the western seaboard of Ireland not as significant a route way, but this may not have been the case. Certainly, as Sharon Greene has recently demonstrated, there is plenty of historical and archaeological evidence for the early medieval inhabitation of Connacht's Atlantic islands and the movement of ships along the western seaboard – as well as hints of connections right around the north-west coast and towards Scotland.

It is generally considered that early medieval boats would have performed poorly when sailing to windward, so hugging the coastline on long journeys would not have been a safe option. Within the Irish Sea, it is likely that most ships would have sailed up along the east Irish coast, avoiding the dangerous coastline of western Britain. This is because the prevailing winds there (as elsewhere in Atlantic Europe) came from the south-west and would drive the craft of the period onto the lee shores of south-west England and Wales. Sailing would also have been a seasonal activity. The best time of the year to set out on a long ocean voyage would have been between April and September, when weather was best and gales were least frequent. Across the Mediterranean and Atlantic Europe, sailing was generally avoided (apart from local voyages on clear days) from November to March.

Tidal currents and cycles were also significant environmental factors in decisions about ocean voyages. Jonathan Wooding has pointed to the fact that the tidal currents in the Irish Sea are quite complex. The tides in the south work clockwise, moving up from the south and down from the north. A different system occurs in the seas between Ireland and Scotland. A knowledgeable mariner can therefore use them to move up and down the coastline, working the tides around the Isle of Man, headlands, estuaries and bays and so on.

Navigation in the early medieval period would have been by dead reckoning – pointing the ship in the desired direction and estimating the distances covered to establish your location. A ship could also be steered 'by the run of the sea' (setting and keeping the ship on a constant direction in relation to the orientation of the ocean swell, which would have followed the prevailing south-west winds).

Clouds building up over land masses can also enable recognition to distant islands. Navigation would also have been aided by the use of prominent landmarks or landfalls. Along the coast of the western sea lanes (Brittany, northern Spain, Ireland and Britain), headlands up to 30m high can be seen from 11.5 nautical miles, while prominences up to 60m in height are visible from 16 miles out. The travel writer Jonathan Raban in his book *Coasting*, describes sailing around Britain in a yacht and has noted an interesting aspect of the seascapes of our part of the world. From about the middle of the Irish Sea, it is possible to see the Isle of Man, Snowdonia in north Wales, the Wicklow mountains and the Mourne mountains all at one time. However, it is also important to remember that early historic mariners would certainly have happily sailed out of sight of land, crossing for example between Gaul and Cornwall.

By the tenth century AD, we should imagine Hiberno-Norse vessels sailing around the Irish coastline, from the north down to the west and also around the south-west coast from Cork and Waterford. Place names around the Irish coast also attest to Norse influenced and perhaps even Hiberno-Norse settlements outside the main towns. Place names such as Strangford, Wexford and Waterford all derive from Old Norse. Similarly, place names on many of the islands and bays around the Irish coast also indicate these prominent landmarks served as navigational points for tenth- and eleventh-century mariners sailing the coastline, such as Dursey Island off Cork and Smerwick Harbour in Kerry.

TRADE AND EXCHANGE ALONG THE WESTERN SEA LANES, AD 500–800

Our archaeological evidence for early coastal trade along the western sea lanes is largely provided by imported pottery, including eastern Mediterranean Red

Slip Ware (A-ware), amphorae pottery (B-wares) and imported French kitchen vessels (E-ware). This pottery tends to be found on high-status settlements (e.g. Garranes, Co. Cork ringfort, Lagore and Moynagh Lough crannogs, Co. Meath) and on ecclesiastical or monastic enclosures (Reask, Co. Kerry, Nendrum Co. Down and around other places on Strangford Lough) even on relatively small sites (such as Kilpatrick, Co. Westmeath in the Irish midlands).

The pottery was not itself always the main focus of trade, sometimes it was a by-product of it, being discarded after its contents (wines, foodstuffs or dyes) had been used. However, it is also likely the pots themselves came to be perceived as high-status goods, being a symbol of prestige and distant connections. Thus pottery vessels would have had a biography, changing in meaning during their use. Even if empty of their original materials, they would have been associated with feasting and exotic foods, providing a material memory for years after of wealth and power. The imported western European and Mediterranean pottery of Ireland and western Britain has been studied in detail by archaeologists such as Charles Thomas and Ewan Campbell and a good understanding of its origins, movement and dating has been established.

The earliest imported vessels found in Ireland are Red Slip Wares, probably mostly deriving from western Turkey in the eastern Mediterranean. These fine bowls and dishes, dated to early sixth century AD, are found mostly in west Wales and south-west England (e.g. at Tintagel, Cornwall). A single sherd of Phocaean Red Slip Ware was found at Garranes ringfort (dating to about AD 500) and a sherd was also found at Garryduff ringfort, Co. Cork. It is likely that these were merely imported as incidental inclusions in cargoes, along with much more numerous B-ware amphorae.

Bi ware or amphorae date to c.AD 500–530. These are globular vessels (particularly the 'Agora' form), with a short neck, decorated with deep lines of grooving in a band on the upper part of the amphorae. Bi wares were imported from the Peloponese islands or the Greek mainland. It has been found at Garranes, Co. Cork, Dalkey Island, Co. Dublin and Clogher, Co. Tyrone. It is rare in Scotland, but it has been found at Dumbarton Rock and Whithorn. In contrast, it is very common in Wales and Cornwall (particularly Tintagel). The pottery then mostly suggests that the major trading links were between Britain and the eastern Mediterranean, continuing on from Iron Age trade in tin and other commodities. This Mediterranean pottery then was brought to Ireland in the sixth century AD as part of ongoing links between these islands.

The second major phase of pottery imports, that of E-wares, occurred in the late sixth and seventh century AD (60). These are found in small quantities at many sites in western Britain and Ireland. E-ware is a fine, grey kitchenware in a range of standard forms. E-ware includes everted-rim wares, small beakers, flared bowls and strap-handled jugs. The most common forms in Ireland are the jars and the beaker. The most likely source of E-ware is western France, on the basis of petrological analysis, although Hodges has suggested different sources, such as

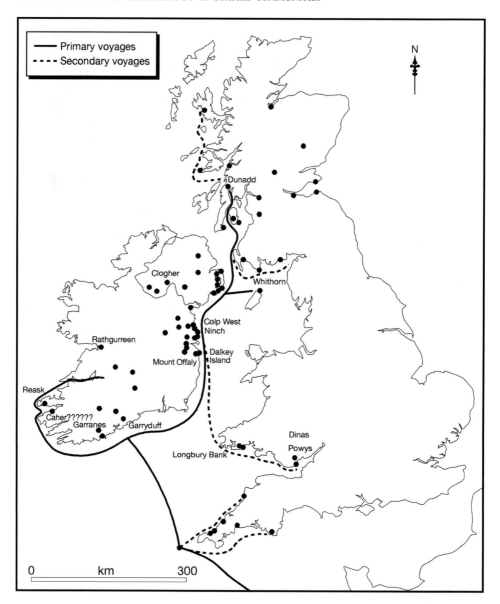

60 Distribution of E-ware pottery in Ireland and reconstruction of maritime trade routes (after Edwards 1990 and Wooding 1996)

Aquitaine and Iberia. In contrast with the B-wares, there is clear evidence that Ireland and Scotland were involved in the direct importation of E-ware, and the dyestuffs, foods, dill, coriander they contained. It is possible that there was a shift in coastal trade towards Ireland in the late sixth and early seventh century AD.

Major assemblages of imported glass bowls and cones are known from Britain and Ireland, particularly from Dalkey Island, Moynagh Lough and Rathtinaun crannogs. This glass has typically been dated to fifth and sixth century AD. It is suggested that its source is northern France/Rhineland. But it is possible that

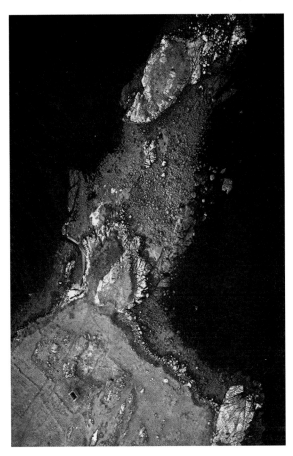

61 Dalkey Island promontory fort
(Marine Institute, National Coastline
Survey)

material reached Ireland via England and south Wales, rather than directly from
the production centre. It is also possible that some glass was imported as scrap,
for glass production, although whole vessels are also known. At Moynagh Lough,
two tiny Merovingian glass vessels probably were used to transport unguents or
perfumes.

Obviously, all this pottery, glass and metalwork from the Greek Islands, France
and northern Europe were brought to Ireland by ships. It seems likely that
imported pottery, metalwork and glass was being brought in by small traders,
working to the demands of coastal communities. The early medieval saints' lives
occasionally mention foreign ships sailing between Ireland and the continent,
using the terms *barca* to differentiate them from local, inshore vessels (see above).

In the early medieval period around the North Sea and the Atlantic, particular
islands or sheltered locations along the coast seem to have been used as places
where pottery and glass were brought ashore by coastal traders. On the other
hand, it may well be that such beach markets were established by maritime
traders along the east coast themselves – in co-operation with local elites or
with the church.

The early medieval coastal settlement at Dalkey Island, Co. Dublin seems to have been one of these places (*61*). Dalkey Island is a promontory fort on this small island on the south side of Dublin bay. It was excavated by David Liversage in the 1950s and produced evidence for Mesolithic, Bronze Age and early medieval occupation. The early medieval settlement on the island was concentrated on a narrow promontory at the north-west end of the island, adjacent to a natural landing place. The promontory fort was probably built in the sixth or seventh century, and probably succeeded a previous unenclosed settlement. The promontory fort has produced the largest amount of imported pottery and glass known from any site in Ireland. It includes fifth and sixth century Bi, Bii, B misc. pot shards and sixth- to seventh-century E-ware pottery, glass bowls and glass beakers. It is unlikely that Dalkey Island was a high status settlement site; neither the enclosure or finds evidence would indicate this. However, Dalkey Island would have been ideal for a trading place. It was strategically situated on the Irish Sea maritime route ways and was also located on an offshore island on the south side of Dublin Bay, where it could have served as a safe and secure landing place for merchants working under the protection of a local king.

E-ware pottery is also found elsewhere up along the Irish Sea coast. Recent archaeological excavations at Ninch, Co, Meath – to the south of the Boyne estuary – have produced some E-ware associated with a multi-period, enclosed settlement on this coastal site, implying the use of natural landing places along the Irish Sea coastline.

The largest concentration of E-ware on the Irish Sea coast is found around Strangford Lough, Co. Down. This pottery may have been introduced into the territory of the local Dál Fiatach via the small island of Dunnyneill Island, situated at the southern end of the lough, opposite its entrance and the mouth of the Quoile estuary. Finbar McCormick and Phillip McDonald's recent archaeological excavations on Dunnyneill Island indicated the presence of an early medieval enclosure, E-ware pottery, Mediterreanean and Anglo-Saxon glass, as well as evidence for high-status feasting, iron-working, copper-working and glass-working. It is likely then that Dunnyneill Island was both a high-status seasonally occupied island, as well as a beach trading station, and was probably also a location for feasting and entertainment.

Both Dalkey Island and Dunnyneill Island as offshore, marine islands could also be seen as usefully neutral places (indeed, this is implied in an early medieval annalistic reference to a royal political encounter on *Inis na Rígh*, another Irish Sea island on the north Dublin coast, which is described as being usefully 'neither sea nor land' and thence capable of being used for negotiating a political agreement). Early medieval trade and exchange was structured around gift giving and reciprocity, so it is likely that local kings or other secular elites sent emissaries out to these islands (or went out themselves) to meet Gaulish traders, exchanging their own locally sourced hides, slaves or other goods for foreign pottery, glass and exotic foods. These exotic goods could then have been brought back to

the royal residence for redistribution to royal kin and clients in local political
territories.

MARITIME TRADE AND EXCHANGE IN THE TENTH TO TWELFTH
CENTURIES AD

By the tenth century AD, Ireland was drawn again into another maritime trading
network, but now with a focus on the North Atlantic. In particular, the Irish
Sea had become a major Atlantic seaway, serving as the axis for sea-going trade
and exchange between the Mediterranean and northern Europe. Dublin was
a particularly significant stopping point or port on the east-west route way
between early medieval Europe and the Scandinavian colonies of the Faroes,
Iceland and Greenland. We can see the role of both the native Irish and Dublin
Vikings in the North Atlantic by the frequent reference in the Icelandic sagas
to Irish slaves and women, while the discovery of Irish type ringed pins at the
tenth-century Norse settlement at L'Anse Aux Meadows also indicates the far
flung maritime connections between Ireland and elsewhere.

Strongly influenced by contemporary annalistic references to Viking raids,
most modern scholars tend to emphasise violence, fleets of warships and raiding
around Irish coastal waters in the ninth century AD. However, it is likely that other,
perhaps even peaceable, types of activities that went under the radar of monastic
scribes were also going on. It is possible that Scandinavian rural settlements
such as the Cherrywood, Co. Dublin site or even the Dublin longphort of AD
841, were the residences of Scandinavian men and women engaged in trade,
manufacturing and rural agricultural labour.

However, particularly striking is the development of Hiberno-Norse ports
and harbours from the tenth centuries onwards in Dublin, Wexford, Waterford,
Cork and Limerick. All these ports appear to have located at places that had a
number of suitable topographic features and landscape characteristics; proximity
to the coast, situation on large natural havens at the confluence of rivers. These
locations would also have provided natural defence, sheltered by the surrounding
topography and the river barriers and with a ready escape route to the sea.
These ports were often at the boundaries of existing expansive socio-economic
and political hinterlands and also provided ready access to a wide and varied
hinterland. This is especially true when one considers the mobility that the
surrounding seascapes gave these Scandinavian peoples.

In any case, by the tenth and eleventh century AD, Dublin was one of the most
important trading ports in Atlantic Europe (62), with its own ships being the key
to trade and commerce with the Baltic, Mediterranean and Russia. Between
AD 920-1170, Dublin had trading links with York, Scandinavia, Anglo-Saxon
England and other parts of Ireland. Gold and silver ingots and a large number of
imported coins indicate the importance of trade with England, particularly the

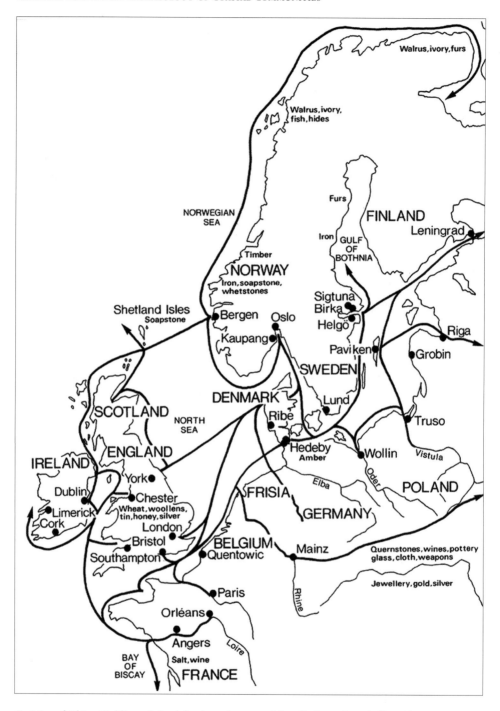

62 Map of Viking Dublin and the Atlantic trade routes (after Graham-Campbell 1990)

Chester area, and with the north-west of France. The presence of walrus ivory (available only in the Arctic circle), soapstone vessels and amber indicates that trade was maintained with Scandinavia while the discovery of silks show that Dublin was part of a trading network which stretched as far as the Silk Road to China. Silver coins from Samarkand, Taskent and Baghdad, Iraq have all been found in Dublin.

What was Dublin exporting? Almost certainly, the town's major exports were wool, hides and slaves (as slavery was to be the source of Bristol's and Liverpool's wealth in the post medieval period). Some slaves were probably obtained in raids, but the most common way of obtaining slaves was by trade. In early medieval Ireland, the lives of captives taken in battle were forfeit to the victors. If the captives were not aristocratic and capable of paying a ransom, it was more profitable to sell the captives as slaves, than it was to kill them. The majority of individuals in the Dublin slave markets then were probably purchased from one victorious Irish king or another. Ireland was not the only source of slaves. England, Scotland and Wales supplied their share. Indeed even in the 1100s the merchants of Dublin were condemned for selling English Christians into slavery in Ireland. Slaves were brought from further afield as well. The first reference to a black man, a *duine gorm* (literally, a 'blue man'), in Ireland occurs in the Viking Age when it is assumed he was a Moor captured from Spain or Morocco – but perhaps he was one of Ireland's earliest African immigrants?

6

Gaelic lordships, Anglo-Norman merchants and late medieval mariners, AD 1100-1550

INTRODUCTION

The arrival of the Anglo-Normans in 1169 heralded the beginnings of a period of landscape, economic and social change in Ireland. In a matter of years the newly arrived colonists from England and Wales had exerted extensive military and political control over much of the country. This was brought about through a process of military subjugation and extensive land redistribution. An essential feature of this process was the development of a network of settlements, fortifications and communication arteries. Existing coastal urban centres were reinvigorated while new ports and settlements were developed.

There was also a large increase in the amount of trade and maritime mercantile activity along the coasts marked by an investment in waterfront facilities and new boat and ship types. The primary difference between this period and the preceding centuries was the formalisation of this activity and the influence centralised controlling mechanisms had. Individual and collective entrepreneurialism was a guiding factor and provided much of the cultural and political impetus for this change, which can be recognised primarily along the eastern and southern seaboards; a large degree of continuity with preceding centuries can also be recognised outside of the major port areas.

Traditional historical and archaeological studies have tended to stress the national-scale changes but have mostly ignored continuing socio-economic activity at a local level. Coastal and fishing communities continued to function and develop along parts of the coast and operated within their own intrinsic local worlds. The sea, coast and physical locality of these communities helped mould their local identities but the sea also brought external influences which provided a broader sense of extended place and belonging, firmly positioning the island of Ireland within the social realm of the Atlantic sphere of influence.

The sea throughout the medieval period acted then as a facilitator and as a constant in coastal lifeways and experience.

LATE MEDIEVAL COASTAL SETTLEMENT LANDSCAPES

Anglo-Norman maritime castles and mottes

The initial years of the colony see a concerted attempt to fortify and protect the coast. This has to be seen in the context of the creation of a coastal frontier, not necessarily in the military sense but in an economic one. The success of the colony depended on its ability to remain a viable economic enterprise. In order to achieve this, the Anglo-Normans needed to maintain the ability to keep their commercial border open. In creating a network of fortifications along the broader eastern seaboard they were ensuring that they had ready and safe access to the communication networks of the Irish Sea and that their modes of communication and trade remained open and secure to England and Wales.

The east and south-east coastline could then be regarded as the economic spine of the country, a role it continued to play for much of the second Millennium AD. The initial construction of a coastal D-shaped ringwork at Ferrycarrig, Wexford, can be seen as the erection of an initial bridgehead into the country in 1169-1171 by the Anglo-Norman forces of incursion. Ringworks are seen here as irregular shaped enclosures, often semi-circular, which are similar in morphology to the rath/ringfort but are substantially more defensive. They are often located at cliff edges and have stone-built entrance features and a deep surrounding ditch. Their position within known Anglo-Norman manors is usually a solid indicator of their original history. Other coastal ringworks are well known from around the country including the site at Dunnamark in the Carew manor at the head of Bantry Bay (63). It is likely that far more of these sites are in existence in a coastal context but have yet to be recognised. These sites would initially have functioned as coastal garrisons erected to provide a military base for invasion and settlement related activities.

The erection of coastal mottes, the distinctive Anglo-Norman artificial mound fortifications with timber palisades and buildings erected on the summit, along the east coast has been seen in a similar vein (64). In particular the concentration of coastal mottes along the County Down coast can be seen as an initial consolidation of the seaboard of the Earldom of Ulster, following John De Courcy's incursions into the north-east in 1177. Traditionally, these type-sites have been viewed purely from a terrestrial perspective, regarded as the fortifications of local garrisons erected to protect the strategic interests of the Anglo-Norman advance and to subdue local populations. However, more detailed site specific survey shows that these sites also played a significant maritime role including monitoring shipping activity, commanding landing places and controlling access into the hinterland.

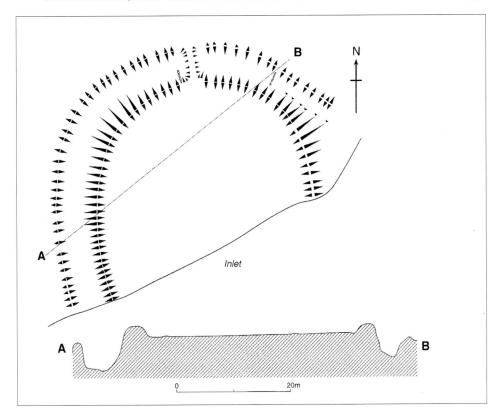

63 Dunnamark ringwork, Co. Cork

The Down mottes, such as Donaghadee and Ballyhalbert, are located at the few established landing places along this coast and are mostly inter-visible, and thus allow for inter-site communication. They overlook the primary shipping lanes and route ways in the northern part of the Irish Sea and are sited so as to be able to observe the movement of marine traffic and control landfall. Kilclief motte, for example, is positioned close to a sandy beach at a sheltered embayment at the mouth of Strangford Lough. Their position at landfalls also meant that they controlled access to the hinterland and played an important governing role in accessing terrestrial communication routes. The density of Down sites is not necessarily reflected elsewhere in the country and may be reflective of the threat that Scottish and Gaelic-Irish shipping posed to the newly established Ulster colony. Excavations at a number of these sites has uncovered the militaristic functions of the sites and exposed the everyday lifestyle of their inhabitants. A large quantity of shellfish was recovered from the excavations at the motte at Clough including cockles, scallops, periwinkles, mussels and oysters. Chris Lynn's excavations at the raised rath/motte at Rathmullan, also in Down, revealed extensive exploitation of foreshore shellfish resources especially in the period post AD 1200.

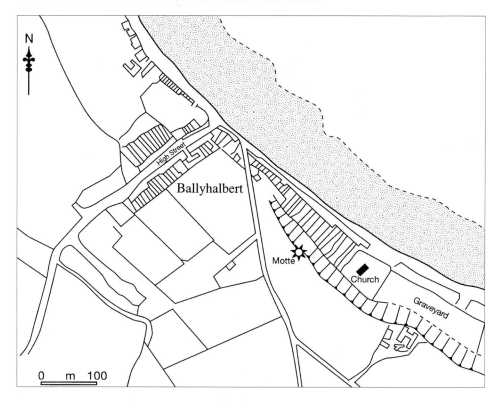

64 Ballyhalbert motte and surrounding landscape

The construction of a number of coastal stone castles can be seen in a related context. The Anglo-Norman lords needed to create centres of power and administration or capita. Large stone castles served this function, and became the focus for political and socio-economic activity in the landscape. Again many of these sites have a specifically coastal context. The large castle at Carrickfergus dominates what is now known as Belfast Lough (65). It is positioned at a natural harbour with safe approaches and anchorages and becomes a convenient port for marine traffic in the north Irish Sea area. A number of other significant castles were constructed in similar commanding maritime locations. King John's castle at Carlingford, Co. Louth was built in a commanding position on the southern shores of the adjacent sea lough. It was probably built in the early part of the thirteenth century with a twin-towered gateway and four square towers on its curtain wall. A settlement developed immediately to the south-east of the castle which was later to be walled. A royal castle was erected at Limerick on the southern shores of the River Shannon again in the early part of the thirteenth century. This seems to have been built on an earlier fortification and commands the head of the Shannon estuary and an important crossing point on the river. In the early years of the fourteenth century Richard de Burgh built a large castle, again

65 Carrickfergus
castle, Co. Antrim
c.1580

with a substantial twin-towered gatehouse, overlooking the entrance to Lough
Foyle. This was a significant gateway into the north-west and its associated
territories.

The construction of these edifices at these locations attempts to do a
number of things. The overt visibility and presence of the sites demonstrates
dual expressions of power and control over the seas and surrounding terrestrial
landscape. These castles commanded this landscape interface, between land
and sea, and were built to accommodate militaristic and mercantile control
over the people who lived, worked and visited their environs. They acted as
architectural connectors between two very different environments and as a
physical conduit for the movement of people and goods through both zones.
They were built to physically protect their respective harbours and to control
both marine and terrestrial access to them. In many cases they also acted as
catalysts for urban development. Certainly by 1229 a planned town had been
established around the castle at Carlingford. This process serves to highlight
the Normans' primary interest in developing economic infrastructure
following conquest.

GAELIC IRISH AND ANGLO–NORMAN TOWER HOUSES

By the fifteenth century, if not before, a new type of building, commonly called a tower house, was evident throughout the Irish countryside and along the coast. Considerable debate surrounds the origins and earliest dates of these buildings which can be described as stone-built rectangular towers with three to five storeys. A number are enclosed by a bawn wall and many are associated with a range of other buildings. Tower houses are found across Ireland with notable concentrations found in the good agricultural land of north Munster and the midlands. Notable coastal concentrations are found in the east coast ports and on the Down and east Antrim coasts. A number of tower houses are also found along the western seaboard where they appear to have been the residence of choice of the leading members of the Gaelic-Irish lordships.

It is important to make the point that tower houses were not just rural monuments but were also a common feature of the urban coastal towns. In these contexts it is more tempting to view the urban tower houses of the ports of Carrickfergus, Ardglass, Carlingford and Dalkey as residences of the mercantile class. The survival of a number of tower houses in the deserted medieval coastal town of Clonmines is strongly indicative of this function. We have much still to learn about these monuments and their role within their respective landscapes. There has been considerable generalisation contained in the literature about their history and function but increasingly local studies are generating a more rounded and in-depth understanding of their histories. It is only through the placement of sites within their local and regional political, socio-economic and environmental context that we can begin to truly understand their role, form and function. At Carlingford, they were obviously situated and oriented towards the sea – and the probable fish catches that were hauled up on the waterfront. We need to think less about these buildings as being military in function, or solely for display of power and social status. They should also be seen as working buildings, oriented towards marine economies. It is becoming increasingly obvious that the towers were multi-functional structures that provided a degree of security and a domestic centre for lord, landowner or merchant. They would have acted as administrative, mercantile and political centres of activity and were an overt expression of lordly and economic presence in the landscape.

MARITIME REGIONAL PERSPECTIVES ON LATE MEDIEVAL TOWER HOUSES

A regional coastal approach is of relevance here. Moira Ní Loingsigh's assessment of the tower houses in the O'Donnell lordship of Donegal showed that they are almost exclusively located by the sea, adjacent to suitable landing places, and were involved in fishery and communications. Rathmullan, Rathmelton and Doe are located beside natural harbours while Inch, Fahan and Balyness are sited on natural landings.

66 O'Malley family memorial plaque on Clare Island, Co. Mayo (DEHLG)

On the Mayo coast the O'Malley tower houses at Klidawnet, Clare Island and Clew Bay in Mayo also control harbours and natural anchorages (*66*). Below these the galleys of the O'Malleys, often reputed to have been pirates, would lie at anchor in safe and sheltered waters.

A regional study of the tower houses on the Beara and Iveragh Peninsulas, associated with the O'Sullivan Beare and the O'Sullivan Mór Gaelic lordships respectively, clearly constituted the residences of the lords of the lordships. They were invariably sited at suitable harbours and landing places and were positioned to control both terrestrial and marine communications and movement. Dunboy castle, for example, is positioned immediately adjacent to a natural sheltered inlet and overlooks the main entrance into Bearehaven.

The fortifications in Castlehaven and Baltimore, Co. Cork under the control of the O'Driscolls, are similarly sited, and appear to have controlled anchorage in particular. This was especially important on the west Cork coast where there are few areas for vessels to shelter and lie at anchor during periods of heavy weather.

The use of the term control is important and is not taken here to imply that the tower houses were heavily armed with cannon etc., but rather implies that they were able to command good vistas over the surrounding seaways and monitor and organise the landing of people and goods. This control manifested itself in a number of different ways, but was centred on the placing of levies and extracting tributes from foreign fishing fleets working in the waters off Ireland. Levies were not only in monetary form but also took the form of goods. The acquisition of wine for instance was especially valued.

A number of tower houses at Strangford Lough in County Down represent individual entrepreneurial enterprises outside of the existing urban centres. Ringhaddy castle was taken by Byran McArt in 1594 and established it as a base for trade with Scotland (67). Eight years later the castle underwent extensive repair before passing to James Hamilton. The castle was ideally suited to command a natural deep sheltered anchorage. It was sited close to a natural submarine drop-off so vessels could almost come directly below the walls of the castle to load and unload. The stone foundations of an original stone jetty are evident on the foreshore below the castle. This consists of two parallel stone linear features running below the high water mark which would have formed basal support for a timber superstructure. An area of cobbling survives adjacent to the structure, which would have functioned as a 'hard' or laid surface to support shore-based activities. A series of steps lead up from the hard to the castle wall.

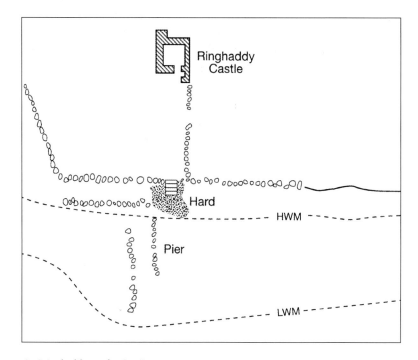

67 Ringhaddy castle, Co. Down

An underwater survey at the site recovered structural stone lying on the seabed below the castle. This stone was probably associated with the refurbishment of the castle at the end of the sixteenth century and may have been lost overboard while unloading at the jetty. Finds of seventeenth-century English pottery and glass reflect trading activity at the site while the recovery of musket balls testifies to its turbulent history.

Individual maritime trading enterprise is also reflected at Mahee Castle further north on the west coast of Strangford where the survival of an extensive waterfront appears to be related to the enterprises of an English Captain, Thomas Brown. Brown obtained a lease from Bishop Merriman in 1560 and subsequently built a tower-house at a cost of 400 marks. The remains of an extensive waterfront complex are evident on the foreshore directly beneath the castle. The remains can be divided into two separate sectors. The eastern sector of the complex consists of two substantial boulder lines, 40m long, representing the foundations of a quay running parallel to the channel. Vessels could come alongside this structure at high water and lie alongside once the tide ebbed.

LATE MEDIEVAL COASTAL VILLAGES

Tower houses survive as the dominant architectural expression of the settlement types and living conditions of the upper social stratas in late medieval society. They were the residences, dwellings and administrative bases for merchants, lords and minor gentry. Their physical survival in the landscape, however, has the potential to falsely suggest that these were the only settlement forms evident in the later medieval landscape. Many other people lived at or near the coast but did not have the finances or political presence to afford these buildings. It is clear from the cartographic, historical and archaeological evidence that there was a range of late medieval settlement forms on the coastline. These varied from large urban port communities, settlement clusters surrounding coastal tower houses, fishing and farming villages, to small groups or single dwelling homesteads.

There are a number of historical records relating to these maritime communities including a listing in the Cloyne Pipe Roll c.1365 that records a number of fishermen as holding cottages at Ballycotton in East Cork. Captain Cuellar's account of his survival in 1588 from a shipwreck of the Spanish Armada makes reference to Gaelic-Irish village near Streedagh Strand on the Sligo coast consisting of a number of huts of 'straw/coarse grass'. An account of a Spanish officer during the course of the 1601 siege at Kinsale refers to similar type dwellings at Castlehaven on the West Cork coastline. He described the land as 'mountainous and without trees … all I can see are straw huts and these are small'.

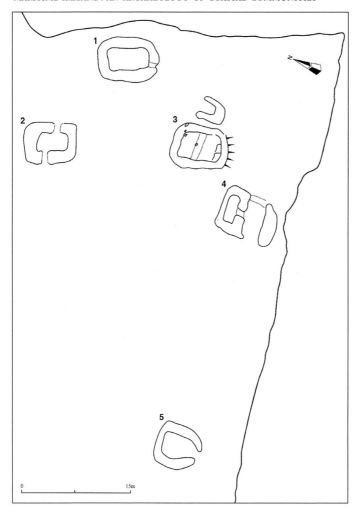

68 Ballynacallagh
settlement cluster on
Dursey Island, Co. Cork

Colin Breen's recent archaeological excavations on Dursey Island, Co. Cork off
the south-west coast of Ireland investigated a settlement cluster of late medieval
date associated with the Gaelic maritime lordship of the O'Sullivan Beare. Here
at least six late medieval house sites are located on the water's edge below a
sixteenth-century earthen artillery fortification (*68*). The remains consist of the
stone footings of rectangular structures with opposing doorways and an internal
division. Interestingly, the material culture recovered from one of the house sites
was dominated by Iberian pottery wares and roof tiles, probably indicative of
the extensive contact the local people had with visiting Spanish fishing fleets.
A similar late medieval settlement cluster with twelve visible house foundations
is visible at the sheltered inlet of Cuanlough, west of Allihies, Co. Cork while
excavations in the grounds of Bantry House, Co. Cork have uncovered the
remains of a small late medieval vernacular house by the shores of Bantry Bay,
beneath the remains of a later sixteenth-century plantation settlement.

A late medieval settlement cluster at Bray, Valentia Island, off the Iveragh Peninsula, Co. Kerry is also of interest. This site, previously mentioned in the last chapter, consists of a complex group of hut-sites, buildings, corn-drying kiln and earthworks which date from across the early medieval to late medieval periods. The site has been subject to archaeological investigations by Alan Hayden and Claire Walsh throughout the 1990s. In the late Middle Ages, it seems to have been a village-like settlement that survived up until the seventeenth century. Certainly, a village called *Crompeol* is shown at this location on a map dated to *c.*1600. The Bray late medieval village now consists of a 70m long 'street' with seven house platforms which in turn overlie high medieval plough furrows. In 1994 one of these house platforms was excavated, revealing a rectangular stone-built building measuring 6.7m by 3.4m internally. The building had a central hearth with opposing entrances and underfloor stone-lined drains. No mention is made of its roof type. Radiocarbon dating from this primary floor occupation level has produced a date of between AD 1410–1620. The house was later sub-divided into two rooms and a second two-roomed structure was built against it. Artefacts from these secondary deposits included a sherd of fourteenth- to seventeenth-century Low Countries Redware. Further investigations carried out in the vicinity uncovered the remains of a further rectangular stone-walled house, dated to the late medieval period on a stratigraphic basis. The Bray late medieval village was located in a spectacular maritime setting, and no doubt there was a maritime element to its economy.

LATE MEDIEVAL PROMONTORY FORTS

The occupation of promontory forts during the later medieval period has rarely been considered although more recent work has shown that some promontory forts were occupied well after the early medieval period. Since T.J. Werstropp's surveys, it has been clear that promontory forts were subject to continual occupation and activity over many centuries. Fourteen promontory forts have been identified in North Kerry, four of which were 're-fortified' with castles or other stone structures in the late medieval period (Ballybunnion, Doon, Pookeenee and Brown's Castle) while two further examples (Meenogahane and Clashmelcon) show potential evidence of later medieval settlement (*69*). Of course without excavated evidence we cannot be sure whether these sites underwent 're-fortification' or were new constructs in the later medieval period. Meenoghane has four sub-rectangular hut sites in its interior while Clashmelcon has two internal rectangular hut sites measuring 13.4m by 7.7m and 13.4m by 4.9m respectively. We cannot naturally assume that these hut sites are high or late medieval in date without excavated evidence, but it does appear from comparative and excavated data generated elsewhere in the country that this may be the case.

69 Late medieval castle on promontory overlooking sea lanes off Rathlin Island, at Kinbane, Co. Antrim (Aidan O'Sullivan)

Eight promontory forts have been identified on the Iveragh Peninsula, Co. Kerry. Reencaheragh has extensive late medieval remains which include a 33.5m section of stone wall incorporating a two-storey gatehouse which cuts off the promontory. The gatehouse has a doorway with a rounded archway, indicative of a fifteenth-to sixteenth-century date on the basis of comparative structural detail elsewhere in the south-west, and two associated lights. The remains of the sod-covered foundations of a rectangular house structure are present south of this feature. Its general morphology, opposing entrances and position within a late medieval monument would all strongly argue for the assignation of a late medieval date for this structure. A second promontory at Cool East shows potential later medieval in the form of a pair of conjoined huts that are roughly square built with drystone walls. These huts share some comparative structural features with the late medieval house sites documented by Alan Hayden on Valentia Island.

The Cork Archaeological Survey has identified forty-one promontory forts in West Cork, five of which are doubtful. Nine of these were witness to later medieval activity ranging from the re-fortification of a headland through to the construction of a tower house. Of three promontories excavated in west Cork by the late Prof. Michael O'Kelly of University College Cork in the 1950s, Dooneendermotmore west of Toe Head is especially interesting. O'Kelly approached the excavation under the presumption that the site was Iron Age in date. However, no primary dating evidence was found, indeed no evidence of Iron Age activity was found at all. Instead the excavator suggested that the promontory ditch was 'recut' in late medieval times in the sixteenth century on the basis of the evidence available, when it was occupied for an 'appreciable time'. The site was positioned on an exposed neck of land separated from the mainland by a very narrow promontory. A stone wall ran across the entrance to the site, c.1-1.5m wide and stood to a height of just over 1m in the 1940s. Excavations in the interior uncovered the remains of a late medieval stone-built house and extensive artefactual evidence for occupation over a 100-150 year period. The remains of roof timbers were also uncovered along with a quantity of roofing slate. Much of the artefactual evidence from the fort is indicative of a later sixteenth- to seventeenth-century occupation. Dooneendermotmore then is perhaps an example of a promontory fort that was occupied and probably even built in the late medieval period.

LATE MEDIEVAL FISHING IN IRELAND

The role of Ireland's fisheries

Fishing represented one of the major industries of later medieval Ireland yet its role is often understated. Much of this is due to the low visibility of surviving archaeological material relating to this activity. Visiting fishing fleets, regardless of their size, leave only a partial distinctive material record behind. The technology relating to offshore fishing is also far less tangible than agricultural or industrial activity. Yet we know from historical records and from an increasing body of archaeological evidence that these fisheries were very productive during the fifteenth and sixteenth centuries. Fynes Moryson wrote in the early part of the seventeenth century that 'no country is more abundant with fish, as well as sea fish in the frequent harbours and upon all the coasts as well as fresh water fish, especially excellent trout in the frequent rivers and brooks'.

A government official in Ireland wrote in 1535 about a fleet of 600 English vessels fishing Herring at Carlingford, while in 1572 it was reported that over 600 Spanish vessels were fishing off the Irish coast. The presence of such extensive fish stocks proved particularly attractive to merchants and fishermen from abroad. This was not a chance occurrence. Certain fish stocks like herring are very susceptible to the slightest change in the oceanographic conditions. A slight rise in water temperature for example will lead to a significant increase in stocks. Recent oceanographic research from Norway is then of direct relevance to this study. Here researchers identified a warm period from AD 1330 to 1600 that had the highest bottom-water temperatures in the North Atlantic during the last 5000 years. The rise in water temperatures in the middle of the fourteenth century also appears to signal the start of a burgeoning fishing industry in Ireland. From this period onwards continental fishing fleets begin to arrive off the coast and begin the systematic exploitation of the fishery resource. It is then no coincidence that fishing ports like Ardglass begin to flourish right around the coast of Ireland at this time.

The archaeological evidence for this type of fishing activity is always going to be difficult to quantify. While it may have involved hundreds of ships and boats at any one time traditional terrestrial approaches will be unlikely to uncover any significant or readily identifiable material. This is related to the fact that the fish catches would be rarely brought ashore and were probably stored and processed on board the vessels. The fishermen would have come ashore occasionally to take fresh supplies and possibly carry out repairs to their nets and boats but this type of activity leaves little evidence in the archaeological record. Along the western seaboard the Gaelic lordships were extensively involved in fishing activity. In Donegal the O'Donnells were known as the 'lords of the fish' given their association with the fisheries off the north-west coast. Elsewhere in the south-west the extensive European pottery recovered from excavations at Dunboy castle in west Cork must be clearly indicative of interaction between the Gaelic lordship and visiting fleets and similar analysis of material cultural evidence from other excavated sites may benefit from this type of examination. The wares included Saintonge ware from central western France, dating to the first half of the sixteenth century as well as a number of sherds of sixteenth-century North French ware and French stone ware. A small number of Valencian lustre-ware vessels dating from the late fifteenth and early sixteenth centuries was also recovered as well as a 'large number of unglazed earthen ware', which may be of Spanish origin and dated to the same period. Sherds of French Bellarmine stoneware, South Dutch maiolica and some Chinese Ming, all dating to the sixteenth century were also present. Other indications of fishing activities can be got from the location of vessels engaged in this activity, investigations of debris fields associated with anchorages and an examination of landing places.

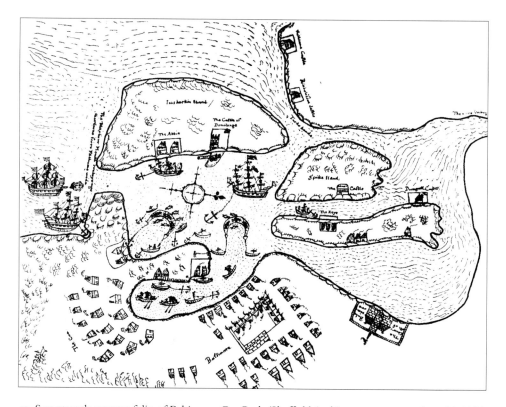

70 Seventeenth-century folio of Baltimore, Co. Cork (Sheffield Archives wwm str p20/100: 8/388/6)

The historical evidence would appear to indicate that fishing along the Gaelic seaboard was largely carried out by visiting fleets with minimal involvement from the local populations. Local groups were probably limited to small localised fishing and to the overall control of the operations. An indication of how this was carried out comes from an Inquisition that took place in 1609 into the extent of the holdings of the neighbouring O'Driscolls of Baltimore and Roaring Water Bay (70). This document outlines in great detail how the O'Driscolls operated and gained monetarily from visiting fishing fleets. They charged each ship four pence sterling to anchor in the sheltered anchorage in Baltimore Sound, while fishing boats were charged an additional nineteen shillings, a barrel of flour and salt, a hogshead of beer and a dish of fish three times a week for use of the fishing grounds and anchorage. Additionally, if the crew were to bring the catch ashore for drying on a 'rock' then they were to be charged six pence and eight shillings. In terms of provisioning the fleet O'Driscoll Mór charged eight pence for every 'beef they [visiting crews] kill … and for every sheep and pig that is killed likewise one penny'. In addition O'Driscoll was entitled to receive four gallons of every butt of wine landed in the area and all goods imported into the area had firstly to be offered to him at a lower rate. All of these tariffs and other licensing rules were enforced by galleys belonging to the lord and through a weekly court held at Baltimore.

LATE MEDIEVAL FISH TRAPS ON THE SHANNON ESTUARY

The last chapter has demonstrated the importance and usage of foreshore fishing engines in the early medieval period. This activity continued uninterrupted across and into the medieval period, a clear indication of the continuity of maritime traditions around the coast. The work of the Discovery Programme's North Munster Project in the Shannon estuary has revealed a large number of medieval fish traps on the Deel and Fergus Estuaries in south county Clare. While many of these structures may have been directly associated with the Norman manors at Askeaton and Bunratty, it is likely that there was Gaelic Irish involvement, especially in the actual working of the traps. These relics of fishing were found on the margins of Gaelic territories and settlements of the O'Briens and the MacNamaras and must have benefited both communities.

Late Medieval fish traps have also been located on the mudflats of the Deel estuary, off the site of a known medieval castle at Ballynash, Co. Limerick (71). This complex went through continuous repair and phases of construction. Deel estuary 1, dated to AD 1037-1188 is a small V-shaped fish trap and has already been described above. A later fish trap at Deel estuary 2 lies directly to the south and is very similar in construction and orientation. It was built using a line of posts erected on a north-east/south-west orientation and measuring up to eight metres in visible or exposed length. This has been radiocarbon dated to AD 1261-1278.

71 Medieval fish trap at Bunratty, Shannon estuary, Co. Clare (from O'Sullivan 2001)

A third, similar wooden fence at Deel estuary 3 is situated yet further to the south and has been dated to AD 1282-1391. The evidence suggests the construction and renewal of fish traps in the area at some time between the eleventh and the fourteenth centuries AD. The Deel estuary fish traps are small structures, and are likely to have been used to catch fish for the locals on the shoreline, rather than for a large, urban population.

Late medieval fish traps have also been recorded on the Shannon estuary mudflats adjacent to the site of the Anglo-Norman borough of Bunratty, Co. Clare (*72*). In 1248, an Anglo-Norman manor was established at Bunratty, at a strategic location on the north bank of the estuary. In 1287, historical sources indicate that the borough of Bunratty had a castle, parish church, a weekly market, annual fair, rabbit warren, a watermill and a fishpond. It also had a sizeable population, with the presence of 226 burgages, implying a potential total of 1000 people resident within the borough. Many of these townspeople would have been 'English' peasant farmers, tenants and merchants, settled on the new Anglo-Norman manors. While the Gaelic Irish social elites had been displaced, this does not suggest that all people of native Gaelic Irish ethnic extraction had departed. In fact, the archaeology of the late medieval fish traps suggests strong continuities in work and practice on the estuary mudflats below the borough. We can see this in the way that the same fish trap types, identical in size, lay-out and construction were in use through the period of socio-political change.

72 Medieval fishtrap at Boarland Rock, Fergus estuary, Co. Clare (Mary Dillon)

A medieval fish trap at Bunratty 4 (radiocarbon dated to AD 1018-1159) was a small V-shaped structure, of post-and-wattle and a horizontal basket supported within a framework measuring 4.6m by 0.8m. There is evidence that it was re-built and repaired on at least three occasions, suggesting that it had been used over decades. It was clearly built and used well before the Anglo-Norman colony was established (i.e. before AD 1248), indicating Gaelic Irish settlement somewhere in the vicinity. Intriguingly, precisely the same style of fish trap can be seen elsewhere on these mudflats, but probably dated to within the general period of the Anglo-Norman colony. At Bunratty 6, dated to AD 1164-1269, a fish trap with a similar post-and-wattle fence, framework and well-preserved woven basket (4.5m in length) was probably placed on the bed of a mudflat creek, and would literally have taken every fish out of the water on the ebbing tide.

Interestingly, then, the Bunratty fish traps indicate that the same types of structure were in use, before and after the Anglo-Norman colony. Similar patterns can be observed elsewhere on the Shannon estuary (and indeed, elsewhere in England and Wales, before and after 1066). On the Shannon estuary, we could explain this in terms of continuities of practice amongst local Gaelic Irish fishing communities. So, while the local Gaelic Irish lordship had been diminished by Anglo-Norman military power and economic investment, with upper social classes removed, we can imagine that the Gaelic Irish fishermen continued to work the channels in the manner of their forefathers. What we may be seeing here is the work of Gaelic Irish *betaghs* (from the Irish word *biatach*, meaning 'food provider') who are frequently mentioned in twelfth- and thirteenth-century historical documents. They seem to have lived in or near the Anglo-Norman manors, working as farmers, unfree tenants and labourers, ploughing land, harvesting crops and herding cattle. At Bunratty, they may also have worked as fishermen, accommodating their work to the new social and political order. It could be argued that these were people who were deliberately working on the estuaries in ways that emphasised continuities with the past.

However, the most spectacular Late Medieval fish traps yet known in Ireland were recently discovered adjacent to an intertidal rock outcrop known today as Boarland Rock, on the Fergus estuary, Co. Clare. These fish traps were identified during an intertidal project carried out on several other archaeological sites on the Fergus estuary by Aidan O'Sullivan and Mary Dillon in May 2004. The Boarland Rock fish traps are situated well out into the middle of this huge estuary, in a vast, almost featureless expanse of mudflats. The traps are situated on the west side of the main channel that carries the river at low tide. Boarland Rock 1 is a large L-shaped fish trap, with two post-and-wattle fences stretching 65m east-west and 130m north-south. The two lines of posts meet at a narrow point *c*.1m in width and run together for *c*.5m to form a funnel-like end – the probable location of a basket trap. It is clear that the fish traps had been repaired on a few occasions, as in places its fences are composed of several parallel rows of upright posts. Two large horizontal post-and-wattle panels were found near the funnel end of the construction and these may be either trackways or falled hurdle panels from the fences. The Boarland Rock 1 fish trap has been radiocarbon dated to AD 1410-1460 (72).

Boarland Rock 2 fish trap situated close-by is smaller in size and actually runs across one of the fences of Boarland Rock 1. It was slightly different in type, as the two converging fences were curved rather than straight and are V-shaped in overall plan. Boarland Rock 2 has been radiocarbon dated to AD 1415-1453. It is likely that the two traps are broadly contemporary but they were probably not in use at the same time. Boarland Rock 3 is another smaller fish trap structure located 300m to the south. It consisted of *c*.80 uprights in a V-shaped arrangement, with little or no horizontal woods visible. In all three structures it was noted that many of the uprights were oak. To the north and south of these Boarland Rock structures, and on the same side of the river, are several post alignments, which are probably also late medieval fish traps.

The Boarland Rock fish traps had not been previously documented, but are well known to the local fishermen who work from boats on the Fergus estuary, who describe them as the 'old eel traps'. The Boarland Rock fish traps are indeed old and have been dated to the early to mid-fifteenth century AD, the first known on the Irish coastline and a useful addition to late medieval rural archaeology and economy. They may have been built and used by the monks of the Augustinian Abbey on Canon Island, also on the Fergus estuary, which is situated *c*.3km further to the south and clearly visible from the site. This abbey was founded by

Donal Mór Ua Bríain in the twelfth century, but there is also architectural and historical evidence for the abbey's expansion through the fifteenth century, when its inhabitants were presumably making use of the diverse resources of the field and shoreline. On the other hand, there are also probable fifteenth-century tower houses on the banks of the estuary, such as at Clenagh, Co. Clare, which may be the lordly or elite residences of local landowners who managed and controlled the estuary's fisheries in the fourteenth to fifteenth centuries AD.

LATE MEDIEVAL STONE FISH TRAPS, GREY ABBEY BAY, STRANGFORD LOUGH

The early medieval wooden fish traps on Strangford Lough have already been described and some undoubtedly date to after the AD 1200 date. At Greyabbey Bay on the eastern shore of the Lough, there are also a large number of stone traps with at least ten identified examples (73). Thomas McErlean has argued that the construction of these stone traps began in the thirteenth century, replacing the earlier wooden traps referred to in the last chapter, and that they continued in operation into the sixteenth century. One trap at Chapel Island West produced a calibrated date of AD 1220-1279 from a post line in a gap on the trap. Their initial construction corresponds with the arrival of the Cistercians in the area and the establishment of monastic foundations at Greyabbey and Comber. The Cistercians had come to Ireland in the twelfth century and had established thirty-three abbeys across the country by AD 1230. Their monasticism was structured and hierarchal which is directly reflected in the physical layout of their buildings and their systematic organisation of their associated estates. The Order was renowned for its land management skills and the exploitation of this foreshore fishing industry was another example of the innovative ways they developed to exploit the natural resources of the landscape.

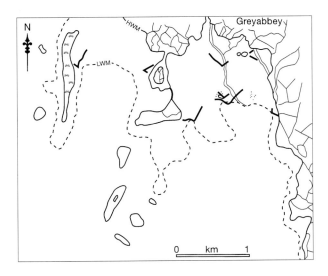

73 Fish trap distribution in Greyabbey Bay, Co. Down (CMA)

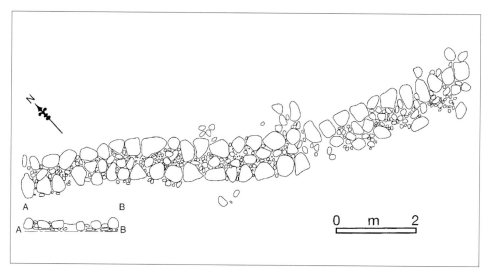

74 Detail of west arm of Ballyurnanellan 149:9 showing double kerb and fill method of construction (CMA)

The Strangford Lough traps have a variety of forms including V-shaped, crescent shaped and 'tick' shaped. Five V-shaped traps are known from the Greyabbey Bay region, three of which come from Ballyurnanellan townland and two from Chapel Island. The three Ballyurnanellan traps utilise the natural landscape, running between two pladdies, to enclose large areas of the foreshore, c.200m², and have leader arms averaging 100m in length (74). Two of the traps display the double kerb and fill construction method which appears to be the most common constructional method on traps of this date in this area. This method involved laying down a foundation layer of stone boulders directly onto the red glacial clay which underlies the sediment in Strangford's intertidal area. This clay provided a solid foundation base for the overlying structure. The stones were laid in two parallel lines and it is this foundation which made up the kerbing. A stone/rubble infill was then piled inside the two kerb lines to provide internal fill. It appears this foundation provided the base for a low-lying wall over 1m in height, or three to four courses high.

It is interesting to note that it was not just fish that were trapped by the traps but they also appear to have been used to harvest shellfish. The low-lying stone walls that made up the traps seem to have had a dual function. Not only could they trap fish but also the hard strata that they provided on an otherwise featureless mud landscape provided an ideal harvesting ground for molluscs. The enormous quantities of shell that inhabit the traps are still immediately obvious when you walk out on these walls at low water. The layout of the traps could then be regarded as an early form of mariculture and the walls were deliberately built with both functions in mind.

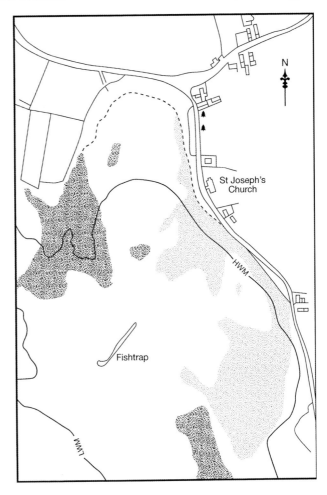

75 Rossglass fish trap, Co. Down

Other fisheries and individual fish traps are known along the Down and Antrim coast. The well-known geographer Estyn Evans recorded a curvilinear stone trap at Swinley Bay, Carnalea and two stone-built traps on the foreshore in Dundrum Bay at Newcastle, while other traps were recorded on the southern shores of Belfast Lough. The taxation of Pope Nicholas lists a church, valued at 2 marks, in the townland of Rossglass on the shores of north Dundrum Bay in 1306. This church is mentioned in a document dated 4 March 1305 when Walter de la Hay, the King's Escheator, gives an account of rents paid into the Irish Exchequer. Included is an account of '£3 16s 6d of the rents of farms, of a mill, of prizes, services, *fisheries*, and of the perquisities of the court of Rossglasse for the foresaid term'. The remains of a stone fish trap, over 50m in length, are visible on the foreshore below the church (75). It is hook shaped and works on the ebb tide and is not unlike the tick shaped trap from Greyabbey Bay. Its lead arm consists of a roughly built stonewall leading to the low water mark.

LATE MEDIEVAL MARITIME TRADE AND PORTS

Political and economic origins of ports and harbours

The late medieval period in general is witness to a significant increase in the volume and type of trade that Ireland is involved in. The majority of overseas trade took place between the ports of the eastern seaboard and individual English ports in the Severn estuary, including Bristol, and Liverpool Bay. Trade also occurred to a lesser extent with the Scottish ports. Later the ports of the French Atlantic coast as well as a number of Iberian cities also became involved in Irish trading networks. Wine, iron, salt and material culture (including ceramics and clothing) constituted the primary imports while hides, timber, wool and agricultural produce made up the majority of the export material.

To facilitate this burgeoning trade a structured socio-economic and political coastal bureaucracy now began to take shape along the eastern and southern coastline of Ireland. This system was based on a hierarchical port structure incorporating both the hinterland and foreland of each individual port and controlled centrally by the English crown and its agents in Ireland. Individual merchants within each port played a pivotal role in their development and commercial success. This system originated in the immediate aftermath of the Anglo-Norman invasion of the country and their selection of a series of harbours and landing places which were suitable for development as ports and centres for economic activity. Selection was based in some cases on existing sites such as the Viking coastal towns.

Other ports developed as a result of their direct proximity to Britain, with access to coastal resources and to the suitability of their hinterland and foreland being key supporting factors. Individual adventurers and entrepreneurs were highly influential in initial site selection, and their investment and subsequent involvement with port towns was a major contributing factor to their success. Carrickfergus, Strangford, Ardglass, Dundalk, Drogheda and Youghal were all ports which prospered and developed in the thirteenth century due to Anglo-Norman involvement. The prosperity of the established towns at Limerick, Cork, Waterford, Wexford and Dublin was especially evident, with new investment and associated commerce ensuring their continuing success.

AN EMERGENT PORT SYSTEM

The first real historical indication of such a national port and customs system dates from 1275 with the introduction of the 'great custom'. The customs returns for the 1275 Great Custom and the subsequent returns over the next 40-50 years list 11 ports Galway, Limerick, Kerry, Cork, Youghal, Waterford, Ross, Wexford, Dublin, Drogheda and Ulster. These port towns essentially represented a dynamic commercial and political link with the ports and economy of England and constituted a fluid economic border along the Irish Sea. These returns clearly show the importance of the south-eastern ports and the secondary role that the ports of Ulster and of the West coast played. The returns do not purport to be from individual actual reports but refer to sections of coastline. Hence the 'port' of Galway refers to the coastline and hinterland of Galway town, the Kerry 'port' refers primarily to Dingle and its adjacent coastline and so forth. The Ulster ports include Coleraine, Carrickfergus, Strangford and possibly Carlingford. By 1402, an English statute of Henry IV recognised a distinction between '*Les grantz ports du mier* [large sea ports] and *petitz crkes* [small creeks]'. The statute differentiated between those ports that carried out international or overseas trade and those that were involved with localised or coastal trade. Over the next two centuries this was to evolve into a three tiered system of head-ports, member ports and creeks. A formal system of port hierarchy was now beginning to emerge although the actual terminology for a head-port system does not appear in Ireland until the sixteenth century.

The appointment of ports was reflected in the development of their hinterland, with subsequent expansion and proliferation of settlement in direct correlation with the importance of the port. Individual sites and ports became strongly protected by fortifications on land and sea while their waterfronts continued to expand to accommodate larger ship and cargo sizes. Archaeological evidence for such an expansion comes from the waterfronts at Dublin, Drogheda, Waterford and Limerick. The surrounding landscape was also influenced by port appointment which influenced the development of an agricultural and industrial hinterland and encouraged the proliferation of secular and ecclesiastical settlement. These settlements in turn, frequently became involved in the systematic exploitation of marine resources.

The factors in individual port development are of relevance here. Each port is influenced by four basic factors: the *land situation, water situation, land site* and the *water site*. It is the final factor, i.e. the physical coastal location, which governs initial site selection and usage. The other factors then influence the subsequent success or pathway of the port. The land site must be suitable to sustain settlement growth and site expansion as well as allowing access to the hinterland. The land situation must be able to provide sufficient resources and support the population to sustain the operations of the port. While the water situation must provide access to the foreland, to the major marine communication routes and to marine resources. Many of these factors are not constants. Economic and political situations can fluctuate greatly while resource availability can also change. Topographical factors can change in some parts of the world but they are broadly stable for the period and region in question. These factors are then given increased value in the context of this study. Every port has then gone through a series of stages from initial usage through to their modern form. These stages can be categorised as follows.

Stage	Form and usage
Informal stage.	Informal use by small boats. No physical structures.
Initial development stage.	Site selection for development. Initial economic and communication activity.
Development Stage.	Established usage of site. Development of waterfront.
Site Expansion.	Formalisation and expansion of waterfront in line with increased economic activity.

Table 1: Development and formalisation of a port

ARCHAEOLOGICAL EVIDENCE FROM LATE MEDIEVAL PORTS

It has already been established that Hiberno-Norse ports established in the tenth and eleventh centuries AD established Ireland as a key location on the widening Atlantic and Mediterranean seaways. A continuity of coastal settlement can be seen with these Hiberno-Norse ports after the arrival of the Normans in the late twelfth century. The new arrivals had a similar need for a series of port towns along the coast and took control of the existing Hiberno-Norse towns. Their requirements were primarily economic and they strived to establish functional port settlements that would provide hinterland and foreland access. The emergence of this formalised port system is now evident in Ireland which was intrinsically linked to developments in England. This formalisation had little to do with the preceding Viking period other than a continuation of appropriate site settlement. It is the Normans who must be credited with the emergence and consolidation of these sites as viable economic and political settlements.

LATE MEDIEVAL DUBLIN'S WATERFRONT

The most comprehensively studied medieval waterfront in Ireland is Dublin (76). The numerous excavations that have taken place in the city since the 1960s associated with urban development have ensured its waterfront evolution has been comprehensively traced.

Pat Wallace, of the National Museum of Ireland, has identified nine stages of waterfront advancement into the River Liffey's foreshore area dating from the tenth to the fourteenth century AD. Bank 1, constructed in c.AD 900 and bank 2, built c.950, consisted of two low flood banks built using the natural boulder clay

76 Medieval timber waterfront at Winetavern Street, Dublin (Andrew Halpin)

and debris from the settlement site. Bank 3, built c.AD 1000, was of a similar but more substantial construction but also contained a post and wattle fence and later a palisade. This possibly served a dual natural and military defensive function. A large stonewall was erected on the foreshore in c.1100. Its excavated average height was 2m, although the excavator suggested that it could originally have stood to a height of 3.5m and was a defensive structure. The Dublin authorities issued a number of grants in the later part of the twelfth-century encouraging the residents of the town to reclaim foreshore land and move downwards towards the river. To this end, a post-and-wattle wall and associated embankment (Bank 4) were erected by c.1200 in an apparent attempt to reclaim more foreshore land and raise the depth of the water level in the river to allow for vessels with deeper draughts to proceed up to the town's waterfronts.

In AD 1210, a front-braced wooden revetment was erected along the extent of the town's foreshore in an apparent municipal project. A section of revetment was extended 20m farther out onto the shore in the same year. Excavations undertaken by Andy Halpin on Winetavern Street in 1993 uncovered further evidence of this section of front-braced revetment and studies of the twelfth-century water-level suggested that vessels could actually berth against this structure (77). This suggestion remains tentative and the evidence for gaps in the structure remain as more convincing evidence for vessels berthing in dock-like areas. It is also thought, through Aidan O'Sullivan's analyses of the waterfront assembly, the woodworking evidence and particularly the joints used, that the

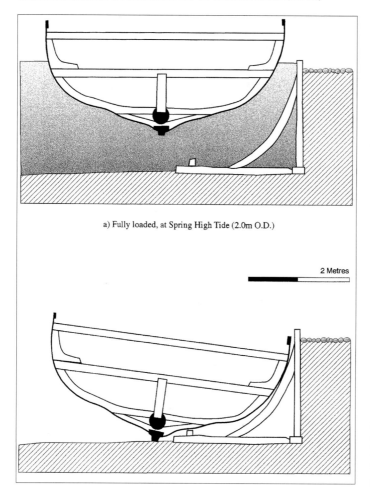

a) Fully loaded, at Spring High Tide (2.0m O.D.)

2 Metres

77 Reconstruction
of medieval vessel
lying against Dublin
waterfront (after Halpin
2000)

Dublin thirteenth-century timber waterfronts were built by English carpenters,
possibly from Bristol. It has been suggested that the Anglo-Norman invasion of
Ireland was funded by Bristol merchants precisely for this reason, to take control
of the valuable maritime trading connections of the Irish port.

Archaeological excavations by Claire Walsh in 1990 had previously uncovered
a further section of Revetment 1 during the course of investigations in
Winetavern Street. Base-plates from a timber revetment were found on a low-
lying stone foundation wall and was dated by dendrochronology to the very
early part of the thirteenth century. Its structural and topographic make up
suggest that it may have been associated with a pier of jetty giving access to high
waters of a depth range of 3.3m O.D. to 4.7m O.D. (springs). The lack of front
braces on the structure would have facilitated the access to boats to its face and
further supports its association with a pier-like function. This structure was later
converted into a dock-like inlet in the later part of the thirteenth century, similar
in construction to the dock at Usher's Quay, excavated in 1991 that predates

1192. Two further revetments were added later in the thirteenth century a further 15m out towards the river from Revetment extension 1, both of which were back-braced with base-plates.

In c.AD 1300 (possibly between 1305-1308) a stone quay wall, which survived to a height of 1.75m and was 2.75m wide, was built at Winetavern Street. A short 2.5m section of this quay wall was also uncovered by Linzi Simpson in 1993 at the Isolde Tower site adjacent to Temple Bar. The wall was built of cut limestone blocks and survived to a height of 1.10m and was 3.05m thick. That this wall also served as a defensive structure to protect the town's waterfront is illustrated by the fact that buildings were taken down in 1317 to help re-fortify the quay wall against a possible attack by the Scots. While this wall would have served as a useful and substantial quay wall for shipping activity, problems with the shallow nature of the Liffey remained. Cargo merchant ships by this date had become substantially bigger with far greater draughts than two centuries previously. Vessels could come in at high water and rest on the foreshore during low tides before being floated off again during a flooding tide but this practice was not especially suitable for a busy mercantile port like Dublin. This system was not conducive to heavy traffic or the rapid turn around of vessels.

As a consequence the deepwater anchorage of Dalkey – a medieval village situated several kilometers south-east of the town – served as an out-port for Dublin where many vessels partially discharged their goods in order to lighten their load before approaching Dublin. This posed a continual problem for Dublin merchants who complained in AD 1358 about the lack of deep-water berths in the town which does not allow for the anchorage of 'large ships from abroad'.

LATE MEDIEVAL WATERFORD'S PORT

Evidence of maritime borne trade and activity at Waterford appears in the documentary sources soon after the Norman invasion of 1169. Much of the subsequent success and prosperity of the town is linked to its proximity to Bristol and the markets of south-west England. Excavations in the city have to-date found little evidence of the nature of the waterfront during the thirteenth century as investigations have concentrated in the town centre and not in the area directly associated with the river. However, the documentary evidence would support the claim that Waterford's port was probably the second most successful port during the thirteenth century after Dublin, as it appears to be the biggest importer of wine and a major importer of wool. Waterford was to face stiff competition in the thirteenth and fourteenth centuries with the foundation of a new settlement and port at Ross in c.1200. New Ross, as it later became known, typifies Norman investment into new settlements and ports in an attempt to develop a commercial enterprise. Old Ross had been located 8km further inland before William Marshall developed the new port on the confluence of the Rivers Nore and Barrow. The siting of the new port was ideally located to take advantage of the surrounding agricultural hinterland, the communication and transport networks afforded by the two rivers and the possibilities of the foreland.

LATE MEDIEVAL CORK'S PORT

Prior to the Anglo-Norman occupation and development of Cork, the city appears to have existed on two separate islands (78). The Hiberno-Norse settlement occupied the south island (the area around modern South Main Street), while a secondary undefended suburb, referred to as Dungarvan, existed on the north island, in the area which corresponds to modern day North Main Street. Recent archaeological excavation work at the South Gate Bridge and 'Sir Henrys' site has uncovered house sites associated with the twelfth-century settlement and associated jetty or quay structures. An intensive period of development of the town began early in the thirteenth century, primarily with the reconstruction of the town walls in AD 1211-12. Details on the town's waterfront are vague with very limited information on early port development in the literature.

A slipway associated with a water-gate in the town walls was uncovered during excavations undertaken by Maurice Hurley and has been dated strati-graphically to the late thirteenth-century AD. The slip-way was later re-paved in the fourteenth century before falling out of use at the end of the century. An interesting aspect of the structure was that it appears to have been designed to allow boats to be dragged inside the town walls. This would be characteristic of an area of the town with limited quayage facilities and implies the use of tenders to off-load larger cargo vessels lying at anchor in the river or estuary. A possible

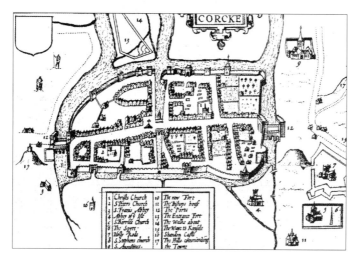

78 John Speed's plan of Cork c.1610

large quay wall was uncovered during the course of excavations at the North Gate Bridge site in the City in 1994. The wall was built using irregular sandstone blocks on a foundation of unworked boulders with a vertical outer face. This fronted onto the river and could have accommodated vessels lying alongside during suitable tidal conditions.

LATE MEDIEVAL PORTS OF DROGHEDA AND DUNDALK

North of Dublin the pattern of town and associated port development in the late twelfth and thirteenth centuries is particularly obvious. Drogheda was an important port from the thirteenth century onwards. Its location was eminently suitable for the development as a port given its position at a narrow bridging point on the River Boyne and the access to the surrounding hinterland that this provided (79). Access to the Irish Sea foreland and safe shelter was also provided by the Boyne estuary. It seems apparent that formalised waterfront structure and storage facilities were constructed early in the thirteenth century with the development of the port. David Sweetman's Excavations at Shop Street in 1981 found the remains of a wooden waterfront structure dating to the first decade of the thirteenth century. The structure consisted of four groups of oak timbers embedded into the riverbed. The excavator suggests that they represent the foundations of a wharf as opposed to the base of a revetment.

79 Maidens Tower at Mornington, a late medieval tower probably built as a navigational aid and look out post for vessels entering the Boyne

Recent important excavations undertaken by Malachy Conway for Archaeological Consultancy Services in 2000 revealed a detailed chronological sequence of the waterfront at Drogheda. Five medieval phases of development were recorded dating from the late twelfth to the late sixteenth century. The earliest phase of the site consisted of a thirteenth-century burgage plot associated with a timber wharf and jetty. The basal platform for a crane or hoisting spars used to load and unload cargo was also uncovered. This find represents the earliest such use of a manual 'crane' used for handling cargoes in Ireland. In the thirteenth and fourteenth centuries, a harbour was created along the waterfront, which the archaeologist suggested was associated with the medieval chapel and precinct of St Saviour's. An enclosed harbour space with a small dock and inlet was built at this time and coexisted with a timber revetment with section bracing. This harbour was filled in late in the fourteenth century and a series of buildings and structures were erected on the site over the following centuries.

Further north, Dundalk was operating as a port from at least the late part of the thirteenth century when the *Mariot* of Dundalk shipped '72 quarters (of wheat), boards, timber and nails' from Drogheda to North Wales. Little is known about the topography of the early port but it must have been a difficult port to access with vessels having to negotiate its shallow tidal estuary with extensive sandbanks and saltmarsh. Sir William Bereton describes the port in 1635 as a 'town seated upon the sea so as barks may come within a convenient distance with the flood; much low, level, flat land hereabout, which is often overflowed in the winter, and here is an abundance of fowl'. These physical limitations would have restricted the size and density of shipping entering the port and the 15 ton *Trinitic* of Murlington which traded with the port a number of times in 1586 must have been typical of the type and size of vessel using the port. To date no physical traces of medieval waterfront structures have been located and the port may have functioned as a tidal beaching facility.

LATE MEDIEVAL PORT OF ARDGLASS

The late medieval port of Ardglass in County Down survives today as an important and almost unique port landscape (*80*). The port town was probably established in the fourteenth century associated with the exploitation of the herring fisheries and the general Europe wide economic upturn later in the fifteenth century. It was established at a sheltered inlet on the Lecale coastline and very quickly became prosperous with a number of tower houses being built around the harbour basin in the fifteenth century. The port was essentially abandoned at the end of the sixteenth century with the collapse of the Irish Sea fisheries and the political conflicts of the time. It was only really resettled in the later part of the eighteenth century with the re-emergence of the herring industry. However, this abandonment phase has resulted in the survival of a large number of later medieval features of the town.

80 Eighteenth-century drawing of Ardglass with the Newark building in the background (Grose, F.1791 *The Antiquities of Ireland*)

The Newark building at Ardglass, recently excavated by Tom McNeill of Queen's University, Belfast, is of most interest in the context of the study of the port (*81*) and is worth exploring in detail as an intensely maritime-oriented building. More than any other within the town, it epitomises Ardglass's role as a port in the late medieval period. There can be little doubt that this building, or series of buildings, functioned within the context of the port during the fifteenth and sixteenth century. Its position relative to the siting of the waterfront, internal divisions and general size and form all strongly argue for such a role. The building was formerly two storeys high, consisting of at least fifteen to sixteen independent units fronting northwards onto the warterfront, with each unit consisting of a square window and an arched door. There is no indication of vertical or horizontal floors or partitions within the structure and the ground floor appears to have consisted of an uneven rock floor both inside and out. Each of the units must be seen as fulfilling a mercantile role, probably acting as individual mercantile booths for those who were buying and selling goods. They do not appear to have had a residential function, nor do they have an overtly defensive appearance. The occupants may have leased them on a short-term basis, or owned the units and acted as intermediaries for the import/export activity which was happening in the port. These may have been leased to individual visiting merchants or companies who were at the port during various fishing and agricultural seasons.

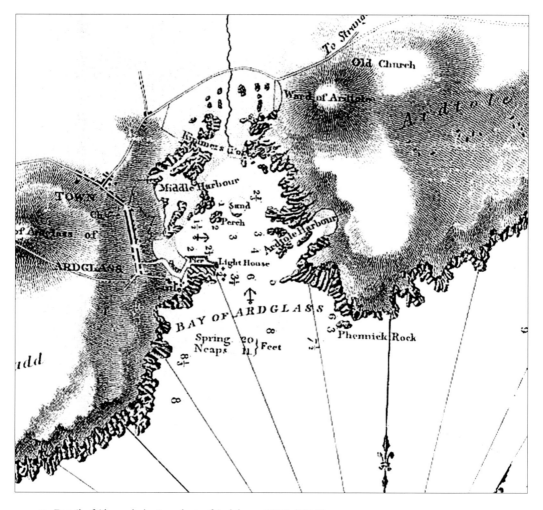

81 Detail of Alexander's 1821 chart of Ardglass – PRO (NI) T234211

The rear, or southern side of the building, which fronted onto the sea, was strongly fortified with no windows, only loopholes. Two towers were incorporated into the structure while a third, a more substantial tower house stood slightly removed from it to the north-west. A fireplace is apparent on the first floor of the east tower while a number of latrines are located towards the eastern end of the southern wall. The presence of the towers is suggestive of defence and the need to protect the activities based at the Newark. The East Tower is also ideally positioned to monitor boat traffic in and out of the harbour. Two splayed windows are positioned on the eastern wall of the first floor of the tower facing straight out to the entrance of the port. Taffe's Castle in Carlingford and the Bridge Castle in Thomastown, Co. Kilkenny share a similar siting with a focus on their late medieval quays. Both castles also have adjoining warehouses although these are more demonstrably used for bulk storage given their size and form.

82 Co. Down tower house (EHS NI)

The actual original port basin area in Ardglass still functions within the modern fishing port but would have been larger in later medieval times. A fifteenth-century tower house, Jordan's Castle, overlooks the basin area to the west (*82*). Mark Gardiner's archaeological excavations at Jordan's castle would appear to confirm this close relationship with the port basin as he uncovered evidence of a medieval hollow way which ran from the castle and Kildare Street down to harbour area. A substantial stone structure excavated on the site has been interpreted as a warehouse. This is an important discovery in so far as it appears to show for the first time a building where bulk commodities could be stored. Certainly the Newark does not seem to have been capable of storing large or bulky cargoes so warehouses of this nature would have been extremely important. The close relationship of this newly discovered 'warehouse' and Jordan's castle is indicative of the inter-relationship of the town's mercantile elite and port operations.

The function of this and the other urban tower houses at Ardglass can then only be fully understood in the context of port operations. Possible functions carried out at the towers would include port based mercantile activity, port administration, security and habitation. Margaret's castle, which is probably of fifteenth century date with its 'gate house' type construction, is also situated in close proximity to the harbour. The entrance to the tower faces onto the harbour and is clearly designed to overlook it. This tower is also situated close to Cowd's castle and the Newark and may originally have been functionally associated with them. Margaret's castle is smaller than Jordan's castle and this differing size can be taken as evidence for different levels of wealth, social hierarchies and tower house functionality within the town. Their physical closeness can also be associated with an urban relationship focusing in on or centring on the economic mainstay of the town, the port.

Cowd's castle, directly to the west, must be viewed as a more functional entity. This small two-storey structure (Co. Down tower houses appear in general to have three storeys) does not appear to have been a merchant or secular residence, but rather functioned as a port security building. Support for this interpretation comes from its siting; positioned strategically to have wide vistas over the harbour entrance, the adjacent fishing grounds on Ardglass Bank, the operations of the port basin and the Newark as well as the south western entrance to the town. The simple nature of the structure (not itself a defining characteristic of a secondary or utilitarian building), the relatively few small loop embrasures and the wall walk at roof level would also lend support to the tower functioning as some form of garrison or port watchtower. One of the interesting features of the building is the absence of a fireplace, which would appear to confirm its non-residential function. The apparent absence of a latrine would also lend support to this. In any case, at Ardglass we have a uniquely surviving maritime urban landscape.

GAELIC PORTS AND HARBOURS

While the Anglo-Norman ports present one image of late medieval maritime activity, those regions in the northern and western seaboard that remained outside of English control in the territories of the Gaelic-Irish lordships did not see the same level of investment into ports and waterfronts. The Gaelic Irish O'Donnells controlled much of Donegal, the O'Malleys and O'Flaherty's dominated sections of the Mayo and Galway coast, the McNamaras were present along the Clare coast while the O'Sullivans, the O'Driscolls and the O'Mahoneys controlled significant sections of the Kerry and Cork coastlines. The ports of Galway and Limerick remained outside of the Gaelic lordships were intrinsically linked to the Dublin administration. It would be a mistake, however, to see this as a strict division between Gaelic and English controlled Ireland. In reality there was a high degree of movement and interaction between the different regions and traditional notions of separation and nationhood have been exaggerated.

Nonetheless, the sections of coast controlled by the Gaelic lordships simply did not have elaborate port facilities. Instead their facilities reflected the types of activities that were in operation along their respective sections of coastline. In the late Middle Ages, the various European fishing vessels that came to the western Atlantic approaches mostly stored and salted their own catches onboard. Where catches were brought ashore it was usually for drying or immediate sale so elaborate storage facilties for bulk commodities was not required. The physical infrastructure that was found on the east coast was therefore simply not needed along the Gaelic seaboard and moreover a centralised customs system (which also requires facilities) never developed. Large quays or waterfronts were not required and instead fishing-oriented settlements developed around areas of natural anchorage and available landing.

It is also increasingly clear that the archaeological evidence supports this model. To date there is no evidence for large waterfront facilities along the coastline of the Gaelic Irish regions. There is, however, a good deal of evidence for small localised landing places, or occasionally piers and harbours, beneath tower houses and around the areas of anchorage. Many of the eastern ports were involved in the movement of goods on a macro scale, such as corn and grain, which would have required extensive waterfront facilities as well as accommodation for the mercantile facilitators. There was of course similar exportation of goods like cereals and wool from the Gaelic regions but it was on a different scale and not centrally controlled. Exportation was on a more localized scale and facilitated on a casual basis. Movement of people and goods across the landscape then becomes a key component of the maritime ability of these Gaelic lordships. For example, one can consider the archaeology of the lordship of the Isles in later medieval Ireland. Here, along the seaboard of western Scotland and north-east Ireland a number of important Gaelic family groupings controlled the seaways. Their presence in Ireland is dominated by the arrival of the McDonnells to north-east Antrim in the sixteenth century and their subsequent occupation and refurbishment of Dunluce castle, Co. Antrim. The subsequent emergence of a sea province did not depend on extensive coastal infrastructure to survive but rather existed on the basis of cultural interchanges, less than formal trading and communication networks and familial connections. All of these were facilitated by settlement centres of power spread along the coast and through their ability for sea travel.

SHIPS AND BOATS IN LATE MEDIEVAL IRELAND

Late medieval European shipbuilding traditions
By the late Middle Ages, a range of ships and boats developed in northern Europe –largely inspired by the massive increase in maritime trade and activity through the twelfth and thirteenth centuries AD. The range of ships (including cogs, hulcs, galleys) reflects both regional stylistic developments as well as the roles these craft played. No finds of either cogs or hulks have been recovered from Irish

waters but there are numerous documentary references to their usage. Clinker construction continued to be used on these vessels and was not overtaken by the carvel construction techniques until nearly three centuries later.

The military function of ships also becomes more obvious with the addition of fore and after wooden castles to the larger vessels during the twelfth century. These castles were essentially raised areas at the front and back of vessels to accommodate both archers and swordsmen during conflict at sea. The raised nature of these platforms would have given the vessel an obvious strategic advantage over smaller craft in much the same way that a parapet on land castle gives the defenders of the site a distinct advantage over foot soldiers below.

The range of archaeological evidence for ships and boats in late medieval Ireland includes depictions on coins, maps, some ship sculpture as well as ship graffiti on the walls of churches and cathedrals. As with the early medieval period, this iconographic evidence should be understood to be symbolic and ideological in intent. However, it can also be used cautiously to reconstruct the forms of ships plying the waters around Ireland.

EVOLUTION OF THE NORDIC SHIPS

From AD 1100–1400, the round-hulled, clinker-built vessels of earlier centuries became broader and deeper, enabling them to carry larger cargoes and crews. Presumably because of their association with mercantile trade, these ships are typically represented on twelfth to thirteenth century civic seals around northern Europe. The ship depicted on the thirteenth century seal of Dublin can be taken as one of these, representing a transitionary phase between the usage of the earlier Viking vessels and the development of the later larger mercantile vessels.

83 1662 Seal of Waterford (Mount Sion Monastery Museum)

The ship retains a Scandinavian character being double ended and clinker built. It carries a single mast set midships with a single large sail. This ship depiction displays a dual functionality of both a military and commercial role which would not necessarily have been evident in the earlier Viking period ships. Similarly the Charter Roll for Waterford City dating to c.1370 shows four clinker-built, wooden vessels lie at anchor in the river by the city (83). Two of the vessels are illustrated with fore and after castles, high sweeping bows and large, central masts with castellated mast tops. Both have end-mounted rudders and one is clearly anchored at its bow. Another clinker-built vessel with an end-mounted rudder and a high, curved bow is shown unmasted at anchor below the city walls.

THE COG

During this period, the flat-bottomed vessels of the northern European, Frisian tradition were developed for trade. Known as a cog, this new form had high sides, with a straight stem and stern post and a stern rudder. The cog's deep draught meant that it could carry large cargoes, while its flat bottom meant that it could easily land on beaches and stay upright. Historical documents indicate that cogs were in use in Irish waters and some were owned by Irish merchants operating out of Irish ports. Cogs are documented historically when Maurice, son of the Earl of Desmond, hired the cog *La Rode cogge,* which was based at Limerick in 1338, for a journey to Gascony. The Book of Ballymote dating to c.AD 1400, in the Royal Irish Academy, Dublin, contains a sketch of a boat which represents Noah's Ark. The vessel has the appearance of a cog, featuring clinker planking fastened with lozenge-shaped nail heads, and a single straight prow slightly curved at its head. Characteristically, the vessel has an end-mounted rudder, secured by two rudder pintles, presumably made of iron. The vessel also carries a single, central, sturdy mast.

THE HULC

The use of hulc is first documented by the Waterford vessel, the *Blessed Mary,* which delivered a cargo of corn to the English army in Gascony in 1297. Two depictions of hulc-like vessels survive on the sides of tomb chests in churches at Thurles and at Cashel. The example from Thurles, which dates to c.1520, shows an ecclesiastic holding a round-hulled ship with a pronounced after-castle in both hands at waist level. A similar representation survives on the north side of a tomb chest, dating to the first half of the sixteenth century, on the western side of the north transept at Cashel. Here again an ecclesiastic is shown holding a clinker-built vessel with a large central mast and two castle-like structures clearly shown at both ends of the hull. Archaeologically a number of timbers from medieval vessels have also been recovered including timbers dredged up from Dublin Bay during a number of recent major infrastructural projects. A large, single curved oak timber was also recovered by fishermen from the Suir estuary near Waterford. It appears to be the stern post of a galley or nef, a vessel type repeatedly referred to in both Irish and north-west European medieval texts.

GALLEYS IN THE GAELIC WORLD

There is little direct archaeological evidence for the type of craft that were in use in the territories of the Gaelic lordships. Information is limited to tantalisingly brief references in the texts as well as to various illustrative sources including memorial plaques, ship graffito and seals. It is suggested here that the Gaelic Irish never adopted the newer larger boat forms introduced throughout north-west Europe after the thirteenth century. Instead they maintained the Scandinavian boat-building traditions that were introduced in the ninth and tenth centuries and developed their own vessel hybrids from this tradition commonly called galleys.

A vessel of this type is illustrated as ship graffiti on a gatehouse at Dunluce Castle on the north County Antrim coast (*84*). It shows a double-ended ship with an animal-headed stern, 22/23 oar ports are visible and the vessel has a single central mast with one yard. It is shown with its sail tied up and rigging lines running from the stern and bow.

84 Galley carving at Dunluce Castle, Co. Antrim

A memorial plague belonging to the O' Malleys on the walls of the abbey on Clare Island contains a depiction of a wooden clinker built, double-ended boat, again with a single central mast. The vessel is shown with six oars on one side indicating a relatively small vessel. A number of seals from the town of Youghal show a wooden, clinker-built vessel, double-ended with a high prow and stern and a single central mast. The sail on these vessels is shown furled on a yard hanging from the mast. The earliest of these seals is from a later medieval document dated 12 June 1527, but they continued in use into the seventeenth century.

All of these vessels retain Scandinavian ancestry and must represent local adoptions to the vessel types introduced during the Viking period. These types of vessels must have been the most common medium-sized vessels seen around Irish waters with the larger mercantile vessels confined to the bigger urban ports, linked to cross channel and European trade.

THE CARRACK

With the emergence of new shipbuilding technology, ship design witnessed some radical changes. New larger vessels emerged and the face of shipping underwent a rapid reformation within a century. The carrack, more than any other ship type, epitomised this change. Although originally developed early in the fourteenth century in the Mediterranean, it quickly evolved and was adopted throughout north-west Europe. Carracks were big, heavy ships with large fore and after castle structures. Initially they were rigged on the fore and main masts with single square sails, but later they essentially became three-masted ships. Important changes in the method of ship construction begin to appear early in the fifteenth-century Europe. Carvel techniques, involving the setting of planks edge-to-edge and caulked to make a smooth finish, became the more common building method employed on larger craft. Larger vessels were now more structurally sound and more economical. As vessel size increased the clinker technique had become overly complex and exhausted large supplies of timber. In contrast, the carvel technique used less timber and required less skilled labour. The carvel technique also allowed larger superstructures to be accommodated upon the ship's hull. This was especially important for military vessels, as larger fighting platforms could be built with integral gunports. This was an important development as naval tactics increasingly depended on artillery. The development of the broadside armament of cannon reduced the sheer of ships' hulls and required consideration of stability and the use of space. Two or three masts were added to ships to increase speed, and bowsprits became increasingly necessary in order to give proper lead to the bow-lines. The fore and after castles were merged into the hull of the vessel, and the after castle in particular became much larger and played a more central role in the internal layout of the ship.

By the middle of the sixteenth century hulls had become much more round-bottomed to increase stability and carrying space. Square sterns were added in order to support the superstructure and accommodate larger end-rudders. These developments also led to a more formalised internal social arrangement within the vessel. The captain and officers' quarters were located in the stern section, while ordinary seamen and supplies were accommodated amidships and forward. Galleons differed from carracks in that they had high, narrow sterns with a lower forecastle and a low beakhead. This distinctive feature protruding from the hull below the bowsprit was used for ramming and later provided a platform for handling head sails. Galleons also had a strongly braced hull adopted for almost continuous use in the strong Atlantic seas. There were many variants of this ship type throughout Europe with different regions displaying characteristics which were adopted to suit local needs. Although primarily associated with naval functions, galleons were also frequently used for mercantile and fishing purposes.

CONCLUSIONS: MARITIME IRELAND IN THE LATER MEDIEVAL PERIOD

Past histories and geographies of Ireland have tended to stress differences and division between the different parts of Ireland which were under English or Gaelic-Irish control. It is clear from much of the archaeological evidence that much of these differences have been exaggerated. Of course the macro-political climate was different but the everyday lifestyles of the people did not differ to any great extent as you moved around the coast. Of course there are extremes between someone living in a small coastal community on the western seaboard and an individual living adjacent to the busy urban ports of the southern or eastern coasts. Fundamentally though, maritime traditions functioned as a constant. It is clear people worked and fished the coastal environment in almost identical ways. The everyday thought and preoccupations of a person working a fish trap in the Shannon estuary must have been very similar to those working in Strangford Lough. Peoples' lifeways were linked inextricably to the sea and its bounty. It was a source of food, transport and it governed local timeframes. These maritime traditions that were evident around the coast epitomise continuity. The continued usage of maritime technology across the chronologies we have developed questions our artificial divisions of the past, broken by political events and specific dates. The increasingly formalised nature of these traditions and their associated expansion linked to the emergent globalised economy become more evident in the following chapter.

Plantation, industrialisation and the modern world, AD 1550-1945

INTRODUCTION

When do the Middle Ages end and the Modern world begin – in an Irish context at least? Traditional historical studies will point to major events such as the Nine Years War of the 1590s or the advent of the English and Scottish Plantation into Ireland as marking the beginnings of a new period. Similarly archaeologists find it convenient to assign a general period-based framework to the past which allows for temporal classification of sites and artefacts. The assignation of chronological terminology is artificial and is reflective of twentieth-century needs to categorise and order the past. In attempting to chronicle and interrogate the past the use of terms like medieval and post medieval by archaeologists and historians would have borne little relevance to the contemporary populations of Ireland at that time. Similarly the progression from the medieval period into the post medieval period was unlikely to have been marked by celebratory events, but yet these time frames continue to influence the modern academic mind.

Much space in learned texts has been taken up with attempting to define the change and transition into post medieval Ireland. A number of writers will simply ascribe a date of major importance to this change. Traditional histories have, for example, used the Spanish Armada of 1588, the Nine Years War of the 1590s or the more long-term plantations as marking the shift into the new era. Structuralist archaeologies similarly have attempted to demonstrate this shift through changes in architecture or material culture. While there is value in these approaches each is too simplistic in itself. There is no doubt that major socio-economic and cultural change takes place in Ireland from the 1550s onwards but these changes were not just related to a single event or to changing political environments. Instead they were part of a broader movement towards modernity and globalisation. It is this period that witnesses the emergence of capitalism in the country and sees the beginnings of Ireland's contemporary coastal landscape taking shape. In this context change can be seen in new economic practices, changing settlement patterns and in the processes of industrial and resource exploitation. Gaelic-Irish power and influence collapses, a wave of new settlers and planters arrive, new towns and villages are established, new industries emerge and the cultural character of the landscape begins a process of rapid alteration and change.

One of the key aspects to the study of maritime activity through the post medieval period is the question of scale. It is easy to generalise on island-wide coastal traditions over the last 400 years but this approach does not do justice to the range and breadth of activities, identities and beliefs which all coexisted along the seaboard. Much of the economy of the east coast was firmly positioned within a developing global economy yet fishing and settlement traditions also survived on a far smaller local scale. This is not to argue that the maritime traditions of the remote past continued unchanged into recent centuries as some more romanticised and idealised commentators would lead us to believe. But there are continuities in terms of fishing practice, vernacular craft and settlement location. The problem then that presents itself with writing an archaeology of the recent maritime past is to try and present a cohesive story of the diversity of Ireland's recent maritime past given its multi-faceted and multi-influenced and multi-dimensional nature. This is not necessarily an inclusive story so is probably best presented in this first instance as a chronological narrative which seeks to set the context of the development of modernity using the main sources of evidence and archaeological survivals.

MARITIME PERSPECTIVES ON THE GAELIC REBELLIONS, THE SPANISH ARMADA AND THE PLANTATION OF IRELAND

The desmond rebellion and Dún an Óir

Throughout the 1570s and 1580s the Gaelic-Irish septs which dominated the western seaboard of the island were engaged in resistance and conflict with the ruling English administration in Dublin which had begun to attempt to assert its authority over a greater part of Ireland. This Gaelic resistance was helped to an extent by the Catholic powers in Europe, most notably the Spanish. This help lead to a number of significant maritime events which continue to play a part in the national psyche of contemporary Ireland. The first event occurred on the Kerry coast and was related to uprisings organised by the Gaelic Desmond lords of Munster. On the 17 July 1579, three Spanish ships under the command of James Fitzmaurice, son of the Earl of Desmond and a known opponent of English rule in Ireland, landed on the North Kerry coast and occupied Dun an Óir overlooking Smerwick Harbour (*85*). This small force made several incursions inland but was met with a great deal of resistance and was forced to over-winter at Smerwick.

85 Detail of seventeenth-century map of
Smerick Harbour engagement (MPF 75, PRO
London)

The following summer reinforcements of 800 soldiers commanded by Don Juan
Martinez de Recalde arrived at Smerwick and set up an artillery fortification at Dun
an Óir. An English naval squadron under William Wynter arrived at the harbour
in order to counter this new threat and set about destroying the fortification with
incessant ordnance bombardment from its larger ships. The three largest ships in
the squadron, the *Revenge, Swiftsure* and *Aid*, carried out the primary bombardment
from their decks while three smaller vessels the *Merlin, Achates* and the *Tiger* sailed
close to shore and subjected the encampment to a lesser assault. The attack finally
ended when the English landed a force of soldiers near the camp and the garrison
quickly surrendered. One of the original ships of the Spanish garrison is depicted
as being broken on the rocks below the encampment on a contemporary map of
the engagement. This small episode in the continuing conflict between Elizabeth
II England and Philip II Spain was to set the stage for a much greater assault on
England by a Spanish Naval force in 1588. However, the English forces in Ireland
were also facing internal dissent with a number of the Gaelic lordships on the
island beginning a sustained period of resistance and revolt against English rule.

EARLY PLANTATIONS

Following the collapse of the one such revolt, the Desmond uprising of the 1580s
in the southern half of the island, the English Crown quickly moved to plant these

newly conquered lands. The initial plan was to people selected areas of Munster with 'loving subjects of good behaviour and account none of the meer Irish to be maintained in any family'. There had been previous attempts to plant English subjects in Ireland most notably through the Leix–Offaly plantation of 1556, Thomas Smith's 1572-5 plantation of the Ards Peninsula in County Down and through a number of other projected or failed schemes. These were low-key and individualistic schemes and were primarily designed as exploratory entrepreneurial ventures.

The Ards scheme resulted in a number of tower houses being occupied on the coast of the peninsula and around Strangford Lough. A Captain Thomas Browne took out a lease on the estate surrounding Mahee Castle in 1570 (*86*). As part of this venture it appears that Browne constructed a series of quays and slipways adjacent to the tower house to facilitate the movement of goods and people from this enterprise. Another jetty with stone foundations can be seen on the foreshore directly beneath Ringhaddy Castle dating to a refurbishment phase of the tower house at this time. This is again indicative of the infrastructural efforts being made to ensure that these sites could accommodate increasing trade activity associated with the new plantation ventures. Elsewhere in the country other plantation schemes were being organised. Surveys began in Munster in an attempt to map out the forfeited lands and design a model plantation for this area. Many of these were coastal lands and schemes were located on the Dingle Peninsula and parts of the Cork and Waterford coasts.

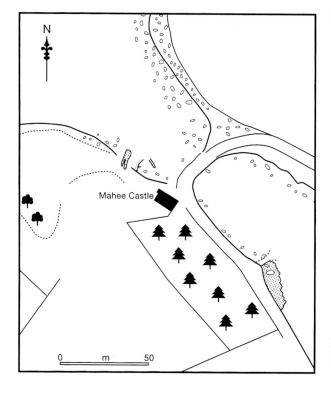

Left: *86* Map of Mahee Castle, Strangford Lough, showing the quay complex to the right of the castle on the foreshore (CMA, UU)

Opposite: *87* The English pursue the Spanish fleet East of Plymouth, 31 July – 1 August 1588

THE SPANISH ARMADA

Against this backdrop of plantation and Gaelic resistance external threats to English rule in parts of Ireland continued. This sense of heightened threat was best exemplified by the so-called Spanish Armada of 1588 (*87*). This was never an invasion attempt on Ireland, but was rather a plan involving a large fleet of ships sailing from Spain to Flanders and meeting with the successful Spanish army in Flanders under the Duke of Parma. The naval fleet would escort the army across to Spain where it would lead an invasion of England. In May 1588 a large armada of ships left Lisbon consisting of 130 ships divided into 10 squadrons, each squadron based on the vessels of origin of its vessels of the type of vessel involved. For a variety of reasons including superior English naval tactics, storm force winds and poor preparation this expedition ultimately failed.

After six days of conflict the Spanish fleet was ordered home. Rather than risk going back into the Channel the fleet instead chose to round Scotland and return home via the West of Ireland. On this passage the home ward bound Spanish Armada had to contend with very stormy weather combined with freezing fog and unfamiliar coastlines. Many of the ships had suffered during the weeklong conflict and were carrying storm damage. Over 30 ships were lost on the return voyage with as many as 26 lost on the Irish coast.

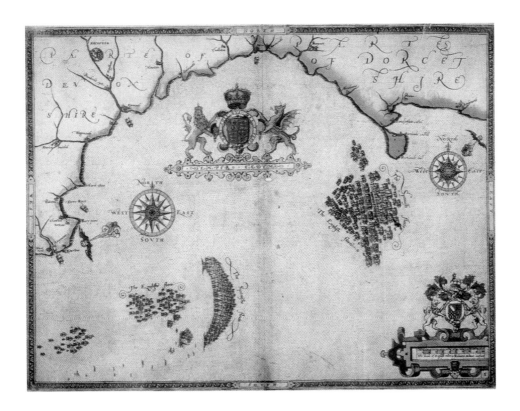

88 Sixteenth-century Spanish vessels
(David Wilkinson, EHS)

A number of the wrecks of the Armada have been excavated in Irish waters and have proved to be of enormous importance (*88*). They provide a unique insight into technology and society of late sixteenth-century Europe. The vessels were essentially small floating towns carrying enough equipment and cargo to keep a substantial sized community going for weeks at sea.

THE SANTA MARIA DE LA ROSA

In the 1960s after many seasons searching a wreck was located 180m south east of Stromboli reef in Blasket Sound, Co. Kerry. Initially the divers thought they had found the *San Juan* but this identification was quickly discounted in favour of the *Santa Maria de La Rosa*. The Santa Maria was the Vice-Flagship of the Guipuzcoan squadron under the command of Miguel de Oquendo. With a tonnage of 945 and carrying 297 men with 26 pieces of ordnance. All that remained on the seabed of the wreck in 1968 was a large tightly packed ballast mound of limestone blocks, 33m in length and 40m wide. The mound lay in 40m of water on a flat shingle bottom and survived to a height of just under a metre. Excavation of the mound, under the supervision of Colin Martin, produced structural elements from the lowermost part of the hull. A section of the scarf-jointed keelson was uncovered with portions of a number of stanchions surviving which would have supported the orlop beams. A complex mast step with a surrounding wooden box survived on the keelson and was excavated during the course of the project. A series of ground timbers and an assortment of artefacts also survived beneath the mound. Lead ingots, shot, arquebuses, muskets and fragmentary skeletal remains of a mariner were recovered during the course of the excavation. Two pewter plates recovered confirmed the identity of the ship. Both were marked with the name 'Matute'. The *Santa Maria* carried on board Francisco Ruiz Matute, an infantry captain, on board. Martin interpreted this section of the remains as being from the bow portion of the ship on the basis of the location of ballast in ships of that period and on the position of the mast step.

LA GIRONA

In 1967 Robert Stenuit, a Belgian salvage expert, came to Ireland in search of Spanish wrecks. He had originally planned to concentrate his efforts on Blasket Sound, but finding the English group at work he switched his attention to the north coast. Stenuit was attracted to a bay near the Giant's Causeway on the Antrim coast (*89*). The ordnance survey maps of the area labelled the bay in Irish Port-na-Spanaigh, or port of the Spaniards, an obvious indicator of a Spanish connection. Two possible wrecks had occurred in this vicinity including *La Girona* – a galleass of the Naples Squadron. The galleass was a relatively new type of vessel originating from an oared Mediterranean galley with three masts and sails.

On his first dive around Lacada Point, Stenuit recovered a number of Spanish coins and noted the presence of a range of other artefactual remains including the distinctively shaped lead ingots which were a common item carried onboard the Armada vessels. These ingots would have later been melted down to make lead shot once the invasion force had landed. He returned the following year in 1968 with a dive team and a range of equipment that would enable him to carry out a large-scale salvage job. Unlike the *Santa Maria* no hull structure was found from the site of the *Girona*. The topography of the seabed at this location, the shallowness of the site and the high-energy nature of this coastline mitigated against the survival of such a large structure. The largest items recovered from the site were three guns, one bronze half-saker and one bronze esmeril and the muzzel of a third gun. The ship had an original complement of up to 50 guns, but many of these were salvaged at the time by local chieftains and by an English salvage operation mounted soon after the wrecking. A large assortment of personal items were found including religious crosses, jewellery and kitchen utensils.

TRINIDAD VALENCERA

The *Trinidad Valencera* was found by the City of Derry Sub-Aqua Club in 1971. The ship, because of its bulk carrier abilities, carried three large siege guns

89 The North Coast (Nigel McDowell, UU)

which were to be used on land once land conflict in England had started. Two of the siege guns were recovered during the course of the excavation bearing the weight marks 5260 and 5316. They had come from a Flemish foundry and fired 40lb cannon balls. The ship also carried 29 other pieces of ordnance with 79 mariners and 281 soldiers. No intact portion of the hull structure survived in the areas of excavation. Oak planking was found on the site and this appears to have been exclusively fastened by iron and treenails and were apparently not used.

STREEDAGH STRAND

Three Armada vessels were lost at Streedagh Strand. The three vessels wrecked, the Sicilian *Juliana* of 860 tons, the Venetian *Lavia* of 728 tons and the smaller *Santa Maria de Vision* of 666 tons, were from the Levantine Squadron. A map drawn by Sir Richard Bingham on 20 April 1588 and subsequently endorsed by Burghley shows the three vessels breaking up in the surf at Streedagh. Three guns were recovered from the site in the 1980s including two pedreros, short barrelled guns with reduced powder chambers used for firing stone shot, and one saker with a foundry date of 1570. A large rudder with its pintles still intact was also uncovered and photographed on the site but this was later reburied by sediment movement.

THE NINE YEARS WAR AND LATER PLANTATIONS

The failure of the Armada and the continued unrest throughout Ireland led to a more intensive and successful phase of plantations in the early 1600s. This was especially true in Ulster where the most ambitious undertakings took place. In the middle of the sixteenth century there was increased tension between the forces of the English crown and the Ulster Irish lords. This period of tension culminated in the Nine Years War in 1594. After years of fighting the English had effectively defeated the Irish forces and many of the leading Irish lords fled to Spain in 1608 in what became known as the 'Flight of the Earls', having failed to live in compromise with the English forces. The English Crown now moved again to grant large tracts of land throughout Ireland to British settlers, with most settling in Munster and Ulster.

The same degree of formality that was proposed for the earlier schemes does not appear to apply to the early seventeenth-century undertakings. One reason for this is that much of the threat from Gaelic insurgents, a factor that hindered earlier settlement in these areas, had now effectively gone. The later undertakings appear to be far more individualistic with the grantee being able to operate without any political interference and to develop their own scheme. There was now much greater diversity of settlement in new settlement and trade centres. A *laissez faire* market had been introduced and individual activity and initiative was actively encouraged. One of the direct consequences of this is that the actual morphology of the plantation settlements outside of the main urban centres is less rigid than that which was proposed for the earlier Munster settlements. A more uniform approach to layout is adopted in Ulster where the large towns at Derry/Londonderry and Coleraine are laid out in a grid-like fashion and enclosed by fortifications (*90*).

ECONOMIC DEVELOPMENT OF MARITIME TOWNS AND TRADE

Port towns

With the advent of the early seventeenth-century plantations and the restructuring of the economy within Ireland a number of new port towns were developed and new infrastructural development is apparent at a number of the older established towns. Ulster in particular witnesses the main thrust of these developments being, as it was, to the forefront of plantation activity. The area east of Lough Foyle was granted to the London companies in the first decade of the seventeenth century and by 1613 two towns at Derry and Coleraine had been established. There had been pre-existing settlements at both of these locations but the arrival of the new settlers sees significant fortified urban settlements being developed. A substantial earthen rampart with a number of small bastions was built at Coleraine by 1612. The town was situated on the River Bann, three kilometres from the sea,

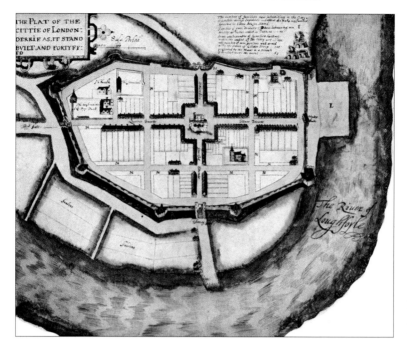

90 Thomas Raven's Londonderry in the 1620s

directly downstream from the important salmon fisheries close to Mount Sandel. However, the port was hindered by its riverine location and never developed as a deep-water port. Derry adopted a more suitable position and its quickly acquired prosperity was reflected in the extensive circuit of defences erected around the town. The approaches to its quays were protected downstream by the triangular artillery fort at Culmore, originally fortified in 1600 by Henry Docwra (*91*).

While the Plantation schemes developed on the eastern banks of the Foyle, parts of Down and southern Antrim were also settled even though they were not part of the formal plantation project. This region attracted mainly Scottish settlers, such as the Hamiltons and Montgomerys. These families began to re-invest in individual port towns which subsequently emerged as central settlements in the broader socio-economic structure of the north-eastern seaboard. New developments included Sir Hugh Montgomery's work at Donaghadee where he built a large stone quay to accommodate vessels engaged in the ferrying activity between Scotland and Ireland from 1616 onwards. Similarly, letters patent were issued to James Hamilton in March 1620 granting him permission to constitute Bangor as a port. He was also made customs collector and built a customs house to facilitate this, which still survives on the quay. This is very distinctively a Scottish style building with its turrets and general form, reflective of the ethnic origins of its patron.

This new investment manifested itself in a number of other ways as well. A tower house was built at Castleward in *c.*1610 while a second tower house was built at Kirkistown in 1618. Killyleagh Castle, on the shores of Strangford

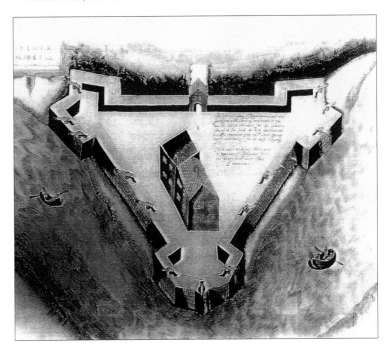

91 Detail of
Culmore Fort
in the 1620s, Co.
Derry

Lough, was built in a Scottish style for James Hamilton by 1624, while Portaferry
Castle was refurbished by James Montgomery in 1635 (*92*). The construction of
the tower houses illustrates a certain sense of continuity with past settlement
traditions in the region and also demonstrates the diversity of the plantation
experience. Settlement was not just concerned with the development of large
new urban centres but was also involved in reshaping landscapes in a more
organised manner but yet maintaining traditionalist elements.

KILLYBEGS AND ROUGH POINT

While the political histories and larger architectural statements of these early
plantations survive, far less is known about the so-called commoners who would
have lived and worked on these newly granted lands. An important site at Rough
Point in Killybegs, Co. Donegal, has recently been published by Frank Coyne
and Tracy Collins, which for the first time investigates a large area of a waterfront
settlement of this period. While there had been Gaelic-Irish settlement around
Killybegs harbour throughout the later medieval period it was in 1615 that a
town was formally established here in the plantation precinct of Boyagh. It was
granted to undertakers from Scotland, from where the inhabitants of the Rough
Point settlement may have come from. The small settlement cluster consisted of
five stone-built structures built in a variety of architectural styles reflecting both
English and Irish vernaculars. The form of the houses reflects the environment of

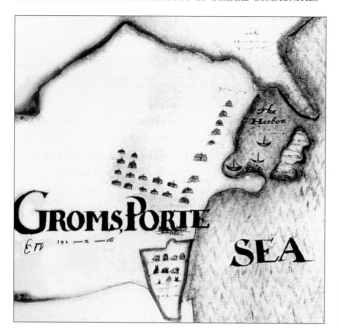

92 Detail of Raven's 1620s Estate map of Groomsport, Co. Down (North Down Museum)

this seaboard and the excavators suggest they were built specifically to endure the harsh Atlantic climate. The structures were all rectangular and ranged between 10-15m in length. A number had fireplaces built into the gables, a building fashion that is common in other British plantation period structures across the North Atlantic sphere. The artefactual and structural evidence are clearly supportive of a plantation period date and origin for these structures but what is less clear is the function of the cluster. It is of course reasonable to suggest that the inhabitants were involved in the extensive fisheries off the coast at this time.

Certainly entrepreneurial fishing activity was a common feature amongst the planters who came to Ireland. Interestingly though no artefactual evidence was uncovered which was directly related to the fishing industry although a number of the red earthenware pieces may have been used as herring jars. It seems likely that an industrial area associated with fish processing, boat repair etc. was located elsewhere around the harbour and this would account for the paucity of fishery remains at the site. Could it also be indicative of new arrivals who had yet to become fully acclimatised to their new holdings? Does their settlement position on an island spit, removed from the mainland, reflect a degree of insecurity and a feeling of separation from the surrounding populations? The material culture recovered from the site is indicative of this difference being largely made up of imported table-wares. These remains represent an important survival and must constitute only one of many of these rural site types yet to be found.

PORTS AND HARBOURS

The seventeenth century saw the re-development and modernisation of the major ports around the coast. Substantial stone quays were erected along the riverfront at Drogheda, Dublin, Waterford, Cork, Limerick and Galway. This century also witnessed the emergence of 'new' substantial ports including Derry, Belfast and Newry. Much of this development is still evident today incorporated into the modern line of the individual quays. Excavations undertaken by Anne Lynch have also uncovered evidence of this development. Investigations at Charlotte Quay in Limerick uncovered the remains of a seventeenth century quay wall which ran parallel to the town wall and appears to have been built to provide boat access to the west Watergate (93). The wall survived to a height of 3.2m and ran along the river for 32.5m. It was built with a core of mortared rubble and faced with ashlar limestone blocks. A stone quay with a series of steps providing access to the waterfront was uncovered in 1981 during excavations at the Shop Street site in Drogheda. The stone structure was located on the north bank of the river Boyne and dated to the seventeenth century. In Munster older ports like Youghal greatly benefited from reinvestment by the planters. Here the port was refurbished and an enclosed harbour was built to accommodate shipping associated with the export trade of pig iron and charcoal as well as cattle and wool. The smaller port towns of Kinsale, Baltimore and Dingle prospered in a similar manner benefiting from the planters involvement with the sea fisheries of the south-west coast.

Ulster ports also began to rise in prominence during this period. William Pitt was appointed as Customer of the ports of Newcastle, Dundrum, Killough, Portaferry, Donaghadee, Bangor, and Holywood in 1625. Thomas Raven's drawings of 1625 clearly show pier structures at Groomsport and Killyleagh

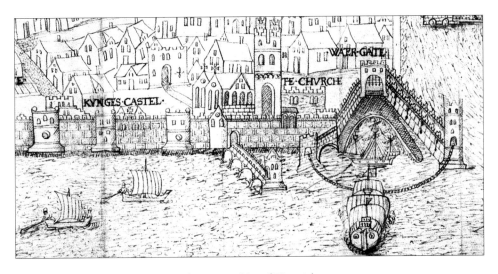

93 Detail of Jobson's early seventeenth-century City of Limerick

94 The 'Old Quay' at Strangford, Co. Down (Rosemary McConkey, UU)

while new investment at Strangford Port resulted in it overtaking Ardglass in importance. Much of this investment came from the Earl of Kildare, whose agent, Valentine Payne, wrote in 1629 '*I have built a key (at Strangford) where there was none before, that the biggest shippe that the Kinge hathe may lay her side beside it.*' This quay, the 'Old Quay' is still in use today with leisure craft mooring alongside it (*94*). The Earl, who also held the majority interest in Ardglass, obviously did not pay as much attention to that port and sold its customs in 1637 as the port had been undergoing a decline for a number of years. Also in 1637 a report was issued by the Surveyor General of Customs which gives an indication of the relative importance of Irish Ports. The list is compiled from accounts of the customs due from each port and their 'subsidiary creeks'. Of the Ulster ports listed Carrickfergus is ranked first, followed by Bangor, Donaghadee and Strangford. Carlingford and Coleraine each had £244 due in customs and had an equal ranking.

POST MEDIEVAL FORTIFICATION OF THE COAST

The onset of the political troubles of the 1640s was ultimately to see the end of the Gaelic land-ownership and power along the western and northern seaboards. The Cromwellian confiscations of land and subsequent re-granting of it to soldiers and undertakers loyal to the Parliament was to have a fundamental impact on the nature and ownership of landholding throughout the country. Architecturally, this change is manifested in the development of a number of new fortifications at strategic locations around the coast, the founding of a number of new planter towns and the development and intensification of coastal industries. A new form of angular fortification was specifically developed to offer increased protection to these places.

In particular star-shaped forts were enclosed structures built of earth and/ or masonry and were used to mount and resist cannon (95). They worked as defensive fortifications through the strategic placement of cannon on salient angles or bastions which aspired to command a full 360° line of fire around the fort. Each bastion was roughly spear-shaped and projected from each of the salient angles on the fort. The walls of the fort were fronted by low thick-profiled ramparts, 4–6m thick, built of earth and sods and reveted with stone, which were built to absorb the impact of cannon. The ramparts were in turn surmounted by a parapet, access to which was gained by a series of steps or ramps from the interior. The forts were also almost exclusively surrounded by a deep external ditch. The size and sophistication of each fort was governed by a wide variety of factors.

Strategic positioning was obviously of primary importance with many of the forts positioned to protect harbours, sea-lanes, communication routes and significant settlements. Local factors also influenced location and design. Topographic suitability was an over-riding concern. Forts had to be positioned on well-drained soils as sandy soils were subject to sliding. Well-drained soils also mitigated against damp and flooding which was of especial importance to a fort

95 Detail of Newtown fort from Thomas Philips 1580s vista of Bantry Bay, Co. Cork

designed specifically for artillery. An elevated position with commanding vistas was an important military requirement as well. Financial resources, personnel, building expertise and tools would all have played a role in determining the nature of the structure. Many of these factors fluctuated so forts periodically fell out of usage while others were re-established or re-fortified.

The combination of all of the defensive and aggressive characteristics of these forts points to structures that were fundamentally different to the tower houses that had been built over the previous centuries. Star-shaped forts were exclusively military structures built to house a garrison of professional soldiers and to engage in artillery warfare. They had no other major role to play within society other than the protection of the surrounding land from hostile forces. This mono-functionality is reflected in the short-term occupation of many of the sites and their subsequent abandonment and decay once a period of conflict ends. Only the larger sites associated with urban settlements or important ports appear to have been occupied for any length of time.

Initially these types of defensive works were built in response to the crises of the Nine Years War. A pentagonal earthwork, James Fort, was built at Castle Park near Kinsale in 1602 while a similar fort was erected on Haulbowline Island in Cork Harbour at the same time. Elsewhere sites such as Duncannon Fort in Waterford Harbour were strengthened in recognition of the pivotal strategic role they played over the previous decades of conflict. This refortification in times of crisis is a feature of many of the forts around the coast. During the Cromwellian wars of 1641-1660 Duncannon again underwent refurbishment. The recent discovery of a shipwreck in the shipping channel near to Duncannon has been provisionally identified by Connie Kelleher as that of the *Great Lewis,* a 400 ton vessel of the Parliamentarian navy sent to relieve the garrison at Duncannon. The vessel was lost in 1645 in an engagement with Royalist forces. A number of cannon, timber structure and artefactual material have been recorded on the seabed at this location. The Anglo-Dutch war of 1651-2 acted as a catalyst for further construction. Two star-shaped forts, for example, were constructed at this time in Bantry Bay to protect and defend the region against Dutch shipping, one at Dunboy and the second at Newtown (1km north of Bantry town). Both overlook shipping routes and important areas of anchorage. Forts were also located on the islands off the west coast, including Mutton Island, Inisboffin and Inishmore.

THE FRENCH TERROR: LATER REFORTIFICATION

While the Spanish constituted the primary external threat to the security of Britain and Ireland in the sixteenth century it was the French who took on this mantle in the later part of the eigtheenth century. In 1789 the French revolution took place and this single event was to have profound repercussions

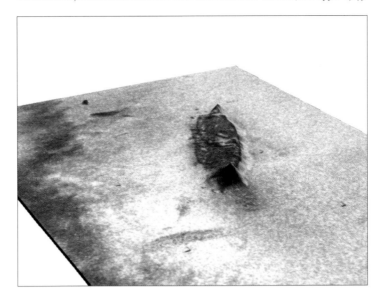

96
3D geophysical image
of the shipwreck La
Surveillante (Rory
Quinn, CMA)

across Northern Europe as the revolutionaries sought to spread their ideals and
overthrow existing monarchies. The newly founded Republic declared war on
Austria in April 1792 and the revolutionary war quickly spread throughout
western Europe. In the Autumn of 1795 a new political regime came to power
in France, the Directory, which made peace with Spain and became its ally
in the war against Britain. Theobald Wolfe Tone, one of the leaders of the
United Irishmen, went to France in 1796 and began to campaign for support
for a French invasion of Ireland. Eventually the French agreed, and a plan was
developed which involved a landing at Bantry Bay where an expeditionary force
would join up with local insurgents and march on Cork (*96*).

On the 16th December 1796, 48 ships and 13,000 troops under the command
of Vice-admiral Morard de Galles left Brest. However, as with so many other
campaigns of a similar nature it was effectively doomed from the outset, plagued
by poor organisation, planning and storm conditions at sea. The invasion force
never landed and a number of vessels were wrecked on the Irish coasts. The
frigate *La Surveillante* arrived in Bantry Bay at the end of December but was so
badly damaged during its passage from Brest that it was dismantled, abandoned
and scuttled. Its well preserved remains lie in 32m of water north of Whiddy
Island and consist of the copper-sheated lower section of the hull which lies
partially buried in the bottom sediments. The frigate *L'Impatient* was wrecked
below Mizen Head. Unlike *La Surveillante* none of its hull survives due to the
high-energy nature of the marine environment at this location. Instead only the
ferrous material from the wreck remains and consists of a number of cannon
spread through a series of rocky gulleys. Two years later three frigates left from
France with 1000 soldiers and landed at Killala. They joined up with a larger
group of Irish revolutionaries and after some initial success surrendered. In

September of the same year ten vessels left Brest and sailed to Donegal where they engaged an English naval force but were defeated and the majority of the vessels, including the ship of the line *Hoche,* were captured.

The English response to these and other smaller scale events was to engage in the extensive re-fortification of the Irish coast in an attempt to protect against any future French invasionary force using Ireland as a bridgehead into Britain. In the immediate aftermath of the 1796 campaign temporary gun batteries were established around Bantry Bay. Later a series of signal towers were erected around the coast between 1804 and 1806 in an attempt to improve military communications and intelligence. The towers were designed to communicate with naval vessels and sometimes other stations through a series of flag signals. They mostly consisted of a single square defended tower, usually two storeys in height and operated and defended by a signal officer and a handful of men. 81 towers were built on the coast from Dublin southwards in a line to Inishowen Head in Donegal but by 1809 the vast majority had been abandoned.

By 1804 a series of Martello towers had been built down the east coast, from Dublin to Wexford, and in the strategically important harbours at Cork, Bantry and in Lough Swilly. Martello towers were designed to function as gun towers to defend the coast against enemy shipping and the landing of troops (97). A large 18-24 pounder gun was mounted on the tower and additional guns were often present in adjacent batteries. The effectiveness of this method in firing on ships offshore has often been questioned and was one of the factors in the eventual abandonment of the sites. However, they would have been useful in a number of locations and they could also have played an effective role in repelling an infantry

97 Martello tower at Magilligan Point, Co. Derry

landing. The towers have a relatively uniform design consisting of a circular two-storey tower with thick stone walls. Entry was usually gained through a first-floor doorway which lead to the living space in the tower.

The establishment of the Coastguard force in 1822 represented the government's shift from protection against external military threat towards trying to protect the coast from smuggling. Such activity was widespread, albeit exaggerated, and was viewed as having a detrimental effect on the Island's economy. Initially these bases consisted of a cottage with a boathouse and watch area, but later in the century more substantial two storey structures were erected. Communication between the bases was carried out through the use of flags. The erection of these stations is interesting in that it represents a form of economic coastal fortification as opposed to militaristic defence. It is also representative of the increased centralisation of power and government in Ireland at this time and of a reassertion of control by the British government. Many of these stations today are private residences, but interesting examples survive outside of the main areas of recent development such as that at St. John's Point in Down, which is associated with a lighthouse and small settlement complex.

THE POST MEDIEVAL FISHING INDUSTRY

Ireland's post medieval fisheries: local and regional diversity

It has been too easy to generalise about the fishing industry over the last few hundred years around the coast with archaeologists and historians dealing simply with fish and boat types and an occasional mention of material culture. However, this was a complex and multi-layered industry with extensive physical operations and social relationships. It was an industry that transcended the land and sea interface, reaching far inland. It was also an industry that operated at many levels from the local to the international and incorporated many nationalities and social levels.

One only has to investigate the local practices of a fisherman working on the Blasket islands in the nineteenth and early twentieth centuries. These islanders operating a locally based fishing system where boats were owned within familial groupings and operated within a loose cooperative community environment. They fished local markets and traded their fish within a local context. As well as fishing, small-scale agriculture also played an intrinsic part in their livelihood. Occasionally, a visiting vessel might engage with them but this type of enterprise was largely local.

At a medium scale we can consider the industry within a slightly larger fishing community environment. The Claddagh in Galway, for example, was a medium sized community largely dedicated to fishing and marine transport (*98*). All levels of society in this settlement were consumed with servicing and operating these activities. In 1834 Henry Inglis observes during his visit to the Claddagh that he went '*and looked into, hundreds of cabins; and there was scarcely one in which I did*

98 Claddagh cottages in the nineteenth century

not see females busily engaged in spinning, making or mending nets'. The majority of the men worked the fishing boats and plied their trade along the extent of the western seaboard. On a national and international level there were the large commercial fishing fleets of the larger ports and the continental fishing vessels which continued to visit these waters slowly over-fishing the available stocks.

Throughout the last four centuries fishing continued to be an economic mainstay. Historically, herring has been the most profitable and commercially exploitable pelagic fish in the Irish seas and has been the most abundant. These fish stocks fluctuated greatly but this was not due to changing spawning grounds, but rather to over-exploitation coupled with subtle changes in environmental conditions and migration leading to a depletion of stocks in certain areas, occasionally accompanied by a boom in others. Even a slight drop of one or two degrees in sea temperature was enough to trigger a depletion in stock. Similarly, if there were an intensive few years of fishing at a specific herring location then stocks would be adversely effected. The population of spawning adults would be severely decreased leading to an overall collapse of the fisheries. This may take many years to re-establish itself. These factors can be used to explain why a herring fishery might be extremely successful for a number of years before failing miserably only to be resurrected many years later. It is this constant state of flux of the stock which gives catches such an unpredictable nature. This unpredictable nature of the herring stocks has been noted by many writers. Harris, writing in 1744, notes that Carlingford and Strangford Lough as well as Quintin Bay and Carrickfergus Bay abound in herring. The pilchard (*Sardinia pilchardus*) also belongs to the same Superorder as the herring and the sprat. They feed in the inshore area in large schools remaining at the surface during the night and going down to up to 55m during the day. Many of the young shoals of the fish will enter and feed in estuaries or large bodies of sheltered water. Breeding season is April through to July for the pilchard in these waters, with larvae hatching at *c.*4mm in length and maturing after four years.

Fish palaces and fish ponds associated with this industry are dotted around the coast. Fish palaces were large stone built structures in which barrels of pilchards were laid under press beams and weights in order to pack the barrels and extract

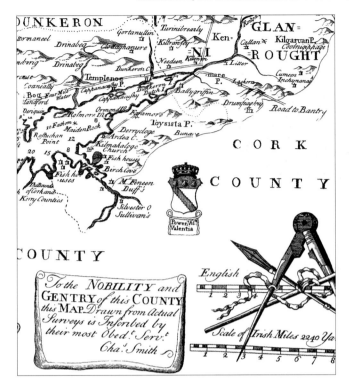

99 Detail from Smith's map of Kenmare River showing fish houses

oil. Independent walls and sections of exposed bedrock cliffs were also used for this purpose. Charles Smith, writing in 1750, records that several fish palaces survived in creeks around Bantry and Kenmare Bays, which were built for the saving, preserving and salting of pilchards, while de Latocnaye, writing in 1798, records that there were many pressing walls on Whiddy Island used for extracting oil from pilchards (99). Other palace locations include one on the southern shores of Reenadisert, a curing house at Gerahies and possible sites in Bantry town and at Gurteenroe. The storage of fish in coastal ponds also took place around the Bay and this activity appears to be associated with the estates. A much dilapidated pond is shown on the OS 1840s map of the area around Dunboy, while a second pond was located on the foreshore in the townland of Ardaturish Beg on the northern shores of the Bay. This second pond takes advantage of a natural break in the exposed bedrock. The narrow entrance on the seaward side of the pond consists of the foundations of a low wall standing 3 courses high at either end built of rough and cut sandstone blocks. A small red brick extension to the sandstone wall marks the location of a 1m wide wooden sluice gate which still survived over 50 years ago. At the land-ward side of the pond, where the bedrock terminates at the beach, a low wall consisting of upright overlapping slates, bonded with mortar, and running around the land-ward edge of the structure is evident. These ponds would have ensured a fresh supply of fish for the estates.

POST MEDIEVAL WHALING ACTIVITIES

On a larger scale whales have always been a valuable commodity on Irish shores. Exploitation appears to be mostly of stranded cetaceans and commercial hunting only really began in the eighteenth century. There are a number of accounts of whaling activity off the west coast in the early part of the century, although most of the early catches were exported to England for processing. In the 1760s the Nesbit brothers of Donegal secured government funding to establish a station in Donegal, probably at Inver, which enjoyed moderate success over the next two decades. The probable remains of this fishery have been recorded by both Rory McNeary and Martin McGonigle, and consist of five buildings situated on the south-facing shoreline. This was a multi-functional site which also catered for the other forms of fisheries on this coast. A salt house was located here as were a number of storage buildings.

It was not until 1908 that a large-scale commercial entity was established on the Inishkea Islands off the Mayo coast when a whaling station was located on Rusheen Island (*100*). Jetties and slipways were built here, as well as a series of storage and working buildings. Fairley describes the stages of processing once the whales had been caught by the station's steamers. They were brought ashore and winched onto a flensing plane where their blubber was removed by a number of experienced cutters. The blubber was then cut into pieces and boiled in huge pots from which the oil was extracted and stored in barrels. The meat and bone was subsequently used for a variety of purposes. This was a short lived complex, but a second station, also established in 1908 at Blacksod in County Mayo, proved more durable. A large complex of buildings and associated whalers was quickly built and some 305 whales were subsequently caught between 1910 and 1914. The station was burnt down after the First World War and it never really recovered from this setback finally closing in the 1930s. In 1937 the government moved to prohibit whaling in Irish territorial waters. The site currently lies in an abandoned state on the northern shores of Feorrinyeeo Bay. A series of brick foundations mark the location of the chimney, boiler platforms and lifting mechanisms. The basal remains of the original slipway and pier which would have lead to the flensing plane are also evident.

Elsewhere along the western seaboard the basking shark fishery was also well established (*101*). By 1740, 'sun-fish' oil was being used for street lighting in Dublin, while the Nesbits were extensively engaged in this fishery by 1761. This was largely carried out by coastal communities, often using curraghs to pursue their catch. It was more organised in Galway and parts of Clare and a large number of Galway hookers from Claddagh village for example were involved in this fishery in the eighteenth and nineteenth century. In more recent years a shark fishery station was established on Achill Island, and the oil containers and foundations of a number of buildings associated with this site can still be seen at Purcheen harbour on the island. A crane was also originally positioned on the site to enable the fishermen to land the sharks.

100 Whaling at the Inishkea Islands

101 Shark fishery off Achill

POST MEDIEVAL FISH TRAPS ON THE SHANNON ESTUARY

Post medieval fish traps are well known around the Irish coastline, largely due to the historical and ethnological research of Arthur Went through the twentieth century – particularly at Castlebellingham, Co. Louth, on Waterford Harbour and on the Munster Blackwater. Post medieval fish traps on the Shannon estuary were recorded during Aidan O'Sullivan's intertidal surveys and these allow us to explore ideas about landscape, practice and identity. In the eighteenth and nineteenth centuries, the economic resources of the Shannon estuary were the focus of some social and class conflict. Limerick itself was of course a major

Atlantic port at this time, with abundant historical evidence for ships and boats moving up and down the estuary on their way to ports in Britain, America and the West Indies. Fish, agricultural produce and timber were exported, in return for salt, lead and iron. The estuary's marshlands were being reclaimed in a significant way, and were used for growing huge crops of barley and oats. Labourers were employed to move cattle, sheep and horses across the salt marshes and islands.

An historical and archaeological review of the Shannon estuary landscape reveals the extent to which it has always been a contested space, with lords, tenant farmers, labourers, mariners and fishermen all negotiating and competing for its resources. We can get an understanding of how these different social groups (i.e. English sailors and Irish sheep herders) were living and working on the estuary through the study of place names, giving a sense of its 'alternative geographies'. On the Shannon estuary, various place names provide information on topography and land ownership. Thence, Tullyvarraga (*Tulach O'Bhearga* – O'Bhearga's hill), Clonmacken (*Cluain Maicin* – Macken's meadow) and Ballycasey (*Baile O'Cathasaigh* – Casey's place) are all of medieval Gaelic Irish origin, indicating mostly farming activities. On the estuary channel there are a whole host of other names of rocks, islands and pools, mostly forgotten today, but preserved in nineteenth-century Admiralty Charts. These place names – Battle Island, Dead Woman's Hand, Kippen Rock – are all of English origin, and testify to the fears and concerns of the eighteenth- and nineteenth-century English-speaking mariners. There are also other estuarine place names that were passed down only through folk tradition, used to designate different stretches of the river to be used by net fishermen. Interestingly, these *enuires* (possibly deriving from the Middle English or Anglo-French term *en cure* meaning 'in use' or 'practice') on the river were not 'owned' in a sense by different families, but by the entire fishing community and were allocated to each by agreement.

The Shannon estuary fisheries were an extremely valuable resource, and their ownership was a complex and torturous subject. Fishing rights were jealously guarded and were often the subject of legal disputes over control, ownership and access, leading to unrest and even violence. By the nineteenth century, ownership of the larger fish traps mostly resided in the hands of local landlords, bishops and the Limerick Corporation. The most obvious of these fish traps are massive wooden ebb weirs, with fences up to 250m in length, located usually on the main estuary channel. Eighteenth- and nineteenth-century references refer to local poor people illegally building smaller structures to poach a resource which required no rent and which provided food and a supplemental income. Some of these can be identified as the smaller creek traps that are often located in hidden places, behind islands, or down in the creeks that dissect the deep muds. Both local landlords and net fishermen were loud in their criticisms of these fisheries, as they argued that fishstocks were being destroyed and livelihoods were being threatened. Ultimately, all of these fisheries were to be banned by legislation in 1864. Although, no doubt, people defiantly continued to use them in poaching activities.

Interestingly, on the Shannon estuary there were nearly always post medieval fisheries close to or beside medieval examples. They are certainly not evidence for 'continuity', but they may not be accidental associations either. We believe that nineteenth-century fishing communities would have experience of deep historical time through the recognition of ancient wooden structures in the muds. In a way, fishing communities would have been experts on the materiality of the estuary. They would have recognised the peculiarity and unusual appearance of these medieval traps, with their small post-and-wattle fences and woven baskets on the mudflats. They might have recognised them as, in a sense, antiquities and used them as a source of information for good fishing places. Thence, we can think again of the intimate knowledge that fishermen had of the creeks and channels, and how past material culture might have actively influenced their economic practices and social identities.

POST MEDIEVAL SHELLFISH GATHERING

Shellfish have clearly played an important part in the diet and social structure of labour for the duration of human presence on this island. We have seen in previous chapters how shell middens are an important archaeological survival demonstrating the importance of this resource. Excavations in the medieval cities around the coast have uncovered large dumps of shellfish with oysters being especially common. These features have been recorded at Custom House in Galway, excavations off North and South Main Street in Cork while a medieval midden was also recorded near the south quay at Carlingford. However, they are also a very common feature of the post medieval urban and rural landscape.

Archaeological excavations by Claire Walsh at Ringsend on the south bank of the River Liffey, at Dublin uncovered a small oyster midden, which would originally have been adjacent to the tidal mudflats and sand banks of Dublin Bay. Pottery from the seventeenth-century provided a date for the site. Such dating evidence is always very welcome on these site types as they can be notoriously difficult to date. Other confirmed post medieval middens include shellfish deposits making up the infill of a ditch of the supposed site of Castlegregory in Kerry, a periwinkle deposit in Kirwan's Lane, Galway. An eighteenth-century midden measuring 13m by 9m, of shells of oysters, winkles and limpets, at Ghan House, Carlingford. The extent that this resource was exploited in the recent past has been demonstrated during exploratory work in advance of road development by Richard Crumlish. Nineteen possible post medieval middens, comprised of cockles, periwinkles, mussels and oysters, were located during work on the Sligo to Strandhill road. Such findings should come as no surprise given the sheer extent of this resource around the coast and increased moves in recent centuries to begin to commercially farm shellfish.

Legislation had been introduced by the early part of the nineteenth century to try and protect oyster beds in particular, reflecting the extent and importance of this industry. The sheer volume of exploitation in some areas is astounding. Take, for example, the Wicklow and Wexford Banks where 34.33 million oysters were removed in 1864 alone. This type of exploitation without rejuvenation could not sustain itself and oysters slowly disappeared from these banks. In recognition of the finite nature of these natural resources official recognition of oyster cultivation begins from the 1840s onwards. By the 1860s artificial ponds for oyster spat were built near Kilrush in Clare, in Lough Swilly and in Dundrum Bay. This type of enterprise quickly took off and most parts of the coast experienced these early forms of aquaculture. In Tramore Bay, for example, a large embankment was built and a number of ponds created for this industry. Oyster tanks were built at Derreen and Sneem Harbour in Kerry. Interest also developed in other types of shellfish and by the 1880s mussel beds began to appear.

THE POST MEDIEVAL KELP INDUSTRY

The production of kelp in the eighteenth and nineteenth centuries was a major industry on the coast and became the primary source of income for many small coastal communities. It was especially common along the north-east and western coasts where it primarily supplied the Scottish market. The term kelp can cause confusion as it is both the biological name for a group of seaweeds and the commercial name for the ash residue produced from burnt seaweed. This residue is a source of potassium carbonate and sodium carbonate (soda). Soda is an important ingredient in the production of glass and soap, and is used to create washing soda for the finishing of linen. Of course seaweeds have also been used as fertiliser and as animal fodder, and it is likely that its use as the former greatly predates its industrial usage.

The archaeology of the kelp industry manifests itself in a number of ways. Kelp was first cut from the foreshore and then carried to dryland by cart or hand. Often the foreshore was subdivided by low walls or boulder lines which delineated individual ownership of the foreshore or the rights of tenants from certain estates to work the kelp resource. This was a valuable commodity and ownership was highly prized. In some cases the foreshore was unsuitable for kelp growth, such as where it was predominantly mud or sand. Here kelp grids were laid out consisting of lines of evenly spaced boulders which encouraged colonisation by brown seaweeds. One such kelp grid at Herring Bay in Strangford Lough covers an area of 2.2ha (102). Once harvested the kelp was brought to kilns where it was burnt. These kilns consisted mostly of stone lined pits averaging 1.5-2.5m in diameter. They were mostly circular, oval or rectangular in shape and have been found, or at least predominantly survive, on the islands off the north and west coasts and along some parts of the eastern and western seaboard. Once the kelp

102 Kelp Grid Mount Stewart, Strangford Lough (Thomas McErlean, CMA)

ash was produced it would then be stored in nearby storage facilities or be sent directly for exportation.

Whole island communities became heavily involved in kelp production in the later part of the eighteenth century. Rathlin Island off the north coast became a major centre for production and its shoreline is still littered with kilns and storage places. This was a commercial undertaking sponsored by the island's landlords and involved the whole community. The industry was also commonplace on Tory and the other smaller islands of Donegal. Other centres of significant activity included the Connemara and Mayo coastlines.

RECLAIMING THE LAND

While a number of the more remote communities were participating in emergent coastal industries like kelp other mechanisms for improving agricultural productivity and the social quality of peoples' lives were also being developed. This was the so-called 'Age of Improvement' where the generation and production of Capital was rapidly replacing traditional social and landscape structures. The reclamation of low-lying lands was one such mechanism employed by the land-holding elite in order to generate more land suitable for agricultural exploitation. This type of process dates back to Roman times in Britain, but in Ireland it appears largely to be a later historical phenomenon. It may be that with future research we can push back the dates for these enterprises into the high and possibly the early medieval periods, but at the present time the evidence largely points to a post sixteenth-century development. Of course it could be argued that the continual outward expansion of the waterfronts in the major coastal cities was a form of land claim, but of greater agricultural significance was the deliberate construction of large-scale embankments along the coast and associated drainage projects, which opened up huge tracts of landscape. By the middle of the seventeenth-century sea-banks with sluices had been erected around the Shannon estuary, reclaiming vast tracts of estuarine alluvium known as corcass. This was very rich and valued land with high yields. Today over 11,000ha of corcass exists around the estuary. Reclamation works also appear to have been encouraged in Strangford Lough in the middle part of the seventeenth-century by the Crown. Between 1720 and 1740 reclamation work consisting of sea walls and sluices was carried out at Greyabbey on the eastern shores of the Lough during the development of the Rosemount estate. 1745 marks the first attempt to drain the Quoile estuary in the Lough through the erection of a tidal barrier. The following two centuries were to see repeated and updated versions of this venture which was largely successful. On the northern shores of the Lough around Newtownards reclamation work began on the Londonderry Estate in the later part of the eighteenth century. Again these works were to see continuous improvements over the following centuries. Elsewhere around the coast other major works took place including much of the north-eastern section of Lough Foyle (103), large portions of the inner section of Belfast Lough and in Wexford Harbour.

SALT PRODUCTION

Salt was an important commodity throughout the historic period in Ireland and was among the staple imports into the country. Salt was used for preserving both meat and fish, and for flavouring the food and as a chemical agent in the manufacture of glass and soap. Throughout the Middle Ages it was largely imported into the country from France and Portugal where it was produced in massive salt-pans through evaporation, but there are also indicators that local production was taking place. This probably took the form of natural evaporation of seawater in shallow depressions in bedrock or artificially created pans which may have been lined with clay. In 1203 the church and monks of St. Mary of Drogheda were granted 'a salt grange' in the land of O'Carroll while the Pipe Roll of 1211-12 records the expenditure of £2 1s 8d on a salt pan which was possibly located at Dundrum. The same source records the cost of freighting a ship, 11s 3d, to Carrickfergus which was carrying salt. In 1282 Richard De Burgh destroyed a salt pan worth 2 marks in the parish of Loughinisland, adjacent to Dundrum.

103 Reclamation at the head of Lough Foyle

By the sixteenth century, visiting French and Spanish fishermen were supplying the O'Donnells in Donegal with salt, although the upsurge in the eighteenth-century herring fishery lead to the development of salt-works along the north-west coast. In the late 1770s the salt-works at Port near Inver, currently a ruined complex of five buildings, was producing nearly 500 tons of salt a year. In 1629 the Earl of Antrim records his salt and coal works on the north Antrim coast in a will. The area around Ballycastle subsequently became a centre for the production of salt over the next few centuries. Here the remains of a saltworks can still be seen adjacent to Pans Rocks at Broughanlea. It originally consisted of a series of wrought-iron troughs with various pipes and rock-cut channels which would have piped hot water to heat the brine. It has been estimated that six to eight tons of coal are needed to produce one ton of sea-salt, so the proximity of Ballycastle's colleries was especially conducive to the development of this industry at this location. Throughout the eighteenth and nineteenth centuries the north-east coast served as the Ireland's primary centre for salt importation and production.

MARITIME IRELAND: AN ARCHAEOLOGY OF COASTAL COMMUNITIES

POST MEDIEVAL SHIPBUILDING AND SHIPWRECKS

The relative peace of the eighteenth century witnessed a significant improvement in the Irish economy. This economic resurgence was one factor in the emergence of the industrial revolution and its associated advances in shipbuilding technology. In particular the development and widespread adoption after 1820 of the steam engine, iron hulls and the screw propeller would transform shipping and hasten the end of the era of sail and wooden ships. Experiments with steam-driven vessels had begun in the late eighteenth century in America, France and Britain, but these vessel types only really became viable in the first two decades of the nineteenth century. Andrew and Michael Hennessy constructed the hull of the first Irish-built paddle steamer at their yard in Passage, Co. Cork, in 1815. A year later in 1816 they built the hull of a second steamer with an engine that was manufactured at the Hive Iron Works in Cork city, the first marine engine to be made in Ireland. By 1820 the first steamer had been built in Belfast with its engine being constructed at the Lagan foundry.

One early Irish-owned steamship, the *Sirius,* secured her place in maritime history (*104*). Built in 1837 in Scotland, she became the first vessel powered by steam to cross the Atlantic from Europe to America. The ship set out from Cork on 14 April 1838, under Lieut. Richard Roberts, and reached New York eighteen days later on 22 April. However, later in 1847 the vessel was lost on the rocks at Ballycotton on the east coast of Cork. In the first half of the nineteenth century composite ships also began to be built in response to the shortage of wood and the developments in iron technology. This method involved the use of iron to provide the inner 'skeleton' of the ship while the outer hull was still planked with wood. The wreck of one such experimentally built composite ship, *Taymouth Castle,* lies off the north-east Antrim coast. Built in July 1865 the vessel was lost in 1867 while on voyage to the Far East. The wreck site lies in 15m of water and its remains consist of a large section of the iron framing from the original forward body of the vessel. A large windlass was attached to this section at its western end, consisting of a large, cylindrical, iron drum with wooden components lying on a horizontal shaft. Significant quantities of pottery, bottles and household goods were recovered from the excavations on the wreck.

THE BELFAST SHIPYARDS

While shipbuilding was carried out in Belfast since the middle part of the seventeenth century it was not until the later part of the eighteenth century that the industry really expanded. In 1791 William Ritchie from Scotland transferred his building yard to the shores of the Lagan and established the first of many wooden shipbuilding firms. Subsequent reclamation of foreshore and the redirection of the Lagan resulted in the development of Queen's Island as

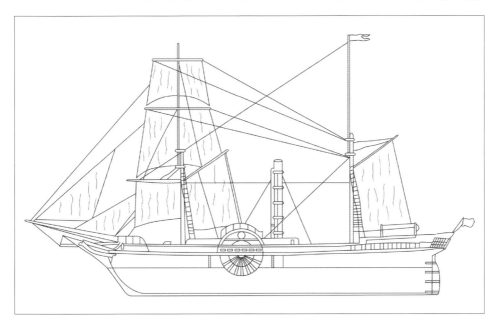

104 SS Sirius

a centre for this type of industry. It was in this area that the Harland and Wolff company was developed in 1862 rapidly expanding into the largest company of its kind in Ireland, an expansion which owed much to the emergence of the north-east as the industrial centre of Ireland. Their expansion led to the creation of the most developed and complex Victorian port landscapes in the country. The Hamilton graving dock was built in 1862, followed by the Alexandra dock in 1889 and the Thompson dock in 1910. Other works included the construction of extensive wharfage and support industries around the area. It was in this area that the *Titanic* was built.

Significantly the massive growth in shipbuilding led to the development of extensive urban areas built to house the thousands of yard workers employed in the industry. Row after row of terraced houses testifies to the tight social communities that serviced the yards. Street and place names, churches and working mens' guilds still bear testimony to this once massive industry. The uniformity of the buildings reflects the communitarian social engineering favoured by the captains of industry with which they could organise their working societies. Religion also served as a fundamental role in ensuring social conformity and good practice. Unfortunately, this outward appearance of cohesion also masked underlying sectarian tensions and social division, which expressed itself in the emergence of contested social space and differing expressions of material culture. This was a pattern that was most apparent in Belfast where division manifested itself primarily along religious lines, but class was also a major factor and is an emergent factor in the other major urban centres.

POST MEDIEVAL SHIPWRECK

The advent of modernity and globalisation was also witness to a massive increase in shipping around the coast of Ireland. Much of this activity was linked to economic interaction between Ireland and Britain, but was also related to the movement of people through emigration, through conflict and through travel. This increase inevitably led to a marked rise in the number of vessels which were wrecked off the coast (*105*). The majority of these were lost as a result of the stress of weather. Vessels which were unseaworthy were particularly vulnerable. Analysis of the wreck data for the coast of Northern Ireland shows that most vessels were lost during the winter months and in times of very bad weather. Nearly 50 per cent of all wrecks were lost in the period of October through to March, with 75 per cent of these wrecks lost during storms with the wind blowing a force seven or stronger. Sailing vessels can quickly become unmanageable in heavy seas and gale force winds, especially if they lose their steering capabilities. They are then left to the mercy of the seas and many of these were driven up unto the coast and wrecked. Closer examination of the wrecks which happened during the summer months shows that in most cases they were lost due to circumstances beyond their control. A large number were war losses, sunk by U-boat action or were lost because of collisions with other vessels.

105 Shipwreck salvage on a vessel at Strangford, Co. Down (UFTM)

A number of vessels were also lost off Co. Down as a result of pirate activity. Throughout the post medieval period, pirate activity was very common off these shores. An exotic perception of pirates has developed over the last 50 years with the advent of cinema. However, the reality of the situation was far different. Most of the coast of Ireland was infested with pirates. These vessels were often acting officially, especially during times of war when British vessels were encouraged to disrupt the shipping of the enemy as much as possible. The same was true for enemy vessels and French, Spanish and American privateers were common off the coast. Shortly after the American declaration of Independence in 1776 many American vessels became privateers. In 1777 the collector of customs wrote to his counterpart at Belfast, asking him to inform the merchants and traders that there were three American privateers – the *Reprisal*, the brig *Lexington* and the cutter *Dolphin*, cruising between Belfast Lough and the Mull of Galloway. The sloop of War *Wolf* was sent along with other naval vessels to counter this threat but the *Wolf* was later lost on rocks at Ballywalter. In September 1777 the H.M.S. *Drake*, with 20 guns also arrived to counter this threat. This vessel was lost after engaging Paul Jones's vessel the *Ranger* off Donaghadee.

Nearly 60 per cent of all wrecks in Northern Ireland occurred on the Down coastline. This reflects its importance as a trade and communications route with a number of major ports located on it. While Antrim accounts for 34 per cent of the wrecks the majority of these occur in North Belfast Lough and along Island Magee in the vicinity of Larne Lough. The north-east Antrim coast was known as a dangerous stretch of coast and was avoided. Wrecking only occurred when vessels were blown onto the shore during gales. Rathlin attracted a large number of wrecks given its position in treacherous tidal waters. Derry accounts for under 10 per cent of all wrecks which is not surprising given its shorter coastline and smaller visiting ship numbers. A number of places along the coast were well noted for the danger they posed to shipping. Concentrations of wrecks are noted at the entrance to the major sea Loughs Carlingford, Strangford, Belfast, Larne and Foyle. Attempting to enter these Loughs in bad weather was particularly dangerous. The entrance of Carlingford has many rocks and pinnacles at its narrow entrance where many vessels have met their end. Angus Rock stands in the centre of Strangford trapping many vessels over the centuries. The problem of passing the narrow entrances of Larne and Foyle was compounded by poor visibility and periods of heavy weather. Dundrum Bay has also had its share of wrecks and has been referred to as a ship's graveyard many times in the past. The many dangers in the Bay include shifting sand-banks and partially submerged rocks like the Cow and Calf.

Most coastal villages along the Irish coast were fishing communities, with each village having its own small fleet. Invariably many of these fleets suffered losses along the coast which survive in folk memory, but were not officially recorded. These communities have always recorded their respect and fear of the sea in stories and song. Ian Wilson writes of one such disaster which happened to the fishing fleets of Newcastle and Annalong in January 1843. Sixteen yawls had left the villages for fishing when the weather turned. In the ensuing storm 14 of these boats were lost in the heavy seas including a rescue boat which had gone to their aid. Only two craft survived – the *Victoria* and the *Brothers*.

The two world wars had a major impact on shipping on the Irish coast with many vessels lost as a result of submarine activity. Four vessels, the *Saint Mungo*, *Derrymore*, *Amber* and the *Morion*, were captured and sunk in Ballyhalbert Bay in May 1917. The vessels were sunk by the U-boat UC 65 commanded by Otto Steinbrinck, one of the most famous U-boat commanders of the First World War. One of the most infamous incidents occurred towards the end of the First World War. On the 30 May 1918, a fleet of Kilkeel fishing smacks was sunk by UB-64 under Captain Von Schrader. The smacks encountered included the *Jane Gordon, Moss Rose, Cyprus, St Mary, Never Can Tell, Mary Joseph, Sparkling Wave, Lloyds, Marianne Macrum* and the motor vessel *Honey Bee*. The vessels were sunk 12 miles off the Down coast. Only the *Moss Rose* and *Mary Joseph* were spared, and the crews returned to shore on these vessels.

Analysis of the wreck data also offers some important economic insights into the nature of coastal trade and communications in the north-eastern counties of Down, Antrim and Derry over the last few centuries. Wreck sites can be taken as a representative sample of shipping as a whole in these waters. Examination of the data shows that *c.*35 per cent of all vessels wrecked in northern waters were carrying coal which appears to have been the primary import product, 18 per cent of wrecks were carrying foodstuffs, while only *c.*3 per cent of wrecks were military craft. Interestingly less than 1 per cent of vessels lost off Co. Down were engaged in fishing, while 14 per cent of wrecks lost off Antrim and Derry were fishing vessels.

An examination of the port of registry and port of origin for Northern wrecks can also offer an interesting insight into where vessels were originating in their trade with Northern Ireland. The majority of vessels seem to have come from the north-west coast of England and western Scotland. There was a surprisingly small percentage coming from what are now the counties of the Republic of Ireland, with only 9 per cent of vessels wrecked on the Down coast originating from what is now the Republic. Wales also has a low percentage represented in both ports of registry and origin. It could be suggested that there was an economic zone in evidence here which consisted of the regions bordering the north Irish Sea. The existence of such a maritime region can be traced back to prehistoric times when there was free movement of goods and people between Ulster, Scotland and northern England. This much later wreck evidence confirms the continuity of maritime activities and traditions throughout the ages.

106 Hook Head lighthouse

LIGHTHOUSES

The earliest known extant lighthouse in Ireland is the impressive stone-built tower at Hook Head, marking the entrance to Waterford Harbour (*106*). It was probably built some time in the thirteenth century, but was refurbished in the seventeenth century when a turret and a glazed lantern were built in the 1670s and 1680s. The present turret was added in 1863 and the tower now stands to a height of 31m with 2.6m thick walls. A number of important lighthouses were built in the closing decades of the seventeenth century, a period corresponding to the modernisation of the Hook light. These did not take the form of tall towers but rather consisted of a series of stone-vaulted cottages with a platform either built on the roof or positioned adjacent to the cottage. A fire was lit on the platform in certain conditions and this acted as the precursor to the light of later centuries. Four of these cottages survive at Howth Head, Copeland Islands, Loop Head and at the Old Head of Kinsale.

One of the earliest of the modern form of tower light was that constructed at Wicklow Head in 1778. This was an octagonal building constructed from bricks and stone work. The earliest rock tower built appears to be that on the South Rock off county Down. It was designed by Thomas Rogers and commenced construction in 1793, eventually standing to a height of 16.75m. However, the vast majority of standing lights around the coast date from the nineteenth century when major concerns emerged about the extent of shipping loss. It is interesting that the primary source of concern from the Government at this time was not the actual amount of lives being lost, but instead the potential damage the extent of the wrecking was having on the economy. Real concerns and strategies for dealing with personal safety at sea only really emerge in the second half of the century. It is the father and son Halpin partnership which is most associated with the design and construction of lighthouses around Ireland during this period. Both built over 50 lighthouses in their time including those built by George Halpin senior at Inistrahull in 1812 and Tuskar Rock in 1815. Others associated with George junior include the Skelligs, the Fastnet in 1854 and Kinsale in 1853.

VERNACULAR BOATS ON THE IRISH COASTLINE

The use of vernacular boats around the coast stands in direct contrast to the large bulk commodity shipping which was now a frequent visitor to Ireland's major ports in the early modern period. These boats bear direct testimony to many thousands of years of usage of certain boat types and reflect the local environment and social economies of the people who used them. The currach or naomhóg as it is known in the south-west is probably the best known and most popular of these traditional boat types (107). It has a predominantly west coast distribution and are lightly built boats consisting of hides stretched over a wooden, ribbed frame. The wooden frame of the boat is flexible yet very strong, and its smooth under hull allows the boat to glide over the water. Currachs were generally used for fishing, kelp gathering or for the ferrying of goods and passengers along the Atlantic coast of Ireland.

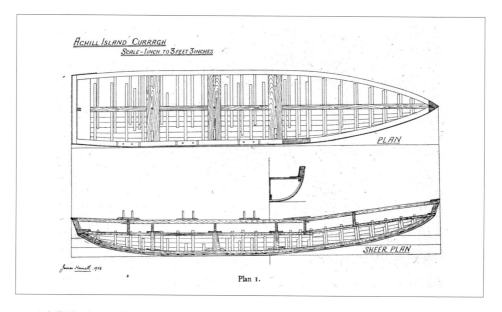

107 Achill Island currach

Regional variations developed probably as a response to local working needs and the waters of their area. The Kerry naomhóg had an average length of 7.6m and width of 1.4m in the 1930s. The sheer of the gunwale curved elegantly both fore and aft, and the boats carried an average crew of three men. Many of the vessels were fitted with a short mast, less than 4m high, set forward through a thwart. The Clare currachs, also termed naomhógs, were very similar in form and size to the Aran currachs. They differed only in their high pointed stern as well as a few minor features. Nineteenth century descriptions of the Aran currach indicate that they varied in length from 2.4m to 7.6m. Cow hides were used to cover the boats. The boats in the Blacksod Bay and Iniskea area had single gunwales and, like the Achill boats, used broad-bladed, feathering oars pivoting on a single pin. Along the coast of Donegal the currachs are particularly distinctive. They are smaller and more rounded than the currachs to the south, and are often designed to carry a single man. The Tory currachs, for example, were originally designed to be paddled and not rowed.

The 1836 *Report into the State of Irish Fisheries* has been used as a base line for the study of these wooden craft used in the fishing industry around the coast. This report was very important as it was the first comprehensive inquiry into coastal communities in Ireland, and it records in great detail their living conditions, maritime activities and boats. Results from the study indicate that the average boat size of the Irish fleet was small and that it was mainly engaged in local inshore fishing. The majority, 73 per cent, of the boats were open rowing boats, while 17 per cent were open sailing boats. Few boats were involved in what could be termed offshore fishing as decked sailing vessels represented only 2 per cent of the total fleet. A noticeable difference in boat-building techniques is one of the most striking aspects of the report. The clinker technique of construction dominated along the north-east coast was also present along the Cork and Sligo coasts, while the carvel technique was more popular and was recorded everywhere except along the north-east coast.

Among the best known wooden vessels were the hookers which were used all along the western and southern seaboards. The boats have a very distinctive shape being sturdily built with a raking transom stern and a deep-heeled keel. They were traditionally open or half-decked and their hulls were blackened with tar. The vessels were smack rigged, the larger boats having a foresail and jib and also carrying a strong weather helm. One of the most interesting areas mentioned in the 1836 report is the Claddagh, the fishing suburb of Galway City. At this time the district had a population of over 2,000 who made their living from the waters of Galway Bay. The community was traditional and went to great lengths to protect its fishing grounds. The fishermen used carvel-built hookers which were open hookers ranging from 6-13 tons burthen. The larger 13 ton vessels were made from oak and had no cabins. They averaged 10.1m long and 9.2m wide. Twenty new hookers were built in the Claddagh in 1835, bringing the Galway fleet to over 100 vessels, and great improvements were noted in the construction methods over the previous 20 years. The boats were predominantly used for fishing and the transportation of turf and seaweed, but they also carried other general cargoes. They fished along the western seaboard and are recorded as fishing off Kerry along with Kinsale hookers in 1804.

SEINE BOATS

Seine net fishing is one of the oldest forms of fishing recorded in Ireland. William Petty, writing in 1672, states that 160 gentlemen in Ireland were engaged in seine fishing. Fishing of this type was usually carried out with two boats: the larger leader (or seine boat) carrying up to 12 oars, and the smaller follower (or 'faller') carrying 4-6 oars (*108*). Both vessels were double-ended, heavily constructed, beamy, open rowing boats and differed only in size. The seine boat was wider and stronger than the faller and had an overall length of *c.*9m and a beam of *c.*2m. Seine boat builders worked on the principle that the boat's length was four and a half times its width. The frames of the boats were made of oak, the keel and stern post of elm, while the rest of its body was made of lighter wood (probably larch). Copper and later galvanised nails held the planking to the frame. The leader boat was directed out to sea by an experienced fisherman, either standing on the shore, or sitting in the stern of the boat. When a shoal of fish was met with the men were instructed to drop their nets. The leader boat then quickly tried to encircle the shoal with the net while the follower took up the free end of the net and brought it around so that both ends would meet. This method of fishing was particularly common in the south-west of Ireland, but was occasionally seen in the rest of the country at different times.

108 Abandoned seine boats in the Beara Peninsula, Co. Cork (Wes Forsythe, CMA)

109 Termon view, Co. Donegal (Wes Forsythe, CMA)

ISLAND AND COASTAL COMMUNITIES IN THE NINETEENTH CENTURY

There has been a tendency in Irish literature to romanticise the lives of the people living on the offshore islands and along the Atlantic seaboard of Ireland (*109*). Indeed, Irish poets, travel writers and artists have long seen the peoples of the west – and those of the offshore islands such as the Blaskets, the Aran Islands and Achill Island in particular – as inheritors of timeless traditions that stretch back into a distant past. Indeed, both cultural nationalists and political republican nationalists saw these western islands as a cultural resource, a wellspring of pure, unalloyed Gaelic culture, that could be used to rebuild a Gaelic Ireland that they thought had been damaged by centuries of English colonization. However, it is certainly the case that this view of the islands as places where an almost prehistoric Gaelic Irish culture had survived is in error. Firstly, there is the fact that some of these islands were only poorly inhabited before the nineteenth century, and that what travelers were witnessing was the outcome of an explosion of island populations and agricultural expansion that had its origins in the early nineteenth century. Secondly, the west coast islands have always been on significant seaways and were arguably always more open to cultural and ethnic exchanges on Europe's Atlantic seaways.

Unfortunately, archaeologists have yet to investigate the settlements, material culture and livelihoods of these peoples during the eighteenth and nineteenth centuries, and in many ways they remain a silent and almost invisible people.

Their own writings (particularly those of the Blasket Islands) and those of island visitors (such as J.M. Synge, Robin Flower, etc.) do provide some insight into the patterns and nature of their everyday lives, but archaeology certainly has the potential to reveal the materiality of these people's lives. Recent historical geographical and ethnological studies have started to explore the nature of these insular landscapes.

On Clare Island, off the Mayo coastline, for example, settlement in the early nineteenth century was originally concentrated along the south- and east-facing slopes of the island, consisting of distinct 'villages' or clachans of clustered dwellings, which were immediately surrounded by unenclosed, infield cultivation strips, while outlying commonage and pasture was located on the mountains above. Lazy-bed cultivation of potatoes was commonplace and small-scale, yet intensive fishing constituted the primary form of subsistence. Similar concentrated communities – known as the clachan and rundale system – can be seen on Great Blasket, on Achill and on Tory Island. However, despite some traditional models, it is now known that this is not a settlement and economic system that stretches back into the distant past – the Middle Ages say. Rather, it seems to have been a particular adaptation or response to the massive growth of population on the western seaboard in the early nineteenth century, and arguably coped well with the social and environmental pressures that this brought. For example, periodic redistribution of cultivation plots (some of which were of better quality than others) enabled the community to ensure that no family would fall into ruin because of the poorer soils that they worked. Kevin Whelan has also argued that the close-knit, communal living conditions within the clachans was to lead to a remarkable explosion of traditional oral culture – with its music, song and dance – and that this was used by these island and coastal communities to live together well and to build distinctive island identities.

NINETEENTH-CENTURY COASTAL DEVELOPMENT

This rundale and clachan settlement system was to fall into disfavour by government authorities in the late nineteenth century – being seen as inefficient and uneconomical by outside English and Irish observers, and was also to become fatefully associated with the disaster of the Great Famine of 1847. Efforts at revitalising the economy of the coastline began to be formulated in the first two decades of the nineteenth century. The Commissioners of Fisheries, or the Irish Fisheries Board, were appointed in 1819 to undertake this task and began to finance and oversee coastal survey and infrastructural construction work. One of their best-known engineers, Alexander Nimmo, was responsible for the building of numerous small piers along the western seaboard and other works including dock works at Limerick and the harbours at Roundstone and Dunmore. The Commissioners of Fisheries were primarily responsible for the administration of funds for pier and boat building, while their engineers' The Office of Public Works was established in 1831 by an Act of Parliament, and took over much of the work of the Commissioners in finishing uncompleted piers and the repair of existing piers. They also became involved in navigation and were responsible for the erection of beacons and lights.

The subsequent failure of the potato crop in the 1840s led directly to the Great Famine of 1845 resulting in the halving of population levels from over 1600 people to 545 people in 1851. People have often questioned why coastal communities should have suffered as much as they did during the famine. The argument is that they would have access to extensive sea and fishery resources, and would not therefore have been as reliant on the potato crop for subsistence. However, this argument fails to take account of the seasonal nature of many of the fisheries, the small and undeveloped nature of fishing infrastructure and the continuing over-reliance that coastal populations had on terrestrial-based agriculture. A degree of acceptance of these factors led to the formation of the Irish Board of Works which was involved in the construction of a number of harbours in the west of Ireland by 1848. The establishment of the Board of Works led to the development and refurbishment of harbours in Donegal, Galway and parts of Kerry.

The work of the Congested Districts Board was to have a major impact on the redevelopment of the coastal infrastructure of Ireland's coastline. The CBD was established in 1891 to encourage the improvement of infrastructure and alleviate famine. In order to achieve this an extensive programme of pier and harbour development was initiated between 1891 and 1914, and a large number of fish curing stations and new vessel types were introduced. The majority of the stone piers along the western seaboard date to this period. As part of this programme the CDB sought to upgrade the fishing industry as well as the fishing fleet. It regarded the Irish fleet as being outdated and as a result it introduced a number of new boat types to Ireland, the main ones being Manx nobbys and Scottish zulus. Both were introduced to provide decked, efficient craft for both inshore and offshore fishing. As well as bringing over these new types of vessels the CDB brought over instructors to educate local shipbuilders in the construction techniques of these new vessels, and by 1909 the CDB total included 100 zulus and 87 nobbys.

TWENTIETH-CENTURY DEVELOPMENTS

The picture of coastal activity during the twentieth century is largely one of decline and neglect. It is marred by conflict, political indifference and economic abandonment. During the World Wars the coast is subject once again to re-fortification. Large artillery forts are built or refurbished in the major sea loughs of Belfast, Derry, Swilly and Cork. These were to see little action and increasingly they became physical signatures of a colonial past. After the war the Irish Free State becomes increasingly isolationist and politically introspective. One of the consequences of these policies was that the mercantile fleet largely collapses and Irish shipping is disbanded. The islands around the coast become increasingly de-populated in favour of re-settlement on the mainland. Traditional fishing is actively discouraged and the vernacular boats around the coast are abandoned and left to rot by old landing places. Many coastal communities were neglected, and they become increasingly difficult to sustain during mass emigration and internal migration towards the major urban concentrations. It is only late in this century that the beginning of a reversal in this trend occurs. The advent of a global environmental movement coupled with increasing awareness of issues of sustainability, inter-dependence and the intrinsic value of heritage have all contributed to this reversal in fortunes. It remains to be seen, however, what the twenty-first century holds for our seas and coasts.

Conclusions: towards a maritime archaeology of Ireland

Maritime archaeology explores the ways that people lived and worked by the coast, how they made use of its maritime resources and how they used the sea as a means of travel, movement and communication. We have shown how Ireland's maritime cultural landscapes have seen thousands of years of human occupation, and also that it is best to imagine our maritime landscapes as encompassing the entire coastline; from the land, across the intertidal zone and out onto the seabed. Indeed, this is generally seen as the way forward for maritime archaeology – moving from the study of nautical technology (e.g. ships and boats) to landscapes and seascapes.

We need more regional, landscape archaeological projects that explore maritime localities and regions across time; focusing on themes of settlement and landscape, economy and industry, trade and exchange, surroundings, time and cultural identity. These projects should aim to be multidisciplinary, combining archaeology, folklore, history, geography, oceanography, marine geophysics, as well as utilising the array of traditional sources (e.g. maps, aerial photographs, documentary sources) that scholars of landscapes use. Indeed, it might be argued that future maritime archaeologists should be trained across institutions and disciplines to provide them with the technical skills and interpretative abilities that will be required. But what questions and themes should future projects focus on?

One thing to explore will be the tensions between continuity and discontinuity, whether that is social, economic or cultural. Continuity is certainly readily identifiable along the seaboards of Ireland – continuity in its broadest and most general sense. There is continuity in terms of a continual human presence, in the exploitation of marine resources and the methodologies employed in the extraction of these resources. One of the striking things about fishing methodologies employed is their durability, and indeed their similarity to techniques found around the globe. The use of fishing engines, baskets and nets, show remarkable consistencies throughout the ages. Also, the design and adaptability of boat types to specific waters and coastlines demonstrates the endurance of technologies that are both locally functional and inherently successful. Much of this continuity is ultimately linked to the fact that the sea is a provider. It produces food resources including fish, shellfish and plants; building material including sand and gravels; and raw materials for industrial processes including kelp for iodine and shells for dying. These have been traditionally viewed as infinite resources, but historical and contemporary exploitation clearly demonstrate that they are not. Climate change, overfishing, pollution and overuse all contribute to the decline of fish stocks and changes in the marine environment.

We could also usefully explore how the sea has been a facilitator for communication, travel and trade. The archaeological manifestations of these activities include shipwrecks, boats, harbour piers and anchorages, as well as the material culture associated with these processes. There are also extensive surviving remains of the waterfronts built to accommodate this activity and a continuity of usage is again apparent in the continual reuse and redevelopment of established landfalls.

Scholars could also continue to investigate how the sea has also been viewed as a source of metaphors and cultural, artistic and literary inspiration on this island. It has been the subject of folklore, stories and superstition as well as being the focus of visual and literary appreciation through art, poetry and literature. We can also see the sea as a more abstract concept, removed from its physicality in the mind of the people who lived by and worked on it. The sea then can be seen as it exists or is imagined by the individual and community. Of course we can never be sure what people thought of the sea over the past millennia, but aspects of it have surfaced and have been expressed through story, poetry, painting and other forms of human expression. In these art forms it has emerged as something to be admired and valued, but most of all respected. It is difficult not to be in awe of its expansive beauty, but there will always be an underlying sense of threat. Increasingly too the sea has become commoditised and this is how it will probably be defined or remembered in the twenty-first century.

With scientific advances in seabed exploration the previously hidden sub-surface energy resources have become highly sought after. Nations compete for ever-dwindling fishery stocks in seas delineated by economic and political boundaries. Increasingly also the sea is being used as a dumping ground for domestic and industrial waste. Somewhat contradictorily, it is also increasingly desirable to live by the sea with its associated vistas and perceived quality of the coastal environment but not work on the sea. In many ways these processes must be seen as a reversal of traditions in previous centuries when life along the coast was perceived, at least in the minds of the urban dwellers of the east coast, as marginal and difficult. The challenge then for present and future generations is to develop sustainable lifestyles for coastal living and working.

Our maritime archaeological heritage faces a range of threats and pressures. Firstly, at a global level, it is clear that our oceans will be subject to significant changes because of climate and sea-level changes. It is thought that sea levels may increase. There may also be increased storms, flooding, and the scouring and loss of intertidal deposits in estuaries and bays. All of these processes will increase pressure on our archaeological sites, either through erosion or through the inappropriate engineering of coastal defences (e.g. extraction of sand, building of sea banks and defences). These engineering works could easily destroy or damage traces of our past coastal heritage.

It is also true that coastal erosion is a natural process, so while some beaches, sand dunes or cliffs are being eroded by the sea today, they may be forming through coastal deposition elsewhere. On estuaries, channels shift back and forth and marshes and reeds grow or disappear in the normal way. Environmentalists increasingly emphasise that such natural coastal processes should not be interfered with by coastal engineering, as this would cause problems elsewhere (a concept known as managed retreat) – and that other places can be developed to provide bird feeding grounds or refuges for plant and wild life. However, archaeological sites cannot be thought of in the same way! Once an archaeological site is destroyed by natural coastal and intertidal erosion, a part of our past is gone forever and it can never be replaced by an alternative one. While we may not always be able to prevent the destruction of coastal archaeological sites by the sea, it is crucially important that we record them before they disappear.

Coastal communities often depend on fishing, fish farming and shellfish farming for their economy and livelihood, and it is appropriate, indeed vital, that this continues for the social and economic well-being of our population. However, the modern re-development of ports and harbours, the use of beaches for shellfish farms and the scouring of the sea-bed by fishing gear can seriously damage intertidal and submerged archaeological sites (e.g. shipwrecks, ancient ports). Archaeologists, working with government authorities, can identify sites of interest and suggest means of protecting them or investigating them prior to their removal.

Other human pressures on coastal landscapes will continue to include urban expansion, tourism developments, caravan parks and the building of links golf courses. Fragile archaeological sites like shell middens may also be damaged unknowingly by people driving their vehicles across them – as we have seen on several sites. Farming and industrial pressures on sand dunes may include intensive sheep or cattle grazing and the quarrying of dunes for sands and gravels. Again, it is appropriate that local communities continue to live and work in coastal landscapes. However, it should also be possible to do this in ways that encourages respect for our coastal archaeological heritage. Indeed, it is suggested that coastal communities could investigate and encourage people to appreciate their coastal heritage for tourists, walkers and other users of our landscapes.

Other future threats will include various offshore developments. Growing energy crises and government concerns about impacts on our economy will lead to the increasing construction of offshore platforms, pipelines and wind turbines for oil, gas and wind-farm resources. Such industrial developments may directly impact on archaeological sites, or indirectly through alteration of currents and erosion patterns. Harbour dredgings, the dumping of spoil offshore and maintenance of shipping channels may lead to the damage or destruction of underwater archaeological sites. Offshore sands and gravel extraction may also be immensely destructive of underwater archaeological sites (e.g. shipwrecks, submerged landscapes).

There are also positives. The establishment of the Marine Institute as a leading world player in marine research and survey has given a tremendous boost to this sector on the island. The continued valuable work of dedicated maritime archaeological survey units both in the respective Departments of Environment north and south of the border will continue. The professional input of these teams into the planning and protection process ensures maritime archaeology is rapidly becoming an integral part of the heritage protection agenda. In recent times, Integrated Coastal Zone Management (ICZM) has emerged as one potential approach to our coastal heritage. In practice, this encourages all the institutions and stakeholders involved in the coast to manage the sea and the land in an integrated way. Archaeologists are involved in ICZM in a range of ways. Many marine developments must be preceded by an archaeological survey or excavation carried out by professional archaeologists. However, given that Ireland has a coastline 7,500km in length, it is also vitally important that local communities are involved in protecting and understanding our coastal archaeological heritage.

A new sense of guardianship needs to be encouraged to ensure both the survival and sustainability of both the natural and cultural resources of the seas around the coast of this small island. Ultimately, we can then begin to reassert our sense of an island identity within the context of the broader social world of the Atlantic seaboard. We can also begin to appreciate that the insular nature of the country did not necessarily equate to isolation in the past. The coast has always been subject to arrivals and departures and their associated multitude of identities and race. This form of cultural fusion has been a feature of society in Ireland for millennia and will continue. The sea then has been a constant, but we must continue to reinvigorate our interest in it to ensure its continued vibrant and healthy presence.

In conclusion, we believe that Ireland's long story of human occupation has been written on its seashore, as much as on its hills, fields and boglands. About ten thousand years ago, our first settlers – hunter-gatherers of the Mesolithic era – came here by boat. Since then, people have lived, worked, travelled and buried their dead around Ireland's coastal landscapes – using the sea as a source of food, raw materials, as a means of travel and communication, and as a place to build communities. However, as might be indicated by this book, Ireland's maritime archaeological heritage remains poorly understood and is largely undiscovered. We hope that this book will enable people to understand our coastal heritage, to help to discover it further and to protect and manage it for future generations.

HOW TO GET INVOLVED IN MARITIME ARCHAEOLOGY

Maritime Archaeology is not just for experts. Given that Ireland has an extensive coastline 7,500km in length (longer that most European countries), it is vitally important that local communities are involved in protecting and understanding our coastal archaeological heritage. Although archaeologists have a good knowledge about some aspects of Ireland's maritime archaeology, inevitably very little is known about the character and current state of archaeological sites along our coastline; for example, whether or not they are under threat from erosion or other pressures. Thousands of archaeological sites are known from coastal districts; more have been recently found on the inter-tidal zone, while there are at least ten thousand shipwrecks from around our coastline. These sites include ancient settlements along the coast and islands, piers, harbours, fish traps, middens on the intertidal zone and shipwrecks and submerged landscapes on the seabed. Yet, it is likely that there are significant numbers of other, unknown archaeological sites on our islands, in coastal sand dunes and on the intertidal zone. Most likely, these will only be discovered by local communities appreciative of their value and role.

Local coastal communities could encourage the appreciation of our maritime archaeological heritage amongst tourists, walkers and other recreational users of our seascapes. You could help to trace the historical development of coastal landscapes using historical sources, folklore, early maps and photographs. Using the Discovery Series 1:50,000 maps you can locate known archaeological sites close to the coast to visit. Sites on private land should only be visited with the permission of the land owner. Your county's RMP (Register of Monuments and Places) is available for consultation in your county library. A database of Northern Ireland's archaeological sites can be consulted at www.ehsni.gov.uk/built/mbr/monuments_database/mons.asp. Many archaeological excavations have been carried out on coast sites (see www. excavations.ie).

One way to get involved is to join a local archaeological and historical society and seek to learn more about your own region's maritime archaeological heritage. You could also enrol in local Adult Education classes in Archaeology that are held in Universities, Institute's of Technology and other centres – perhaps you might even become a professional maritime archaeologist!

WHERE CAN YOU GET FURTHER INFORMATION?

Further information on archaeological monuments in the maritime and coastal zone may be available in the Republic of Ireland from the National Monuments Service of the Department of the Environment, Heritage and Local Government, Dun Scéine, Harcourt Lane, Dublin 2 (website at www.environ.ie).

In Northern Ireland, information may be available from the Environment and Heritage Service at Historic Monuments, Waterman House, 5-33 Hill Street, Belfast, Northern Ireland, BT1 2LA (website at www.ehsni.gov.uk/default.asp).

If you discover a previously unknown monument in the Republic of Ireland, you should report it to the National Monuments Service, phone 01-8882000 (website at www.environ.ie).

If you find an archaeological object in the Republic of Ireland, you must report it to the National Museum of Ireland, Kildare St, Dublin 2, phone 01-6777444 (website at www.museum.ie).

OTHER WEBSITES ON MARITIME ARCHAEOLOGICAL PROGRAMMES

Heritage Council, Rothe House, Kilkenny: www.heritagecouncil.ie/
UCD School of Archaeology, University College Dublin: www.ucd.ie/archaeology
Centre for Maritime Archaeology, University of Ulster at Coleraine: www.science.ulster.ac.uk/cma
Submerged Landscapes Archaeological Network: www.science.ulster.ac.uk/cma/slan

A GUIDE TO FURTHER READING

We have hopefully written this book as a readable, accessible introduction to maritime archaeology, and so we have not included any distracting in-text academic references (although we do attempt to acknowledge our colleagues inspiring research as much as possible). So, we do not provide here one of those dry, daunting list of books and articles that always looks more like a to-do list rather than a resource. Instead, we have tried to provide a brief bibliographical essay on further reading, with our advice on how the reader might tack between different ideas, approaches and archaeological sites. Any readers hoping to explore Ireland's maritime heritage in further detail can depart on their own journey of research by delving in the various bibliographies of the publications below.

CHAPTER 1: INTRODUCTION

Ireland's coastline has been the subject of generations of scholarship across the humanities and sciences. For a recent general introduction to its physical, environmental and cultural histories, we suggest the splendidly-illustrated book, R. Nairn, *Ireland's Coastline: exploring its nature and heritage* (Cork, 2006). For other introductions to the Irish landscape, see F.H.A. Aalen, K. Whelan & M.

Stout, *Atlas of the Irish Rural Landscape* (Cork 1997) and G.F. Mitchell and M. Ryan, *Reading the Irish landscape* (Dublin 1997).

Recent pioneering regional coastal archaeological studies in Ireland include A. O'Sullivan, *Foragers, farmers and fishers in a coastal landscape: an intertidal archaeological survey of the Shannon estuary* (Dublin 2001) and T. McErlean, R. McConkey and W. Forsythe, *Strangford Lough, an archaeological survey of the maritime cultural landscape* (Belfast 2002). These surveys range across prehistory to modern times, providing a sense too of the archaeological potential of the rest of Ireland's coast. For an illustrated guide to the archaeology of one small island, see G. Cooney, T. O'Keeffe, A. O'Sullivan and B. Leon, 'Dalkey Island – an island on the tides of time', *Archaeology Ireland Heritage Guide* 16, 2001.

For general studies of European maritime archaeology, we recommend that readers begin with B. Cunliffe, *Facing the Ocean: the Atlantic and its peoples* (Oxford 2001). Ships and boats are well described in S. McGrail, *Ancient boats in north-west Europe* (London, 2nd edn 1998) and G. Hutchinson, *Medieval ships and shipping* (Leicester 1994). For a review of Ireland's nautical heritage, see C. Breen and W. Forsythe, *Boats and shipwrecks of Ireland* (Stroud 2004).

CHAPTER 2: MESOLITHIC

For a general account of Irish prehistory (from the Mesolithic to the Iron Age), see J. Waddell, *The prehistoric archaeology of Ireland* (Galway 1998). General studies of the Irish Mesolithic include P.C. Woodman, *The Mesolithic in Ireland* (Oxford 1978). For an ecological approach to Mesolithic Ireland, see M.J. Kimball, *Human ecology and Neolithic transition in eastern County Donegal, Ireland* (Oxford 2000). For recent inspiring discussions of Mesolithic hunter-gatherers' perceptions of the ocean and inhabitation of coastal landscapes, see G. Warren, *Mesolithic lives in Scotland* (Stroud 2006) and various papers in C. Conneller and G. Warren, *Mesolithic Britain and Ireland: new approaches* (Stroud 2006).

For reports of the archaeological excavations of two key Mesolithic sites, see P.C. Woodman, *Excavations at Mount Sandel 1973-77* (Belfast 1985), and P.C. Woodman, E. Anderson and N. Finlay, *Excavations at Ferriter's Cove 1983-95: last foragers, first farmers in the Dingle Peninsula* (Dublin 1999). Other coastal Mesolithic sites mentioned include P.C. Woodman and G. Johnson, 'Excavations at Bay Farm 1, Carnlough, Co. Antrim and the study of 'Larnian' technology', *Proceedings of the Royal Irish Academy* (1996, 96C, 137-235).

For a recent review of shell middens across time, see P.C. Woodman, 'The exploitation of Ireland's coastal resources – a marginal resource through time?' in G. Morales and G.A. Clark (eds), *The Mesolithic of the Atlantic façade: Proceedings of the Santander Symposium*, (2004), 37-56, Arizona State University Anthropological Research Papers no. 55. Earlier studies of Mesolithic shell middens include G.F. Mitchell, 'Further investigations of the early kitchen midden at Sutton,

Co. Dublin', *Journal of the Royal Society of Antiquaries of Ireland* 1972, 102, 151-9; G.F. Mitchell, 'Further early kitchen middens in County Louth', *County Louth Archaeological Journal* 12, (1949) pp. 14-20; G.D. Liversage, 'Excavations at Dalkey Island, Co. Dublin, 1956-1959', *Proceedings of the Royal Irish Academy* 66C, (1968) 55-233. For a recent re-interpretation of the Mesolithic (and Neolithic) middens on Dalkey Island, see B. Leon, 'Mesolithic and Neolithic activity on Dalkey Island – a reassessment', *Journal of Irish Archaeology* 14, 2005, pp. 1-22.

For a previous discussion of Mesolithic burials, rewritten for this book, see A. O'Sullivan, 'Living with the dead amongst hunter-gatherers', *Archaeology Ireland* 2002, 63, 10-13.

CHAPTER 3: NEOLITHIC

For an accessible and comprehensive introduction to the Irish Neolithic, see G. Cooney, *Landscapes of Neolithic Ireland* (London and New York 2000). The Neolithic landscapes of Céide, north Mayo are described in S. Caulfield, 'The Neolithic settlement of north Connaught', in T. Reeves-Smith and F. Hamond (eds), *Landscape archaeology in Ireland*, British Archaeological Reports British series 116 (Oxford 1983), pp. 195-215. A range of papers on Neolithic dwellings and houses can be obtained in I. Armit, E. Murphy, E. Nelis and D. Simpson, *Neolithic settlement in Ireland and western Britain* (Oxford 2003). The Neolithic houses at Ballygalley, Co. Antrim are reviewed in D.D.A. Simpson, 'The Ballygalley houses, Co. Antrim, Ireland', in T. Darvill and J. Thomas (eds), *Neolithic houses in north-west Europe and beyond* (Oxford 1996), pp. 123-32.

Other Neolithic coastal occupation sites are described in P.C. Woodman, 'Excavations at Mad Man's Window, Glenarm, Co. Antrim: problems of flint exploitation in east Antrim', *Proceedings of the Prehistoric Society* 58 (1992), pp. 77-106. For Neolithic sandhill dwellings, see A.E.P. Collins, 'Excavations in the sandhills at Dundrum, Co. Down, 1950-51', *Ulster Journal of Archaeology* 1952, 15, 2-26; A.E.P. Collins, 'Further excavations in the Dundrum sandhills', *Ulster Journal of Archaeology* 22, (1959), 5-20. For the Culleenamore shell middens, see G. Burenhult, *The archaeology of Carrowmore, Co. Sligo, Eire* (Stockholm 1984).

For stable isotope analyses that reveal dietary change in the Neolithic, see R.J. Schulting, 'An Irish sea change: some implications for the Mesolithic-Neolithic transition' in V. Cummings and C. Fowler (eds), *The Neolithic of the Irish Sea: Materiality and traditions of practice* (Oxford 2004), 22-8. For a discussion of the occurrence of marine shells in Neolithic megalithic tombs, see F. McCormick, 'Animal bones from prehistoric Irish burials', *Journal of Irish Archaeology* 1985/86, 3, 37-48. The Neolithic site at Carrigdirty rock, Co. Limerick is described in A. O'Sullivan, *Foragers, farmers and fishers in a coastal landscape: an intertidal archaeological survey of the Shannon estuary* (Dublin 2001), pp. 73-91. For a discussion of Neolithic movement around the Irish Sea, and particularly the role of its islands, see G. Cooney, 'Neolithic worlds: islands in the Irish Sea', in V. Cummings and C. Fowler (eds), *The Neolithic of the Irish Sea: Materiality and traditions of practice* (Oxford 2004), 145-59.

CHAPTER 4: BRONZE AGE AND IRON AGE

For an account of the Dún Aonghusa excavations, see C. Cotter, 'Western Stone Forts Project: interim report', *Discovery Programme Reports* 1 (Dublin 1993), pp. 1-19; C. Cotter, 'Western Stone Forts Project: interim report', *Discovery Programme Reports* 4 (Dublin 1996), pp. 1-14; For analyses of the fish and bird bone from that site, as well as other later prehistoric sites, see M. McCarthy, 'Hunting, fishing and fowling in late prehistoric Ireland: the scarcity of the bone record', in A. Desmond *et al.* (eds), *New agendas in Irish prehistory: papers in commemoration of Liz Anderson* (Bray 2000).

For an account of Carrigillihy, see M.J. O'Kelly, 'An early Bronze Age ringfort at Carrigillihy, Co. Cork' JCHAS 56 (1951) 69-86. For a discussion of Bronze Age occupation and use of estuarine marshland environments, see A. O'Sullivan, *Foragers, farmers and fishers in a coastal landscape: an intertidal archaeological survey of the Shannon estuary* (Dublin 2001), chapter 4. For a recent detailed investigation of Bronze Age and early medieval shell middens at False Bay, Co. Galway, see F. McCormick, M. Gibbons, F.G. McCormac and J. Moore, 'Bronze Age to Medieval coastal shell middens near Ballyconneely, Co. Galway', *Journal of Irish Archaeology* 7 (1996), pp. 77-84.

For a discussion of the long-term maritime seaways in the 'Irish Sea region', see J. Waddell, 'The Irish Sea in prehistory', *Journal of Irish Archaeology 1991-92*, 6, 29-40.

CHAPTER 5: EARLY MEDIEVAL

For general accounts of early medieval Ireland, see N. Edwards, *The archaeology of early medieval Ireland* (London 1990) and H. Mytum, *The origins of early Christian Ireland* (London 1992). F. Kelly, *A guide to early Irish farming* (Dublin 1997), describes the early Irish historical evidence for fishing, shellfish gathering and other marine activities. T. McErlean, 'Early medieval period, c.400-1177', in T. McErlean, R. McConkey and W. Forsythe, *Strangford Lough, an archaeological survey of the maritime cultural landscape* (Belfast 2002), pp. 57-89 provides a landscape study of the region for this period.

For early medieval promontory forts discussed here, see T. Barry, 'Archaeological excavations at Dunbeg promontory fort, Co. Kerry, 1977', *Proceedings of the Royal Irish Academy* 1981, 81C, pp. 295-330 and V.B. Proudfoot and B.C.S Wilson, 'Further excavations at Larrybane promontory fort, Co. Antrim', *Ulster Journal of Archaeology* 24-5, pp. 91-115. For studies of early medieval maritime resource exploitation, see E. Murray, *Early evidence for coastal exploitation in Ireland,*

Unpublished PhD thesis (Queen's University Belfast 1999); E.V. Murray, F. McCormick and G. Plunkett, 'The food economies of Atlantic island monasteries: the documentary and archae-environmental evidence', *Environmental Archaeology* 2004, 9, 179-88.

Some studies of early medieval shell middens include R. Ó Floinn 'Sandhills, silver and shrines: fine metalwork of the medieval period in Donegal', in W. Nolan, L. Ronayne and M. Dunleavy (eds), *Donegal History and Society*, Dublin 1995, 85-148 (this also includes a discussion of the Dooey complex); for some other midden sites, see B. Ó Ríordáin, E. Rynne, 'A settlement in the sandhills at Dooey, Co. Donegal', *Journal of the Royal Society of Antiquaries of Ireland* 1961, 91, 58-64; D.D.A. Simpson, M.G. Conway and D. Moore, 'The excavation of a shell midden at Minnis North, Co. Antrim', *Ulster Journal of Archaeology*, 1993, 56, 114-119 and J.P. Mallory and P.C. Woodman, 'Oughtymore: an early Christian shell midden', *Ulster Journal of Archaeology* 1984, 47, pp. 51-2.

For a range of general reading on Scandinavian peoples' impact on Ireland, see the various papers in H.B. Clarke, M. Ní Mhaonaigh and R. Ó. Floinn (eds.), *Ireland and Scandinavia in the Viking Age* (Dublin 1998) and A. Larsen (ed.), *The Vikings in Ireland* (Roskilde 2001). M.J. O'Kelly 'An Island Settlement at Beginish, Co. Kerry' *Proceedings of the Royal Irish Academy*, 1955-6, 57, 159-94. For recent ideas about Scandinavian rural maritime-oriented settlement in Ireland, see J. Sheehan, S. Stummann Hansen and D. Ó Corráin, 'A Viking Age maritime haven: a reassessment of the island settlement at Beginish, Co. Kerry', *Journal of Irish Archaeology* 2001, 10, 93-120 and E.K. Gibbons and E.P. Kelly, 'A Viking Age farmstead in Connemara', *Archaeology Ireland* 2003, 63; for alternative explanations, see M. Gibbons and M. Gibbons, 'Hiberno-Norse ringed pin from Omey Feichéin, Connemara', *Journal of Galway Archaeological and Historical Society* 2005, 57, 151-65. For a general account of Viking Dublin, see R. Johnson, *Viking Age Dublin* (Dublin 2004).

For early medieval monk's perceptions of the ocean, see T. O'Loughlin, 'Living in the ocean', in C. Bourke (ed.), *Studies in the cult of Saint Columba* (Dublin 1997), 11-23. For an introduction to the archaeology of early medieval Atlantic monasteries, and an account of High Island in particular, see J. White Marshall and G.D. Rourke, *High Island: an Irish monastery in the Atlantic* (Dublin 2000); for some other sites, see M. Herity, *Studies in the layout, buildings and art in stone of early Irish monasteries* (London 1995); M.J. O'Kelly, 'Church Island, near Valencia, Co. Kerry', *Proceedings of the Royal Irish Academy* 1958, 59C, 57-136; J. White Marshall and C. Walsh, *Illaunloughan Island: an early medieval monastery in county Kerry* (Dublin 2005).

For early medieval fish traps in Britain and Ireland, see A. O'Sullivan, *Foragers, farmers and fishers in a coastal landscape: an intertidal archaeological survey of the Shannon estuary* (Dublin 2001); A. O'Sullivan, 'Place, memory and identity amongst estuarine fishing communities: interpreting the archaeology of early medieval fishweirs', *World Archaeology* 35, 449-68 and R. Van de Noort and A. O'Sullivan, *Rethinking wetland archaeology* (London 2006, pp. 79-88). The spectacular early medieval tidal mill at Nendrum is summarised at T. McErlean and N. Crothers, 'The early medieval tide mills at Nendrum: an interim statement', in T. McErlean, R. McConkey and W. Forsythe, *Strangford Lough, an archaeological survey of the maritime cultural landscape* (Belfast 2002), 200-211.

For early medieval Irish ships and boats before the Vikings, see J. Wooding, *Communication and Commerce along the western sea-lanes AD 400-800* (Oxford 1996); For Viking and medieval ships, see S. McGrail, *Medieval boat and ship timbers from Dublin* (Dublin 1993). Skuldelev 2 – The 'Irish' Viking ship from Roskilde – has been recently published in detail in O. Crumlin-Pedersen, *The Skuldelev ships I* (Roskilde 2002); The Dublin ship models and graffiti are described by A.E. Christensen, 'Ship graffiti and models', in P.F. Wallace (ed.), *Miscellanea* (Dublin 1988), pp. 13-36.

For recent discussions of maritime trade and exchange, see J.M. Wooding, 'Cargoes in trade along the western seaboard', in K.R. Dark (ed.), *External contacts and the economy of Late Roman and Post-Roman Britain* (Woodbridge, 1996), pp. 67-82; E. Campbell, 'The archaeological evidence for external contacts: imports, trade and economy in Celtic Britain A.D. 400-800', in K.R. Dark (ed.), *External contacts and the economy of Late Roman and Post-Roman Britain* (Woodbridge, 1996), pp. 83-96; I.W. Doyle, 'The early medieval activity at Dalkey Island, Co. Dublin: a re-assessment', in *Journal of Irish Archaeology* 9 (1998), pp. 89-103; Viking Age Dublin's maritime trade is comprehensively described in P.F. Wallace, 'The economy and commerce of Viking Age Dublin', in K Düwel *et al.* (eds) *Der handel der Karolinger – und Wikingzeit,* part 4 of *Untersuchungen zu handle und Verkehr derv or – und frühgeschichtlichen Zeit in Mittel – und Nordeuropa* (Göttingen 1987), pp. 200-45.

CHAPTER 6: LATE MEDIEVAL IRELAND

For some general introductions to the archaeology and landscapes of late medieval Ireland, see T.B. Barry, *The archaeology of medieval Ireland* (London and New York 1987); B.J. Graham and L.J. Proudfoot (eds) *An historical geography of Ireland* (London 1993) and K.W. Nicholls, *Gaelic and Gaelicised Ireland in the Middle Ages* (Dublin 1972). Recent archaeologies of the period include, T. O'Keeffe, *Medieval Ireland. An archaeology* (London 2000) and K.D. O'Conor, *The archaeology of medieval rural settlement in Ireland* (Dublin 1998).

For a discussion of late medieval castles, see T.E. McNeill, *Castles in Ireland. Feudal power in a Gaelic world* (London and New York 1997). For a regional, maritime-oriented study of towerhouses, see M. Ní Loinsigh, 'An assessment of castles and landownership in late medieval north Donegal', *Ulster Journal of Archaeology* 1994, 57, 145-58.

For maritime perspectives on Gaelic Ireland, see, C. Breen, *The Gaelic Lordship of the O'Sullivan Beara, A landscape cultural history* (Dublin 2005) and C. Breen,

'The maritime cultural landscape in medieval Gaelic Ireland', in P.J. Duffy, D. Edwards and E. Fitzpatrick (eds), *Gaelic Ireland c.1250-c.1650, Land, Lordship and Settlement* (Dublin 2001, pp. 418-37). This book is an invaluable starting point for any archaeological or historical study of Gaelic lands during this period. Trade and communication from an island-wide perspective is well covered T. O'Neill, T., *Merchants and Mariners of Ireland in medieval Ireland* (Dublin 1987).

Two regional surveys which the reader may find useful include A. O'Sullivan, and J. Sheehan 1996, *The Iveragh Peninsula, An Archaeological Survey of South Kerry* (Cork 1996) and L. Proudfoot (ed.), *Down: History and Society* (Dublin 1997).

CHAPTER 7

An historical overview of the Spanish Armada is provided in C. Martin and G. Parker, *The Spanish Armada* (London 1988). A detailed historical context for plantation Ireland can be found in N. Canny *Making Ireland British, 1580-1650* (Oxford 2001); R. Loeber, *The Geography and Practice of English Colonisation in Ireland from 1534-1609*, Group for the Study of Irish Historical Settlement, (Dublin 1991) and in M. McCarthy-Morrogh, *The Munster Plantation: English migration to Southern Ireland 1583-1641* (Oxford 1986).

A number of publications deal with aspects of the archaeology of this period including F. Coyne and T. Collins, *Excavation of a Post-Medieval Settlement at Rough Point, Killybegs, County Donegal*. Aegis Archaeology Reports 2, (Limerick 2004) and P. Kerrigan, *Castles and Fortifications in Ireland 1485-1945* (Cork 1995). The archaeology of boats and shipwrecks is dealt with in C. Breen and W. Forsythe, *Boats and Shipwrecks of Ireland, An Archaeology* (Stroud 2004) and in C. Breen, *Integrated Marine Investigations on the Historic Shipwreck 'La Surveillante'*. Centre for Maritime Archaeology Monograph Series No. 1, (Coleraine 2001).

The nineteenth-century life ways and ethnology of Clare Island are discussed in C. MacCarthaigh and K. Whelan, *New Survey of Clare Island*, (Dublin 1999). The Inishkeas are dealt with in B. Dornan, *Mayo's lost islands: the Inishkeas*, (Dublin 2000). For a brief study of the economic state and abandonment of Ireland's Atlantic islands in the twentieth century, see S. Royle, 'Leaving the 'dreadful rocks': Irish island emigration and its legacy', in *History Ireland* 7.2, (1999), pp. 34-7.

An important and comprehensive account of industrial aspects of maritime Cork is presented in C. Rynne, *The Industrial Archaeology of Cork City and its Environs* (Dublin 1999). Important developments in fishing are dealt in A.E.J. Went, (1946) 'The Irish Pilchard Industry', *Proceedings of the Royal Irish Academy* 51B, 81-120 and in N.P. Wilkins, 1899 *Ponds, Passes and Parcs; Aquaculture in Victorian Ireland*, (Dublin 1989).

Index